ON THE LINE

ON THE LINE

Inside the U.S. Border Patrol

ERICH KRAUSS
WITH
ALEX PACHECO

CITADEL PRESS
Kensington Publishing Corp.
www.kensingtonbooks.com

CITADEL PRESS BOOKS are published by

Kensington Publishing Corp.
850 Third Avenue
New York, NY 10022

All Kensington titles, imprints, and distributed lines are available at special quantity discounts for bulk purchases for sales promotions, premiums, fundraising, educational, or institutional use. Special book excerpts or customized printings can also be created to fit specific needs. For details, write or phone the office of the Kensington special sales manager: Kensington Publishing Corp., 850 Third Avenue, New York, NY 10022, attn: Special Sales Department; phone 1-800-221-2647.

CITADEL PRESS and the Citadel logo are Reg. U.S. Pat. & TM Off.

First printing: February 2004
First paperback printing: February 2005

10   9   8   7   6   5   4   3   2   1

Printed in the United States of America

Library of Congress Control Number: 2003108053

ISBN 0-8065-2544-4

The opinions expressed in this book do
not necessarily reflect the position
of the U.S. Border Patrol.

For those who patrol the line . . .

Acknowledgments

My first debt of gratitude is to border patrolmen Ab Taylor and Joel Hardin; without their insight and willingness to share their vast experiences about guarding the United States's borders over the past fifty years, this book could not have been written. Never have I met two men more proud to serve their country.

I am indebted to the members of BORTAC, the Border Patrol's national tactical team, who, for the first time, opened the doors to their world of Special Operations. I thank Allan Booth for taking me through the rigorous BORTAC Selection Course, and I thank Kevin Stevens, Kevin Oaks, Robert Coleman, and Charles Whitmire for taking me up to the front lines.

Countless people made this book possible. Among those who helped illuminate the harsh realities of the border, I thank Manny Garcia, Keith Jones, Rodger Barnett, Congressman Silvestre Reyes, Thomas Hammond, Paul Christensen, and Dave Khron.

Bruce Bender at Kensington supported the project from day one and Ann LaFarge shepherded it through.

Finally, I'd like to thank Frank Scatoni and Greg Dinkin, my friends and agents at Venture Literary, who guided me every step of the way and provided support when I needed it the most.

Alex Pacheco thanks his wife Karla for putting up with the months detailed away from home, the midnight shifts, and the stresses associated with being a U.S. Border Patrolman.

Contents

Prologue: On the Verge

A<small>T THE</small> Border Patrol Academy in Charleston, South Carolina, I learned how to clear a building as efficiently as any member of SWAT, track a suspect for miles over inhospitable terrain, and arrest up to fifty criminals at a time. I spent six hours a day in the classroom, studying immigration law, naturalization law, statutory law, and criminal law. I expended thousands of rounds of ammunition on firing ranges and in simulators, and I mastered the vehicles I'd be using in the field on a variety of racetracks. But even after graduating from the most rigorous training academy of any federal law enforcement agency in the country, I still had only a vague conception of the dangers and unsettling realities that plague America's last frontiers.

The reason for this was simple—the bloody events transpiring along the trailing edges of the United States are the country's best-kept secrets. Only along the border can the death of fourteen men, women, and children not make headline news. Only along the border can a frustrated American citizen sling an AK-47 over his shoulder to protect his property and hardly garner a second glance. Only along the borders can a foreign military cross onto U.S. soil, open fire on a U.S. federal agent with assault rifles, and then head home without suffering the slightest repercussion, which is exactly what happened to me in the spring of 2002 while stationed at the Ajo Border Patrol Station in Why, Arizona.

Although I was normally assigned to the San Diego sector, I had volunteered to temporarily leave my home and future wife to reinforce the line in Ajo. Since San Diego and El Paso had placed lights, fences, and hundreds of patrolmen along their borders with Mexico, Arizona had become a hotbed for narcotic smuggling and human traffickers. Grossly understaffed, the patrolmen responsible for guarding the rugged stretch of Arizona desert between Coronado National Forest and Organ Pipe Cactus National Monument routinely encountered the most ruthless criminals operating on U.S. soil, and they needed all the help they could get.

My first week at the new station held no surprises—long hours tracking drug runners across the desert, three high-speed chases, and over a hundred arrests. My second week began in the station's muster room shortly before I was to head out on evening patrol. While I was chatting with a few of the other agents, in walked the field operations supervisor. Along with going over the usual pre-shift intelligence, such as alien traffic patterns and the location of the last dope seizure, he began handing out index cards with the acronym SALUTE printed at the top.

S A L U T E

Military Incursion

Immediately communicate the following:

Size of the unit (Number of personnel)

Activity

Location and direction of travel

Unit (Identify if possible)

Time (If reporting an earlier encounter)

Equipment of the personnel

Always remember to communicate!

Then I flipped the card over and began to read the back:

> **Remember**
> Mexican military are trained to escape, evade, and
> counter-ambush if it will affect their escape.
>
> Secure detainees and pat down immediately
> Separate leaders from the group
> Remove all personnel from the proximity of the border
> Once scene is secure search for documents
> Keep a low profile
> Use cover and concealment
> Don't move excessively or abruptly
> Use shadows and camouflage to conceal yourself
> Stay as quiet as possible but communicate
> Hiding near landmarks makes you easier to locate

The fact that the Mexican military had made so many armed incursions onto U.S. soil that someone had seen fit to produce flashcards listing a patrolman's proper response if faced with such an encounter did not faze me. What shocked me were the contradictory suggestions printed on the card. How were patrolmen supposed to "secure detainees and pat down immediately" if they were also supposed to "use shadows to camouflage and conceal themselves"?

I turned to a patrolman who had been stationed in Ajo for a considerable amount of time. "This is crazy."

"Tell me about it."

"How often does this occur?"

"More often than anyone would care to admit," he said. "On the books there's been 118 incursions, but those are just the ones we know about. We've got the Mexican military crawling all up and down the border, claiming to be fighting the war on drugs. When we spot them coming across, they say they got lost. It's funny, you know, wherever you see the Mexican military, you'll most likely find smugglers close by."

"Are they hauling drugs themselves, or just providing security?"

He shrugged his shoulders and smiled. "Supposedly they're just lost."

"And what happens when you catch them north of the border?"

"They don't get caught—just as the card says, they do everything in their power to evade."

Again I looked at the scrap of paper. "It sounds an awful lot like an act of war. What's our government's stance on this?"

"I guess as far as this goes, what happens on the border stays on the border. Just in our area alone we spot the Mexican military jumping the line at least once a month, and yet how many times have you heard about it in the news? With all our government's future plans with Mexico, I guess they're trying to make everything appear warm and cuddly down here."

I nodded, tucked the index card into my pocket, and then gathered up my gear to head out on patrol. An hour later, my partner and I had driven thirty miles due south to the Menagers Dam area, located near Gu Vo village on the Tohono O'odham Indian reservation. After making a few sweeps of the area and chasing a pickup truck back across the line, we parked our patrol vehicles parallel to one another only a few feet north of the Arizona-Mexico border.

It was the kind of night patrolmen dream about. The moonless sky birthed an endless sea of stars, so I rolled down my driver's window, welcoming the bite of the easterly desert wind. Before me I had a clear view of a dirt road that cut deep into northern Mexico's sagebrush-spotted plains. According to the intelligence we had received, drug runners and immigrant smugglers had been using the dirt track to cross illegally into the United States for the past week, but for the moment the only movement on the horizon came from random swirls of dust and the occasional desert critter skittering amongst the brush.

Despite the overwhelming feeling that a threat lurked just out of view, I cherished such moments, ones void of chaos. I took a deep breath, listening to the sounds of the desert.

Far to the east of me lay El Paso, a city steeped in patrol history. Over seventy-five years prior, the first group of country boys had signed up to enforce the laws of immigration along the Rio Grande, but instead they found themselves in nightly shootouts with mescal runners. Not much had changed since the bloody years of Prohibition. The smugglers still existed, only rather than driving a pack train of mules loaded with liquor barrels over the border, they now drove 4X4 vehicles loaded with satchels of cocaine, marijuana, and methampetamines. They had also grown more devious in their tactics. The Juarez drug cartel, grossing an estimated two hundred million dollars a week from narcotic smuggling, supplied their runners with state-of-the-art weapons and surveillance equipment. They sent scouts dressed as gardeners into downtown El Paso to monitor the whereabouts of law enforcement agents, dug tunnels a half-mile long to move freely from one country to the next, and offered a two-hundred-thousand-dollar reward for anyone who could put a U.S. border patrolman in the grave.

To the west lay San Diego, nestled up to the border and its Mexican sister city of Tijuana. Blood had spilled there as well. In 1967 it had been two youthful patrolmen who were kidnapped and savagely executed by a gang of criminals hauling marijuana across the desert, signaling the start of the Border Patrol's long-lasting war on drugs. In the seventies, thousands of naive immigrants blindly crossing the no-man's-land separating the two cities were raped, robbed, and murdered by Mexican bandits in search of easy game. Then it was the bandits themselves, hunted down by a unique task force comprised of border patrolmen and San Diego police officers. The death toll continued to increase into the eighties, when the Arellano brothers took over the drug trade in Tijuana and hired American youth gangs to carry out their drawn out executions. It wasn't until 1994, when the San Diego patrol received the funding to launch the labor-intensive Operation Gatekeeper, that the killing between the two metropolitan areas began to dwindle. But since it was nearly impossible to step foot over the line in San Diego without getting apprehended, the illegal immigrants and drug runners simply moved east, pushing north through more desolate regions and carving such routes as the dirt road that lay before me.

To the north, along the U.S.-Canada border, lay five thousand miles of dense wilderness, protected by fewer than four hundred patrolmen.

There was no question about it—the borders were being overrun, and the majority of the American public knew absolutely nothing about it. While reporters were fixated on celebrities and the stock market crash, we were fighting a war in America's backyard. In the course of an hour, a patrolman could go from a gun battle with a band of notorious drug smugglers to saving a group of terrified immigrants huddled behind a cluster of rocks, grieving over their family members who had perished from dehydration. The everyday battle to keep the madness from spilling north could be thrilling, intense, gut-wrenching. It also had a way of burrowing down into a patrolman's subconscious and clinging on.

Over the course of my career, I had been attacked with knives and stoned by fist-sized rocks. More than once I'd stared into the face of a driver who'd decided to turn his vehicle into a battering ram. Such encounters lingered long after they had been played out, and at times it seemed as if there was no escaping the line. High-speed chases, criminals scattering into the night, and drug runners toting burlap sacks infiltrated a patrolman's dreams. No matter how optimistic a patrolman may be, sooner or later he begins to wonder what the line has in store for him and the country he tries so gallantly to defend.

But it was nights like this, gazing out over an open range unused except by the creatures of the desert, that allowed me to believe for just a moment that all was well along America's borders.

For several hours I listened to the dry gusts of wind and the occasional howl of a coyote, dreaming of my girlfriend back home and how I would propose when I returned. Then, at 0300 hours, a familiar sound forced me back to the present. I leaned my head out the window, eyes squinting into the dark. Vehicles were approaching—one from the south, and the other from the southeast.

I called out the window to my partner, who was lost in a world of his own. "You hear that?"

He nodded, his entire body straightening, like a gopher searching for danger. "Maybe we'll catch a load tonight after all. It could be that pickup trying to slip past us with one of his buddies."

I leaned my head farther out the window. "I don't think so."

Suddenly he heard what I was hearing.

There was no mistaking the low gurgling rumble of two well-tuned diesel engines growing more distinct as they made their way toward the U.S.-Mexico border. As a rule of thumb, smugglers used inexpensive vans, trucks, or rental cars to haul their loads, vehicles that could easily be replaced if seized by the U.S. Border Patrol. In the back of my mind two words began to form: Mexican military.

While scanning the horizon, I remembered a bit of news I received years before, something I hadn't remembered back in the muster room while looking at the little index card. On March 14, 2000, two Mexican military vehicles blazed over the barbed wire fence marking the international border and drove onto U.S. soil near Santa Teresa, New Mexico. A patrolman roaming nearby attempted to inform the nine heavily armed soldiers in the lead vehicle that they were no longer in Mexico. The soldiers' response had been to open fire on the federal agent and chase him for more than a mile north of the border, where a rather bizarre Mexican standoff occurred.

I squinted harder into the darkness before me, wishing now that there was a moon by which to see. "Can you make out anything?"

"I don't see squat."

"Are you thinking what I'm thinking?"

"Do you still have your SALUTE card?" he asked with a laugh. "I think I left mine back at the station."

I smiled, but it vanished quickly. Together we were responsible for protecting this strip of land, and neither one of us planned to retreat without knowing who or what we were dealing with.

"If it's the Mexican military," I said, "I'll light up to let the drivers know that we're U.S agents."

"Sounds like a plan."

I turned to look at him, but his eyes were still focused ahead. As the advancing rumble grew louder, I unfastened the button securing my 40-caliber Beretta 96d sidearm in its holster.

Just as the headlights of the approaching vehicles could be seen on the horizon, they vanished. The racket from their diesel engines, however, continued to grow clearer. Sweat beading my brow, I made out the silhouette of two military Humvee-style vehicles racing directly toward us, their lights blacked out.

The one coming from the south was in front. Kicking up a trail of dust, it slowed as it neared the border. For a moment, I thought the driver had seen us and was going to turn around. Then the vehicle sped up again, blazing over the cattle guard separating the two nations, and then crossing onto U.S. soil.

I lit up my overhead lights, and the tires of the Humvee locked up. When the vehicle came to a screeching stop, it was no more than a car's length before my front bumper. Over thirty miles from the nearest backup, I found myself staring into the wild eyes of four Mexican soldiers, their faces caught in the swirling red and blue lights. All of them were dressed in olive drab fatigues, and they were all heavily armed.

For a split second a name popped into my head—Alexander Kirpnick, a patrolman who had approached a group of drug runners outside of Nogales, Arizona, and got shot at close range in the head. It's unnerving how images and names leap to the front of consciousness during moments of stress, but I didn't let the distraction linger long—I had a job to do.

Putting on the stern face I use when confronting a truckload of immigrants, I leaned my head out the window to inform the Mexican soldiers in Spanish that they were no longer in Mexico, as if the cattle guard they had driven over, the flashing lights, and the Border Patrol decals on the sides of my vehicle weren't explanation enough. But before I could utter a word, the soldier in the driver's seat threw the Humvee into reverse.

Watching the intimidating vehicle begin to back up, I thought that would be the end of the matter. Then one of the soldiers in the backseat extended the barrel of what appeared to be an AK-47 machine gun out his window.

Instinctively, I reached for my Beretta, but before I could jerk it free of its holster, the soldier with the assault rifle opened fire.

Out of my peripheral vision, I saw the sagebrush to the left of my vehicle being ripped apart. Sand kicked up by the bullets showered my windshield. Under normal circumstances, I wouldn't have hesitated to answer the assault with gunfire of my own, but these were not what I considered normal circumstances. The men before me, trying to the best of their abilities to end my life, were not your run-of-the-mill drug runners or a group of desperate immigrants willing to risk it all for entrance into the Promised Land. They were soldiers of a neighboring country, one that was supposed to be friends with the United States.

According to the flashcard tucked into my pocket, I had a choice to make—*separate leaders from the group* or *use shadows to camouflage and conceal myself.*

At the moment, both options seemed preposterous.

Just as I began raising my sidearm to take aim, the second Humvee appeared—it also had four soldiers, all armed with assault rifles. I had seen the damage such guns could inflict. My partner and I were out manned and outgunned, and if we exchanged fire, the battle would only end up with two more border patrolmen in the grave.

With a burst of bullets slipping into the earth all around me, I watched my partner throw his vehicle into reverse, and then I did the same. Using the driver's training we received both in the academy and in the field, we maneuvered across the rocky terrain and made a desperate escape to the north.

Some distance from the border, as I looked into the rearview mirror and saw the taillights of the Humvees disappear back into Mexico, a swirl of emotions hit me, the most prominent of which were relief and anger. I felt relief because by God's grace my partner and I were still alive and well. I felt anger because, once again, the Mexican military had driven north of the border, fired on two federal officers, and then retreated back to Mexico, free to accomplish their mission at a later date, which could have had something to do with the delivery of a large shipment of narcotics. I would file a memorandum and an Assault on a Federal Officer Charge the moment I got back to the station, but the chances were good that it would receive no more attention than the 118 Mexican military incursions before it. No preventive measures would be taken, and I felt anger because situations such as these, ones that occurred in America's backyard, were some of the country's best-kept secrets.

Just as I expected, news of my little encounter did not garner the attention it deserved, and just a few weeks later, three Mexican soldiers in a military Humvee jumped the line and fired upon another Border Patrol agent who was patrolling near Menagers Dam. One bullet shattered the rear window of the agent's vehicle, and then deflected off the prisoner's partition located directly behind his seat. Not surprisingly, earlier that day twenty-two hundred pounds of narcotics had been confiscated in the immediate vicinity.

The agent was lucky, just as my partner and I had been lucky, but along the borders luck only goes so far. In August 2002, Chris Eggle, a park ranger assigned to Organ Pipe Cactus National Park in Ajo, attempted to assist Border Patrol agents in the apprehension of two suspects who had illegally crossed the border. During the pursuit, he was shot and killed.

All three of these incidents occurred along a thirty-mile stretch of border between Lukeville Port of Entry and Menagers Dam—the U.S.-Mexico border is over two thousand miles long.

Patrolmen are faced with life-threatening situations like these on a daily basis, and since the terrorist attacks on September 11, 2001, our job has only gotten harder. Along with being tasked with the enforcement of immigration, customs, and drug interdiction, we are now on the front line of defending the United States from terrorists with half the number of people in most metropolitan police departments.

Few of the American public know just how easy it is for terrorists, immigrants, and drug smugglers to illegally cross the borders of the United States. Congressmen, senators, and political activists have voiced their opinions on this matter in recent years, and yet few of them have visited the front lines of America's most important war.

The U.S. Border Patrol is the first and last line of defense in the mountains, deserts, and forests that mark America's boundaries. Unlike politicians, patrolmen know where America's defenses are the most vulnerable, exactly what needs to be done to plug the holes, and just how deep the problems of drug smuggling, illegal immigration, and terrorism run. Because of this, we are very concerned about America's future.

Historically, the patrol has voluntarily remained in the shadows, gladly allowing other agencies to earn credit for our greatest victories. While the FBI and DEA fight for camera time, BORTAC, the Border Patrol's national tactical team, covertly travels around the world, breaking up riots, infiltrating smuggling organizations, and training foreign drug police. Patrolmen are not glory hunters. We're outdoorsmen, patriots—proud men and women who truly feel we are guarding our country's border. But now, with the increased threat of terrorism, many patrolmen realize that avoiding the spotlight is no longer an option. Securing the United States's borders plays a major role in securing America in general, and so the public has a right to know exactly what is happening along the line.

We have a story to tell—one that details our history, our methods, our concerns, and the reasons why the United States's borders remain an open freeway for foreigners who wish to exploit and hurt the American people.

—Alex Pacheco

ON THE LINE

Chapter One

THE COWBOY DAYS

LONG before agents of the United States Border Patrol had all–terrain vehicles, snowmobiles, motorcycles, helicopters, and armored sedans at their disposal, they guarded the eight thousand miles of America's boundaries on foot and horseback. They managed this without the aid of night-vision goggles, body armor, infrared scopes, motion detectors, two-way radios, or even an official uniform. Armed only with a badge and the firearm of their choice, they spent weeks hiking and riding alone through the backcountry in search of smugglers, combating harsh weather and even harsher terrain. Their sole duty was to enforce the laws of immigration, and they accomplished this task by using whatever means necessary.

In the case of our southern land border, where smuggling, cattle rustling, and general lawlessness was common practice during the latter part of the nineteenth century, only a handful of agents were responsible for patrolling an imaginary line that stretched two thousands miles from a point on the Pacific Ocean just south of San Diego, California, to another point on the Gulf of Mexico, east of Brownsville, Texas. This was a daunting task, for that imaginary line ran across the blistering Arizona desert, over bleak mountain ranges of rock and brush, and eventually along the rough and tumble country of the Rio Grande. The vast border landscape was a no-man's-land, virtually uninhabited save for the occasional border town such as El Paso, Texas, or Nogales, Arizona. But despite being relatively free of civilization, the area was fraught with danger. In the late 1800s, the line harbored not only some of the country's most ruth-

1

less criminals, but also some of America's most menacing critters, including bears, wolves, and rattlesnakes. Water holes were few and far between, and during the summer months, the heat could kill both a man and his horse in a matter of days.

Needless to say, it took an exceptional individual to do the job. One man who fit the bill was Jefferson D. Milton. Although the Border Patrol as we know it today did not come about until 1924, the agency widely recognizes Milton, whose service began in 1904, as the first border patrolman. His adventures were as colorful and fantastic as those of Wyatt Earp or James "Bat" Masterson, and it is through his story that one can best understand where the first patrolmen came from—and why their legacy still serves as the backbone for this unique federal agency.

MOUNTED GUARDS

Despite the dread he instilled in outlaws while patrolling America's wild West, Jefferson Milton was not born into a life of gun slinging. His childhood home was a plantation called Sylvania, deep in the woods of Florida, and his father was a former Confederate governor of the state. Before Jefferson's birth, the Milton family had been influential and wealthy, but that all changed with the victory of the North in the Civil War. Like many well-to-do Southern families, the Miltons found themselves locked under an oppressive carpetbagger government that drained them not only of their riches, but also of opportunity. As a result, Milton grew up on the war-torn remnant of his family's estate. By the time he was fifteen, prospects at home were only growing darker, so he decided to pack his bags and head out west in search of adventure. Roughly three years later, on July 27, 1880, his hunt landed him in the Texas Ranger Headquarters in Austin, Texas.

He was a boy standing amongst seasoned pistoleers who, during this period in history, tended to be a very determined group of lawmen. The rangers had proudly served the citizens of Texas as a paramilitary force since 1823, protecting the territory's first settlers from renegade Indians and outlaws, and yet shortly after the end of the Civil War the United States military forced them to disband. Their former duties were delegated to Union soldiers, who quickly fell into the hands of corrupt politicians. Soon the open plains became a haven for criminals and bandits, forcing Texas into a dark era of range wars, feuds, murder, and robbery. The rangers helplessly watched the mayhem for almost a decade, until honest politicians once again gained control of the Texas Legislature in 1874 and managed to reinstate their companies. They had been working to restore law and order for six years by the time Milton walked through their door, and yet they still had a long way to go.

It was at this time that legends could be made—and Jefferson Milton was determined to become one of them.

Before he could be sworn in as a ranger private, however, he first had to meet two demands. The first one dealt with age; all recruits had to be at least twenty-one years old. Not willing to wait to get the job, Milton simply tacked on three years to his application.[1] When they didn't ask to see proof, he was free to move on to the next requirement—only this one he couldn't maneuver around by telling a white lie. Due to the dangerous nature of the position, he had to prove that he had above-average prowess with a pistol—a prerequisite implemented not so much for his own safety, but rather for the safety of his fellow comrades. A gaggle of veteran rangers gathered around to watch the demonstration, and when Milton jerked his Colt .45 from its holster, most of them couldn't believe their eyes. As it turned out, the teenager had a natural trigger finger and could shoot with the same quickness and accuracy as some of the notorious outlaws who would soon find themselves in the history books.

With a .45 single-action handgun dangling from his hip, another .45 secured in a holster under his coat, and a Winchester rifle tucked into his saddle, Milton rode out onto the open plains. While he rounded up criminals and cattle rustlers in Texas, Congress was conducting their own form of reform in Washington. For decades Chinese workers had come to the United States to escape the poverty and famine in their own country. Encouraged by news of California's gold rush, they came in droves, hoping to stake a claim or find a favorable niche in the country's booming economy. Most of their hopes, however, were never realized. Stranded in a foreign country and ostracized by a large portion of the populace, the majority of them found their only niche working on large-scale public projects, railroads, or in mines.

By 1879, anti-Chinese sentiment was on the rise. The foreign laborers were working for wages that could scarcely provide them with food, and although industry welcomed them with open arms, as more American citizens were ousted from their jobs the Federal government began to hear the complaints. In an attempt to solve the problem, the Chinese Exclusion Act was passed in 1882, outlawing Chinese immigrants from entering the United States for a period of ten years.

Congress considered the matter taken care of, but that was far from the reality of the situation. For the first time, the United States had barred certain individuals from entering the country, and Congress would shortly come to realize that simply passing a law was not enough to keep the excluded foreigners out. Many Chinese immigrants were desperate to find work, to provide for their families back home, and when they couldn't obtain legal entry into the United States, they began arriving on the west coast of Mexico by boat. After hiking to the interior of Mexico, they then hopped on the Mexican Central Railroad, which took them all the way up to Ciudad Juarez just south of El Paso. Once there, Mexican smugglers were more than happy to skip them over the border for a small fee.

Even though they were often treated on a sub-human level once they reached American soil—utilized when needed, discarded when not—they continued to pour in by the thousands. Milton witnessed hordes of illegal Chinese migrating north during his three years with the rangers, but at the time his duty did not include enforcing immigration laws, so he let most of them pass without so much as a word.

For the time being, he focused his attention on the tent cities that had sprung up along the Southern Pacific railroad slowly being laid into El Paso. Patrolling makeshift towns, where an atmosphere of gambling and booze attracted numerous outlaws, was anything but dull. He drew and fired his weapon often, laying more than a few criminals in the ground. But it was his quickness on the trigger that almost ended his career as a lawman for good. While patrolling Mitchell County, Milton and two fellow rangers heard gunfire and rushed toward the Nip and Tuck Saloon. Instead of discovering a robbery in progress, they found two intoxicated ranchers standing in the street, bullet holes pocking the buildings around them. Even though their guns were still smoking, they denied shooting up the town. The rangers had no intention of backing down, however, and when they asked to examine the suspects' weapons, one of the cattlemen drew his pistol and opened fire. Milton acted instantaneously, and a few seconds later the rancher was lying dead.

The event caused quite a stir in Mitchell County. Due to the fact that many of the townsfolk knew each other on a first name basis and guarded one another's backs, Milton found himself on trial for an unrighteous shooting. But having the Texas Ranger face murder charges wasn't enough for the dead rancher's friends and family. When Milton was brought before the judge to state his case, a lynching party gathered out before the courthouse. Their intentions were to dispense some vigilante justice, but they quickly came to their senses. Milton might have been unarmed, but the two rangers protecting him certainly weren't.[2]

After a lengthy three-year trial and plenty of menacing looks from townsfolk, Milton was acquitted of all charges. Despite this fact, he hung up his badge and headed for New Mexico. He tried his hand as a rancher, sheriff, and cattle-thief detective, but eventually found his way back to El Paso where he was hired on as a U.S. Customs Collector. In this new line of work, he roamed the inhospitable deserts from El Paso all the way to the Gulf of California, collecting Customs duties and bringing contraband smugglers to justice. During this time, riding alone through Arizona's hot, dry Sonoran desert, Milton had several encounters with the Papago Indians, a semi-sedentary, agricultural tribe that had thrived in the lifeless desert conditions for centuries. They helped him track down fugitives who hoped to escape their fate by wandering deep into the desert's harshest territory, and taught him how to locate food and water—skills that would come in handy later on.

Milton lost his position with Customs when the entire service was temporarily disbanded in 1889, but by this time he had already earned a daunting reputation that kept him steadily employed as a keeper of the peace. In 1894, he was hired on as the chief of police in El Paso, a town that had become a haven for rowdy gamblers. Determined to clean up the streets, Milton used a local ordinance outlawing gambling to oust a majority of the burly card players from town. As one might imagine, this process was not without conflict, but due to Milton's quickness on the trigger—and the fact that he was dealing with gamblers—most of the men he ousted were wise enough to realize that in a firefight the odds were not in their favor. And in those few cases where Milton's reputation didn't dissuade his unruly subjects from fighting, his Colt .45 solved the matter.[3]

Milton's trigger-finger form of law enforcement was considered too violent by many of the townsfolk, and they voted him out in an election. Not to be stopped, Milton tried his skill as a U.S. Marshal and then a Wells Fargo Express messenger on the Southern Pacific railroad, which proved to be his most dangerous position yet.

Responsible for valuable shipments of gold bullion, Milton personally saw to his cargo's safety by locking himself into the train compartment with an ample amount of food and an arsenal of weapons. By this time, most desperados knew about Milton's prowess with a pistol, and despite the temptations of robbing his cargo, few dared challenge the former Texas Ranger. Burt Alvord, however, a former lawman who had turned outlaw, decided that the benefits were worth the risk. His elaborate plan was to divert Milton so that he wouldn't be on the train on the day of the heist, but his diversion tactics failed. When the train door slid open, Alvord and his gang found themselves staring into the eyes of Jeff Milton.

The gang opened fire, and Milton was shot in the left arm by a high-powered rifle. Bleeding badly, he snatched up his shotgun in his right hand and began blasting, instantly dropping two of his aggressors. Milton was outmanned and outgunned without the use of his other hand. He closed the train door, locked the vault to his cargo, concealed the key in the safe, and then passed out from blood loss. The gunmen continued to fire on the compartment and eventually forced their way inside. They searched for the key to the vault, but since Milton had locked it in the safe, they were forced to retreat without their booty.

Milton spent the next few years seeing to the capture of Alvord's gang and rehabilitating his arm. During this time, the Federal government began making changes in immigration law—changes that would forever alter Milton's path. Only three years after the Chinese Exclusion Act was passed, Congress passed another law that prohibited a company or an individual from bringing foreigners into the country under contract to perform labor. In 1891 they levied a head tax of fifty cents for all immigrants coming to the United States; they then added to the list of limitations, barring prostitutes, idiots, lunatics, convicts, and people suffering from dangerous and contagious diseases. But at the turn of the twentieth century the government came to realize that although they had created numerous laws, they had no real means to enforce them.[4]

The government decided it was time to delegate all matters concerning immigration to one agency, which led to the creation of the

Immigration Service in 1891. Originally placed in the Treasury Department but quickly moved to the Department of Commerce and Labor,
the newly formed agency opened its first immigration station on
Ellis Island on January 2, 1892. Inspectors were hired to interview
all immigrants who came to the United States, and reject those who
weren't qualified for admittance.[5]

The issue of naturalization was also addressed when Congress
learned that each of the five thousand naturalization courts, spread
out in various states, were issuing citizenship to applicants as they
saw fit. Realizing there had to be standard procedures for gaining
citizenship, Congress broadened the Immigration Service's responsibilities, making them the Bureau of Immigration and Naturalization.
Although this massive agency would temporarily split up when the
Department of Commerce and Labor divided in 1913, they would
reunite in 1933, forming the Immigration and Naturalization Service
(INS).

The creation of the Immigration Service in 1891, however, did
little to solve the problem of immigrants illegally crossing the borders. Sheriffs, Texas Rangers, and other law enforcers had their
hands full tracking down killers and cattle thieves and maintaining
order.[6] They had no time to be burdened with illegal immigrants
heading to work in mines or on railroads—and yet greater numbers
of undocumented workers were creeping over the southern border
every month.

The general consensus of both Congress and the Immigration
Service was that the country needed a group of agents whose sole
responsibility was to track down the criminals who smuggled Chinese
immigrants up through Mexico and over the U.S. borders. After di-
viding the border regions into three districts—the Texas District,
the New Mexico-Arizona District, and the California District—they
began searching for agents to patrol them. This, however, was not
an easy task. With thousands of square miles of harsh terrain to patrol, the agents not only had to have a keen grasp of the lay of the
land, but they also had to be prepared to defend themselves against
bandits and smugglers.

As it turned out, the customs officer who had brainstormed the
idea of having such a patrol, Sam Webb, was stationed out of Nogales,
and after years living on the front line, he knew the perfect man for
the job—Jefferson Milton.[7] With numerous years under his belt as a
customs official, Milton knew the border terrain from Arizona to

California like the back of his hand. He was already familiar with the trails smugglers most frequently used, and had proven himself as a man who could single-handedly control large groups of criminals during his time with the Texas Rangers.

In 1904 President Theodore Roosevelt appointed Milton as "Mounted Chinese Inspector" for the Immigration Service. As it was when he was a ranger, he did not receive a uniform. With the sole task of stopping smugglers from bringing Chinese laborers into the United States, he was given only a badge and then sent out into the deserts on his own horse with his own guns. His salary was a meager twenty-four dollars a month, from which he had to pay for his horse's feed.

The poor wages were compensated for by job liberties. Officially, Milton was operating under a district immigration inspector, but rarely was he requested to report in. Early on, government officials realized that they were in no position to dictate rules and regulations concerning this new position. Milton, a man who'd roamed thousands of miles on horseback in hostile territory, knew better than anyone what needed to be done. It was left up to him to decide where to ride and how to break up human smuggling operations.[8]

At the beginning of his long career as a border patrolman, Milton spent considerable time traversing the deserts of southern Arizona. Because the heat and militant landscape dissuaded many lawmen from entering its fiery clutches, it was prime territory for smugglers to bring their human contraband up into the United States. Milton put the desert survival skills he had learned from the Papago Indians to use, sometimes tracking his suspects for days on end. His skills with a gun were also tested, and soon word began to spread that a sharpshooting former Texas ranger was prowling the border.

A major part of his duty was searching for the trails that smugglers used to bring Chinese immigrants to meeting points, known as Chinese Farms, located on U.S. soil. At these locations, the workers would be shipped all over the nation to meet the demand of cheap labor. Milton spent weeks following these trails to their destinations, and a short while into this exploration he learned that a good portion of them led to the town of Tombstone, Arizona. Smuggling operations were far more elaborate than anyone had ever guessed, and upon further inspection he learned that almost every legal Chinese immigrant in Tombstone had a basement dug under his house. They would hide their illegal countrymen while awaiting dispersion. Soon everywhere became a potential hiding place, and

Milton began inspecting mining shafts and caves on the outskirts of town, where he often flushed out hordes of illegal workers.[9]

In just a few short years, Milton and his fellow inspectors had developed an intricate system to both detour and apprehend smugglers. A few of them camped out on the banks of the Rio Grande, seizing smugglers and their paying customers the moment they crossed the line. The border was large and barren, however, and of course there were those that slipped through. To round up the stragglers, inspectors on horseback would track them overland to cut them off before they could reach Chinese Farms or other dispersal locations. But even if a band managed to elude capture and reach one of the many inland railroad stations, they were not yet in the clear. Inspectors were placed at strategic locations along the railroads that ran north and south of the border to conduct surprise searches. This last measure worked well for a time, but the more ingenious smugglers soon learned where these inspection points were located, and they would unload their human cargo and trek on foot to avoid them. Not to be defeated, yet another crew of inspectors was eventually stationed further into the U.S. interior to yet again search both passenger and freight trains.

Milton worked all lines of defense and soon learned every trick smugglers used to get their contraband safely into the United States. With the more elaborate smuggling rings, papers were supplied so that the illegal immigrants could travel without harassment on the railways. For some of the others, deals were struck with railroad workers to stow the immigrants in boxcars. It was a rather ingenious plan, because Milton and his fellow inspectors couldn't demand to search the compartments without just cause. This bothered Milton, and soon he came up with a plan to remedy the situation. While walking down the tracks, he'd hold a bee smoker under the boxcars so that smoke would seep through the cracks. When he heard hacking emerge from cars that were supposed to hold only cargo, he had the evidence he needed to demand that the doors be opened for his inspection.[10]

After skipping from one job to the next for two decades in America's wild West, Milton had found a home as a border patrolman. The nature of the job gave him all the freedom and adventure he was looking for. During the first five years he watched the number of illegal Chinese flooding across the border increase tenfold, while his fellow inspectors never totaled more than seventy five.[11]

This was due, in part, to the unromantic mission of his job. The nation's attention was focused on notorious outlaws, gun-toting sheriffs, and the happenings of dangerous towns such as Tombstone. Little attention was left over for illegal immigrants and the inspectors hunting them down. In the early part of the twentieth century, most Americans cared little about who or what flowed over the U.S. borders, and, in turn, only a handful of peacekeepers were delegated to protect a border that was still to be marked.

That would all change, however, six years into Milton's duty. A new threat began to show itself on the horizon, one that would forever change America's policy concerning our borders.

BANDIT RAIDS

When Porfirio Diaz claimed the presidency of Mexico in 1876, his primary concern was generating foreign investment. In order to accomplish this, however, he first had to eliminate the bloodthirsty bandits who had plagued the countryside for decades and made progress virtually impossible. Simply killing them off proved too risky, because the peasant population generally regarded bandits as their heroic avengers. To solve the matter, Diaz hired a large number of the bandits as rural police, and then ordered them to hunt down and kill the bandits who had decided to keep their former profession. The scheme worked well, and through an "iron heel" Diaz remained in power for thirty-five years, his well-trained bandit-army squashing any peasant uprising before it could gain momentum.[12]

Foreign investment moved in, but it would ultimately lead to Diaz's downfall. When some of Mexico's wealthiest landowners and businessmen felt compromised by Diaz's ties to foreigners, a revolution soon got underway. The heavy-handed president was ousted from power in 1910. As a result, bandits who had been kept under wraps for years by the militant government once again ran rampant in northern Mexico. It did not take them long to find their way over that imaginary line and into the United States.

At first, Mexican bandits targeted the ranches sprawled across the Texas border. Then, with a few victories under their belts, they grew bolder and began midnight assaults on the towns of the Lower Rio Grande.[13] The United States government knew something had to be done, but instead of sending the military to the border they

hoped to solve the problem by supporting the new Mexican government of Venustiano Carranza, which promised to restore order in
central Mexico as well as along the border.

This did not sit well with Francisco "Pancho" Villa. The bandit-
turned-revolutionary had helped orchestrate several uprisings, and
his blood lust both on and off the battlefield made him feared and
respected among a majority of peasants. He'd been determined to
become the next president of Mexico by enlisting the support of
the United States, but when America put its faith in Carranza, Villa
poured his heart and soul into revenge. In a letter to a fellow bandit
in 1915, Villa declared: *We have decided not to fire a bullet more against
Mexicans, our brothers, and to prepare and organize ourselves to attack the
Americans in their dens.*[14]

Villa's plan to devastate border towns in the United States wasn't
fueled only by hate. Still determined to become the president of
Mexico, he hoped his bandit raids would force President Woodrow
Wilson to send troops into Mexico, humiliating Carranza and adding
more credibility to his own campaign.[15]

As Villa and his bandits swept across the line to pillage border
towns in Arizona, New Mexico, and Texas, the job of protecting our
southern boundary became too great for seventy-five mounted inspectors. Under orders of President Wilson, the War Department
sent Brigadier General John Pershing and his Eighth Infantry
Brigade to guard the Mexican-American borders of Arizona and Texas.
Their presence succeeded in pushing Villa and his men back over
the Rio Grande, but the bloodthirsty bandit then simply shifted his
attention to slaughtering American citizens in Mexico. On January
11, 1916, Villa hijacked a train bound for the Mexican mining town
of Santa Ysabel. The seventeen American businessmen on board
were pulled from their seats and forced to kneel by the side of the
track. After each received a bullet in the back of the head, their bodies were horribly mutilated.[16]

The massacre made headline news across the nation, and for the
first time the topic of how to defend the U.S. borders and citizens
abroad became a serious debate. But despite the American loss of
life, President Wilson still neglected to send troops into Mexico to
bring the outlaws to justice. Determined to draw America's armies
south, Villa once again crept over the line, only this time the havoc
he wreaked was far beyond the government's worst nightmare.[17]

During the two months following the train massacre, Villa and his followers, known as Villistas, slowly moved north through Mexico, pillaging every town they entered. They burned houses and murdered innocents, preparing themselves for the confrontation that lay ahead. Then, in the early morning hours of March 9, 1916, Villa and five hundred Villistas attacked the unprepared U.S. Thirteenth Cavalry, which was stationed at Camp Furlong, just outside of Columbus, New Mexico.

Despite being caught by surprise, the cavalry managed to scramble into formation and return gunfire. After dozens of bandits were wounded or killed, Villa decided he had made his statement and retreated. But he didn't go far. His next stop was the town of Columbus, where for several hours he and his men stormed through the streets, looting stores and killing civilians. It wasn't until the sun began to rise that they decided they'd had enough. After setting the town ablaze, they headed for the sanctity of the mountains in their homeland, leaving scores of Americans lying dead on the ground.

As the citizens of Columbus extinguished the fires and buried the bodies of their loved ones, news of the slaughter swept across America by newspaper. The country was outraged, with much of the blame falling upon the U.S. government. President Wilson could no longer delay the inevitable, and he ordered twelve thousand national guardsmen to be stationed along the U.S.-Mexico border. In addition, Brigadier General John Pershing was instructed to take almost five thousand troops into the heart of Mexico and hunt down the most dangerous outlaw the United States had ever known—one who not only knew the lay of the land, but also had a nine-day head start.

No expense was spared in the quest to pay the bandit and his army retribution. Along with an abundance of troops, Pershing had a small fleet of primitive aircraft buzzing through the sky, offering support for the troops on the ground. Although it was one of the most elaborate military operations conducted by the United States, it soon met with disaster. Unfamiliar with the terrain, the pilots wrecked most of the planes while attempting to land them in the countryside. In addition, Carranza's troops threatened to attack the Americans as they moved southward, despite the fact that they were there to destroy Villa, Carranza's arch nemesis. All this and Villa was nowhere in sight, for he and his Villistas had already found refuge deep in the mountains of Mexico.[18]

Determined to accomplish his mission, Pershing divided his

forces to cover more ground. The soldiers that marched to the east found themselves moving through open desert, while the forces in the west had to maneuver rocky fields. Both teams scoured the Mexican countryside, only to reconvene months later empty handed. Pershing established a permanent command post in Colonia Dublan, but did not see serious battle until June 21, when he received a bogus tip that Villa was camped out in a village to the northeast of his command post. Eager for battle, Pershing led his men into the village on a rampage, but shortly thereafter learned that the Mexican troops he was fighting were not part of Villa's army, but rather part of Carranza's. As the two sides drew blood, Villa was rumored to have watched from a nearby hilltop, utterly delighted.[19]

The few times Pershing and his soldiers came close to capturing Villa they were hindered either by the Carranza troops or by local scouts who fed them false information. The drive of American soldiers began to falter in the latter part of the crusade, and with many of his men finding refuge from the long hours of the day in local cantinas, Pershing created a rigorous combat training program to keep them in shape. Even though they would never use this training against Villa, it would come in handy in the near future. While they were desperately searching the Mexican countryside, another threat to America was brewing thousands of miles away in Germany.

Pershing and his forces were called back in January, 1917. Villa considered it a victory, but before he could restore his former power among his people, he met a brutal demise when attacked by a group of unknown gunmen. But his legacy carried on; the only foreign leader to have successfully invaded the continental United States became a hero in his homeland. In America, however, his legacy was a painful reminder of just how vulnerable its boundaries were.

The same year that troops were called off the southern border, the illegal crossings of immigrants immediately resumed. The battle with Villa had brought the borders national attention, and the U.S government was growing more concerned about those people illegally crossing the borders, including those who were being legally admitted into the United States through Ellis Island. Unskilled immigrants from Europe, forced to work for next to nothing, were devastating the economies of cities positioned on the Atlantic seaboard. To remedy the problem, another immigration law was passed, one that required all immigrants to be able to read and write in their native language.

The law did not affect the Chinese, who were already streaming across the border illegally in record numbers, but rather people from all European nations who previously had no restrictions. Since the escapade with Villa, the U.S. government had become aware of one very important thing—not everyone played by the rules. They expected that the passing of the literacy law would bring even more banned individuals over the borders, and they were right. Less than a year later, Milton and his fellow mounted guards were no longer primarily searching for Chinese, but rather for uneducated Europeans in search of employment in the Northeast.

The small band of mounted guards hired to protect the southern boundary was grossly understaffed, but with America stepping foot onto battlefields overseas, no immediate assistance was given. Other than being supplied with a few new recruits, the mounted guards were left to fend for themselves and protect the border with their own guns and horses. This they might have been able to handle, at least to a point that suited the Immigration Service, but in the coming years the mass influx of Europeans was not the only additional burden they had to deal with. While many American men were off to war, another war raged on American soil, one that would put the lives of mounted guards in serious jeopardy for the first time.

A DRY SPELL

When the Eighteenth Amendment to the United States Constitution went into effect on January 16, 1920 prohibiting the importation, transportation, manufacture, or sale of alcoholic beverages, much of the American drinking public considered it an outrage, a nightmare, and an injustice. But for the smugglers both north and south of the border it was a golden opportunity. For every legitimate saloon that closed shop, an underground drinking establishment popped up, opening a vast market for illegal booze. To meet the demand of hundreds of speakeasies across the nation, many distributors turned to Mexican cattle thieves who had become overnight alcohol smugglers. Tequila and Mescal began to flow north, on mules and on the backs of the smugglers who led them. To protect their precious cargoes on the long journey across the U.S.-Mexico border, liquor-runners often brought along a heavily armed contingent of bandits who were willing to gun down any Texas ranger, sheriff, or mounted guard who got in their way.

Dealing with alcohol smugglers was not part of the mounted guards' duty, but because they patrolled the line, they were inevitably drawn onto the battlefield. Patrolmen had not suffered a single death in the line of duty since their appointment in 1904, but that was no longer the case once Prohibition was enacted. In the early twenties, local border town newspapers were filled with gory details of shoot-outs, in which smugglers and patrolmen routinely lost their lives.

By 1923, both Congress and the Immigration Service recognized that the situation was a crisis. They were concerned not so much for the patrolmen who were injured and killed in the line of duty, but rather the illegal immigrants sneaking north while patrolmen were busy battling smugglers. Legal immigration had also gotten out of hand, and so for the first time in American history Congress decided to place a quota on immigrants entering the United States by passing the National Origins Act in 1924. The Immigration Service would regulate the influx by requiring all foreigners to obtain a visa, which the State Department could issue to whichever countries they deemed most desirable.

Congress and the Immigration Service were well aware of the certain ramifications of such a drastic change to United States immigration policies. No longer could they put off the inevitable; the country needed an official agency with the manpower to police the borders. On May 8, 1924, Congress created the U.S. Border Patrol, which was to establish its own command structure within the Immigration Service.

The days of the roaming mounted guards were over, at least as far as Washington was concerned. The country's border regions were broken down into districts, and, within time, each district would be broken down into sectors. In the early years, a sector might have one or two Border Patrol stations, each with just three or four patrolmen assigned to it. But as time went on, additional Border Patrol stations were built to plug the gaps, both along the border and miles inland. More patrolmen were hired. Stations developed their own hierarchy, led by a patrol agent in charge.

Standing at the helm of the Border Patrol was the chief patrol agent in charge. As the commander of the law enforcement arm of the Immigration Service, his job was to oversee the Border Patrol's strategy, pry funding out of the Immigration Service, and send orders downward.

With the details worked out, Congress delegated approximately one million dollars to the agency, and the Border Patrol began its search for recruits. The first place they looked was in border towns, speaking to those who'd earned reputations as fearless lawmen. As a result, the first to sign up for duty were former Texas rangers and town sheriffs. Next they made sure that word of the new opportunity reached the ranches along the border, bringing in cowboys who'd been raised in the countryside and were familiar with firearms. To fill the last positions, the Border Patrol rounded up a number of men formerly employed by the Civil Service Register of Railway Mail Clerks. Although many of them weren't accustomed to border life, they carried guns and were used to working long hours while delivering over 90 percent of the United States's non-local mail.[20]

A few months later, four hundred and fifty men, all of whom met the mandatory bachelorhood requirement, began the official training of the U.S. Border Patrol. Stationed and housed in old military barracks in El Paso, they were tutored by men such as Jeff Milton. There were no guidebooks or instruction manuals indicating how best to perform their job, and despite being the official law enforcement branch of the Immigration Service, they were really only much needed reinforcements for the Mounted Guards. Riding their own horses and packing their own firearms, recruits were simply issued a badge and expected to use their ingenuity to protect America's boundaries—all on an annual salary of $1,680.[21]

The newly trained agents were sent to various posts along the U.S.-Mexico border, with the majority of them being placed in El Paso and southern California. Many of them had no idea what they were getting themselves into when they signed up. The nature of their job demanded that they be outdoors in all conditions, which can be extreme in the desert. The summer heat can leach a man of fluids in a matter of hours, and the biting winds of winter can burn his skin the moment he steps out of shelter. For border patrolmen, there was no escaping the weather. If they wanted to get the job done, they had to be prepared to bear the worst, twenty-four hours a day, seven days a week.

If the weather wasn't enough to scare away the faint of heart, then the blood that spilled across the borders during the first several years certainly was. Their job description was to apprehend illegal immigrants, but during Prohibition, patrolmen spent a majority of their time apprehending heavily armed bandits smuggling alcohol in barrels and goatskin bladders. Hardly a week went by without a serious gun battle. This was not what many had signed up for, and a large percentage of those stationed on the southern border quickly resigned.[22]

The ones who stuck it out, however, became the legends and foundation of the Border Patrol today. Guarding the line day after day, night after night, this closely knit group of federal agents did whatever it took to get the job done, and soon became the most effective and efficient law enforcement agency in the United States. There wasn't another agency whose officers could shoot, ride, or single-handedly take down large groups of criminals with the clocklike precision of those in the Border Patrol.

This was never truer than with the agents stationed in El Paso. Just across the border lay Ciudad Juarez, a bustling Mexican city that attracted smugglers of all kinds. Every night one or more smuggling operations attempted to cross the Rio Grande with their shipments. After fighting in many revolutions, the smugglers not only knew how to use a gun, but they were also aggressive when it came to battle. Some of the more elaborate rings even managed to bribe Mexican fiscal guards, who for all practical purposes were the Mexican version of the Border Patrol. Situated on the south side of the Rio Grande, the guards would open fire on the opposite shore, trying to pick off U.S. patrolmen as smugglers made their getaways.

One patrolman who was called in to help protect the El Paso border was Fletcher Lee Rawls. He had been a scout on the Mexican border when Pancho Villa and his men slinked over the line to pillage small communities, so he knew the terrain well. Once stationed in El Paso, he spent a majority of his time on the northern shore of the Rio Grande. He worked fifteen hours a day, seven days a week. In November 1967, Rawls told the *Valley Evening Monitor* what guarding the line had been like during those dangerous years. "The smugglers had been keeping us so busy, day and night, that we were getting pretty short of sleep. But we were certain those smugglers we were watching for were just waiting for us to take a really good snooze to sneak past us. Then we located a narrow trail across the mountains that looked like it had been used pretty recently, and we figured out a scheme that would allow us to get some sleep and still not lose our smugglers."

The scheme involved tying a string across the trail that would rattle a tin plate when it was triggered. Once Rawls and his partner had the booby trap set up, they lay down out of sight to catch some shut-eye. A few hours later, sometime after midnight, Rawls was jerked up out of sleep by the sound of men cursing in Spanish. He grabbed his rifle and fired a few shots in the air to let them know he was there, but the gunfire spooked the smugglers' horses. "With the smugglers trying to hold them and hollering at us to let us know that they were dropping their firing irons and surrendering, their pack train got so tangled up that two of the pack mules skidded off down into the arroyo with their heavy loads of liquor. Anyway, they didn't put up a fight, and after we'd turned a flashlight on them we found there were three smugglers, and they had six burros loaded with sacks of tequila."

Rawls went on to have a long career as a border patrolman, but not so much can be said for his partner, Miles Scannel. Although he was regarded as one of the best scouts and marksmen in the patrol, he was killed by Mexican liquor smugglers on September 9, 1926 near Presidio, Texas.

Scannel was not the only experienced patrolman to meet an untimely death during Prohibition. In the first year alone, half a dozen agents were killed in the line of duty. Emanuel A. Wright, who joined the patrol in 1925, recognized the danger of his duty and reflected on it later in life. "This was one of the most vicious times in the history of the border," he told the *El Paso Times* on May 28, 1974. "Smugglers had pretty much of a free hand and knew how to handle horses and a gun. They knew the brush country and you were dealing with a man who was equivalent to you. We lost a lot of men—we killed a lot of smugglers."

Another patrolman lost in the line of duty was Lon Parker. A native of Tombstone, Parker had joined the Border Patrol after serving in the army during World War I. Shortly after taking the agency's examination in Los Angeles, he began roaming the deserts of southern Arizona in search of anyone illegally crossing the line. Not only was he familiar with the countryside and its dangers, he was also fearless when it came to face-to-face confrontations with bandits. His chief patrol inspector, Walter Miller, once said that Lon Parker was so fearless, in fact, that he would gladly face the devil himself.[23]

This fearlessness led to success right from the start. Only a few weeks after receiving his badge, Parker used his knowledge of the land to track a group of suspected smugglers hauling a shipment of mescal across the desert and into a canyon. With his eyes pinned on their prints, he suddenly found himself the target of heavy gunfire. Not willing to retreat, he jerked his pistol and returned six shots. When his gun was empty, he didn't bother to reload. Instead, he charged one of his assailants and tackled him to the ground. After wrestling away the bandit's shotgun, Parker turned it on the other two attackers and shot them both through the leg.

The gunfire happened to draw several other Border Patrol agents who were in the general vicinity, but when they arrived the conflict was already over. They found Lon Parker relaxing in the shade, a smile on his face. He told them, "Sorry, but you're too late for the fun."[24]

Lon Parker encountered more of what he called "fun" on April 23, 1926, but this time it ended in tragedy. For the past several months he had been closing in on a smuggler ring operating out of Nogales. When he received a tip as to their trafficking route, he and five of his fellow agents concealed themselves in the brush along the smugglers' trail, waiting to ambush them.

Shortly after nightfall, three smugglers on horseback came down the trail, driving six packhorses weighted with rum. The agents sprung out from their cover, demanding that the suspects turn themselves over. The smugglers did no such thing. They were already aware of the Border Patrol's policy concerning their agents' usage of firearms: unless agents were in grave immediate danger, which translated to being shot at, they were not permitted to draw their weapons.

The smugglers fled, abandoning their packhorses along the trail. The agents responded quickly, and after loading the contraband into their vehicle, they gave chase. Roughly three miles into the desert, however, the bandits surprised them. Finding themselves caught out in the open under fire, the Border Patrol agents pulled their guns and returned a hail of bullets, once again causing the smugglers to flee. Lon Parker gave chase, but the smugglers were mounted on faster horses and managed to elude capture. When Parker returned to the scene of the shooting, he found one of his fellow agents dead on the ground, shot through the heart.[25]

It was part of the job, but that didn't stop Parker from personally hunting down the fugitives over the course of the next several months and seeing to their arrests. The shooting only made him that much

----

more dedicated to patrolling the line, and on July 26 of that same year, he too would meet an unfortunate end.

While attending an afternoon picnic with friends and family, Parker was informed by a rancher that a rider had been seen leading a train of packhorses north. Although it was Sunday and Parker wasn't on duty, his loyalty to protecting the line kicked in and he set out on his horse just before five o'clock to see if he could cut the smuggler off. It was the last time his friends and family saw him alive. An hour and a half later, when the Wills family returned home from the picnic, they found the dead patrolman lying on top of their woodpile.

Border Patrol inspectors soon uncovered the mystery of his death. After discovering a dead smuggler and his packhorse only two miles north of the Wills ranch, they concluded that Parker had, in fact, caught up with his outlaw, but while preparing to apprehend him, he was ambushed by another smuggler hiding somewhere off the trail. After getting shot, Parker managed to kill one of the smugglers and his horse before riding two miles through the night and dying on top of the woodpile.

The years of Prohibition quickly became the Border Patrol's dark years. Day and night patrolmen put their lives on the line to stop liquor smugglers from crossing the border, but in many cases they received harsh penalties for doing so. In 1931, Phil Farrell learned just how deeply politics were embedded in America's dry years. "When I worked with Phil many years later, he looked like an old man because of what he had been through, even though he was still relatively young," said Ab Taylor, who joined the Border Patrol in 1949. "Back during Prohibition, Phil was new to the job. He was working with two officers, and they had set up a roadside checkpoint. You would do this to surprise smugglers—you would pull your car off and angle it toward the highway so you could stand by the fender and not be out there where they could run over you. And you put up a stop sign, stood out there with a gun, and made them stop. Well, this one smuggler ran through Phil's checkpoint. So they got into their vehicle, turned around, and then gave hot pursuit. Now hot pursuit in an automobile that was made in the twenties or thirties was something like you see in Keystone Cops, but they seriously went after him the best they could. The guy turned back toward them, and I'm not sure if he shot first, or they shot because he was trying to run them down. But the patrolmen did fire and killed the smuggler. And for a little while Phil was a great hero—they decided that he was the marksman who had delivered the fatal shot. But as it turns out, the smuggler was the relative of a congressman or senator, and they got on Phil. They indicted him for murder, and succeeded in doing so. He went to prison, and his two sisters spent all the money they had to keep him from being electrocuted. He was in there for five years, and then somebody in the Immigration Service, when the heat was off, got him pardoned and released. I worked with him then in the fifties; he was the radio man for us, and he sat in the office and ran the communications."

Luckily for the patrol, the mayhem that ruled the border for over a decade finally came to an end on December 5, 1933. Prohibition was repealed, making alcohol once again legal in the United States. But even though illicit booze no longer flowed over the borders, patrolmen still found themselves continuously under fire. This time, however, it wasn't from the guns of armed bandits, but rather from policymakers in Washington.

In June 1933, the Bureau of Immigration and the Bureau of Naturalization once again combined, forming the Immigration and Naturalization Service (INS). Now that the dangers along the border had been heavily reduced, policymakers who had never before been to the southern boundary thought they knew not only how patrolmen should do their job, but also who was right for the position. Many of the seasoned patrolmen such as Jeff Milton, who'd earned reputations as tough gunmen who acted first and asked questions later, lost their jobs in an attempt by bureaucrats to create a gentler atmosphere. The ones who chose to stick it out under this new regime had to take a detailed Civil Service examination, which consisted of arithmetic, writing, and knowledge of the Spanish language. If they failed to take the test, they were promptly fired.[26]

Along with the examination, new recruits also had to be approved by a group of administrators. If they passed the preliminary screening process, they then attended classes at the first Border Patrol Training Academy that opened in Camp Chigas, El Paso, in December 1934. There were thirty-four students in the first class, and, although they attended classes in both immigration and international law, they also had to fulfill the requirements that had made the first patrolmen so successful. Along with having to prove his prowess with a firearm, a recruit was not allowed to step onto the line until he demonstrated his ability to control a horse. To do this, the men were taken out to the rugged, nearly vertical incline of Mount Cristo Rey, located on the outskirts of El Paso. To pass the test, recruits had to ride up the dangerous mountain and descend without falling off their horses.[27]

Although the carnage along the border was largely a thing of the past, patrolmen still had their work cut out for them. A new wave of immigrants was now illegally crossing the border, and they came in numbers the Border Patrol had never imagined.

Chapter Two

A NEW DILEMMA

DESPITE the current situation along the U.S.-Mexico border, mounted guards patrolling the line in 1904 were not on the lookout for illegal Mexican workers. The reason for this was simple—very few Mexican workers were heading north. At the turn of the twentieth century, Chinese laborers had constituted the bulk of those creeping past the southern points of entry, and a decade later immigrants from various European nations—struck hard by the literacy requirement—had joined their ranks. The first major wave of Mexican workers that came to the United States didn't occur until 1917. This new influx, however, had more to do with recruitment practices of employers in the United States than it did with Mexico's struggling economy. During World War I, the United States experienced a massive labor shortage. With a majority of American laborers fighting overseas or working in wartime factories, agriculture and industry were in dire need. To solve the problem, they began searching for workers living south of the line.

Lobbyists representing agriculturalists and industrialists expressed their concerns in Washington, and soon the Commissioner-General of Immigration tried to help remedy the situation. With the approval of the Secretary of Labor, a special departmental order was issued, lifting many of the laws. Mexican immigrants were suddenly excluded from having to pay a head tax that had been levied in 1882, and the literacy requirement was temporarily waived. To solve the labor shortage that came about during the war, the United States opened its borders wide for Mexican immigrants desiring work.[1]

Leaving their families and homeland was not on a priority for most Mexican workers, but because many of them were slaving for wages so small they could hardly put food on the table, the notion of guaranteed employment in the United States slowly drew them north. Soon they came by the thousands, moving through El Paso and other border towns. When they returned home months or years later, the money they had earned encouraged others to make the journey. From 1917 to 1924, almost a hundred thousand Mexican workers came to the United States legally and were temporarily employed on farms and in factories.[2] And when the war was over and American workers returned home, the jobs didn't run out, even though many of the immigration laws that had been temporarily lifted once again fell into place. Those who couldn't gain entry into the United States due to the head tax or literacy law simply crossed the border illegally.

Few raised a fuss about the massive influx of Mexican workers, but when the Great Depression hit in 1929, attitudes changed overnight. With so many American citizens struggling to find jobs, there was not only a national call to put a halt to those crossing the line, but also to remove the Mexican workers already in the United States. On March 4, 1929, the Deportation Act was passed, authorizing the Immigration Service to round up Mexican workers across the United States and ship them back to Mexico. In the coming years, almost half a million Mexicans were pulled off farms and out of factories by Border Patrol agents and transported south of the line. To keep them from slipping back across the border illegally, another law was passed, one that made it a felony for any deported alien to re-enter the United States. The open border that Mexican workers had traversed so freely for over a decade was closed in the blink of an eye.

The Border Patrol was not responsible for creating the laws of immigration, they were just responsible for enforcing them. And so after Prohibition had been repealed, patrolmen went from tracking down gun-toting bandits to tracking down illegal workers. Twenty-foot-tall lookout towers were erected along various stretches of the border where patrolmen could peer through binoculars and spot anything moving on the terrain. Although thousands of Mexicans were apprehended for illegally crossing the line, the masses of Mexican workers remained home, waiting for America's employers to demand their services once again.

The Border Patrol fell out of the spotlight, and their funding was cut to the bone as America struggled through the depression. But as the decade drew to a close, the U.S. government's interest in the borders began to revitalize. With Hitler gaining power in Germany, and the threat of war looming on the horizon, securing America's borders from terrorists or foreign spies suddenly became an issue of national security. In 1940, President Franklin D. Roosevelt decided to lift the entire Immigration and Naturalization Service out of the Department of Labor and drop it into the Department of Justice. It was time to worry less about those who needed jobs, and more about those who wanted to do America harm.

THE WAR YEARS

Shortly after graduating from the University of Idaho with a degree in Business Administration, Richard Bachelor took the Border Patrol's written examination, went through an oral review, and then hopped on a bus and traveled to the Border Patrol Academy in El Paso. He received his badge in April 1941, just a few months after the attack on Pearl Harbor. "It was trying times there because when the bombs dropped on Pearl Harbor everybody was shook up," said Bachelor. "There was actually fright in the country, and a lot of it was focused on the border."

The Border Patrol was dragged into a new era. By 1942, patrolmen were no longer mounted on horses, but sitting behind the wheels of newly issued government Jeeps. Attached to the vehicles' dashboards were radios that used Morse code to communicate with headquarters. "Using those things was kind of tough, because I was stationed in South Texas and headquarters was ninety miles away," said Bachelor. "You'd begin tapping on the key, trying to raise headquarters, and you would raise New Orleans. Then New Orleans would have to relay your message to headquarters in South Texas." Many of the old school patrolmen didn't take to the strange devices, and just a few weeks after they had been installed half of them mysteriously turned up broken.

New technology, however, was not the only change the patrol had to get used to. "We had coastal patrols out along the Florida Coast, looking for submarine activity," said Bachelor, "and we camped out on Padre Island. We also interned the Japanese, German, and Italian Embassies by taking the people out and putting them in the Homestead Hotel in Virginia and the Greenbrier Hotel in West Virginia. Mainly it was for their safety—people weren't really happy with them, and they didn't want to get caught out in the open. After the arrangements were made, we took them up to New York and shipped them out. That expanded into taking seamen and other nationals that had been caught with the outbreak of war and transporting them to internment camps, some of which were located in New Mexico and North Dakota."

But Bachelor didn't toe the line for long. Like hundreds of patriotic patrolmen, he left the agency to fight overseas. By 1943, the Border Patrol was in dire need of temporary recruits. The Immigration and Naturalization Service began advertising in newspapers and magazines, trying to entice men by offering a hefty annual salary of $1,800.

For Hubart Hubbard, born and bred in Mississippi, the offer was too good to pass up. "I was raised in the depression, and it was a hard life," said Hubbard. "I was always looking for regular work, and I knew I would have to leave the county if I was to get anything decent. Well, I was working a construction deal up in Utah, and I read in the paper that the Border Patrol wanted employees. So I went to have an interview with them in Salt Lake City, and told them I would like to have a job with them. I didn't know if I would get a job or not, and so I went back to Mississippi. Two or three months later, I got a letter from them telling me to report to El Paso, and so that's what I did. They said they would hire me for the duration of the war, plus six months."

The moment Hubbard arrived in El Paso, they stuck him out on the line to look for anyone illegally crossing the border. Sometimes he would drive along the border or through the downtown streets of El Paso, and other times he would grab a blanket, spread it out on the most frequently traveled route, and then wait for an illegal crosser to stumble upon him. Although apprehensions were rare his first year on the job, the majority of those he did catch were Mexican workers hoping to cash in on the lack of laborers in the United States at the time.

Once Hubbard had illegal immigrants in custody, he brought them down to headquarters for processing. They were fingerprinted, questioned about why they were coming over the border illegally, and then sent off to county or city jails where they usually served several months for breaking one or more of the U.S. immigration laws. Little did Hubbard know, however, that the laws were about to be relaxed in a big way.

Once the war was fully underway, agriculturalists and industrialists turned to the U.S. government for help, and, in turn, the INS turned to the Mexican government. This time, however, the labor exchange was handled more formally. In the past, many of those who came north to work on farms were exploited by their employers. This had led to many grievances between Mexico and the United States, so in an attempt to solve the matter, both governments began negotiating a policy that would help protect migrant workers. The talks went well, and soon the Bracero Program was formalized by Congress, allowing Mexican immigrants to be lawfully employed in the United States. Each worker would receive a contract for a designated amount of time, and in exchange for their labor, employers would provide them with fair and lawful wages, transportation costs to and from Mexico, and health benefits.

Just as they had done during World War I, thousands of workers left their agricultural communities in Mexico and headed north to Ciudad Juarez for seasonal jobs. During the coming years, an average of eighty thousand Braceros moved through El Paso each year, where they were legally distributed to farms across the nation.[3] The new labor force proved to be beneficial to farmers nationwide, but it created a nightmare for patrolmen. They now had to distinguish between the Mexicans who were entering the country legally, and those who were entering illegally. And despite the thousands of jobs being offered to Mexican nationals by the U.S. government, there were those who still illegally crossed the border in the night. Among them were all those who did not qualify for the Bracero Program due to having criminal pasts or contagious diseases.

U.S. farmers were required to hire only Braceros, but this did not always happen. Bracero workers proved to be expensive, at least compared to the illegal immigrants they had hired in years past. Many farmers, particularly those in Texas, didn't see the point in hiring these government-sponsored workers when there was much cheaper labor to be found. Word quickly spread south of the border that they were willing to hire any Mexican who could walk, crawl, or swim across the border.

The problem was all but ignored except by those in the Border Patrol. As far as the ranchers and farmers were concerned, the more illegal workers the better, for it drove down the wages they had to pay. Local politicians, who depended upon agriculturalists, often took a similar stance, and so word of the dilemma rarely reached Congress. And the Immigration and Naturalization Service, an agency that thrived on being politically correct, just turned the other cheek. As the war progressed, it became evident that the INS was not a real advocate of apprehending illegal immigrants, and so they delegated only minimal funds to their law enforcement branch. "They tended to be more admissions-type people," said Bachelor. "They didn't think too much for the patrol."

But the Border Patrol had a job to do. "When it got to be so many coming in, we had to build up camps to hold them because it got too expensive to put them in city jails," said Hubbard. "For example, when I left Presidio, Texas, and transferred up to Calexico, California, we had a camp where we could hold up to a couple hundred people. It had a circle of prison-type wire around it, and it was pretty secure. But it just kept increasing, and as time went on we were picking up thousands of them. So we had to just turn them loose." America's great revolving door had been set in motion, and in the coming years it would only swing faster.

But despite the fact that many of the illegal immigrants apprehended along the border received little or no punishment for breaking U.S. immigration laws, patrolmen didn't abandon their mission. As the number of border jumpers increased, patrolmen realized that there was no way they could apprehend all illegal immigrants the moment they crossed the line, so they altered their tactics. Instead of guarding certain stretches of the border, which would open gaps to both the east and west, patrolmen would focus on catching the illegal crossers as they hiked across the countryside toward U.S. highways or bus stations. They did this by implementing the age-old art of tracking, known as "sign cutting" in the Border Patrol.

AB TAYLOR AND HIS MASTER TRACKERS

As far as the type of men guarding the line in the late forties, not much had changed since the early years. Those who gravitated to the agency were generally country boys who had been raised on a ranch or farm, as was the case with Ab Taylor, who began his long career with the Border Patrol in California's Imperial Valley in 1949. While growing up on a farm outside of San Angelo, Texas, he had

been taught primitive tracking skills to round up lost cattle and retrieve wounded game. When he joined the Border Patrol, he was
encouraged to use his skills to track humans.

It did not take long for Taylor to realize that tracking people was
a much more formidable task. The majority of border jumpers were
well aware that they were being sought, and they often went to great
lengths to disguise or camouflage their trails. They brushed out
their tracks with branches, crossed dirt roads while stepping on
their jackets, walked backward, tiptoed, and crab crawled. They did
whatever they could to throw the inexperienced tracker off their
paths. Because there were no books to read on the art of man tracking, Taylor gleaned what he could from the elder patrolmen and
then began the tedious process of learning through experience.

First he had to learn how to spot a set of tracks. On sand, where
prints were often perfectly preserved, it was relatively easy, but when
dealing with hard, rocky ground or terrain thick with vegetation,
the ordeal became a little more complicated. To learn how to recognize "sign" naked to the untrained eye, Taylor spent countless hours
walking along the San Diego-Mexico border, searching for any dis-
turbance in the natural terrain. Soon broken twigs, displaced peb-
bles, and vegetation that had been trampled by a passing foot leapt
out at him. Sometimes the only evidence was half of a toe print,
and, although such scant markings could easily be mistaken for the
hoof of an animal, Taylor became a master at discerning the difference.

He was quick to realize, however, that the difficult part of tracking was not locating sign, but rather determining its age. This was
imperative. With the Border Patrol grossly understaffed, an agent's
time in the field was too valuable to be wasted following tracks that
were weeks or months old. And so Taylor found himself on his
hands and knees, comparing old tracks with those that had been recently made. He discovered that natural elements changed sign on
an hour-by-hour basis. On sand, wind and rain dulled the contours
of a print; on hard ground, any upturned soil caused by a boot or
overturned rock also experienced a change in appearance due to
the drying effects of sunlight and temperature. After thousands of
hours of analysis, Taylor had the art down to a science. Being able
to pinpoint the exact time a set of tracks was made not only told
him if they were worth following, but also just how far ahead his suspects might be.

Because dating tracks could be a time-consuming business, especially for those new to the art, the Border Patrol was constantly searching for ways to make the task more efficient. One method they devised involved using brooms to brush away all footprints on frequently used trails. That way, when they encountered a set of tracks they would automatically know that they were somewhat recent, eliminating the process of dating them. This method worked so well that they began to do the same with dirt roads that ran parallel to the border. With massive brooms tied to the backs of Border Patrol Jeeps, they drove the roads at least twice a day, wiping the slate clean. The night shift spent a majority of its time working along the shoulder of the roads, and any tracks found were relayed to the morning shift so it could begin tracking down the groups.

Apprehending illegal aliens once their signs had been discovered, however, was the true feat. In many cases it was unrealistic for patrolmen to try to catch up to a group of illegal aliens, especially if they had an eight to ten hour head start. In order to reduce the number that got away, the Border Patrol created a system known as "leap frogging." This tactic required patrolmen to work in groups of at least two, and the process began once they spotted a set of tracks and determined in which general direction the group or individual was heading.

Before pursuit began, they studied the tracks, picking out any distinguishing traits such as the length of the stride or the print pattern of the shoes. Armed with this information, one of the officers began following the tracks while the other leapt ahead in a vehicle to see if he could pick up the prints a mile or two away. If the officer in the vehicle happened to locate some prints, he had to first make sure that the sign belonged to the original maker, and not a different group that had passed through the area, before the hunt was picked up at this new location. This could be verified not only by dating the tracks, but also by analyzing the print patterns of the shoes. Once a positive identification was made, the officer would start tracking the new prints, while the first officer went ahead to see if he could cut even more miles between them and their suspects. This method of sign cutting allowed agents to cover large distances in a short amount of time and to apprehend illegal immigrants who otherwise would get away.

Taylor quickly became adept at all forms of tracking, and soon his ability to follow anyone over almost any kind of terrain landed him in a position to teach others. "Tracking and sign cutting was something that men gravitated to, but not everyone liked it because the step-by-step procedure was damn tedious," said Taylor. "It's a challenge that will either turn you on, or make you so frustrated that you quit. But there were those of us in the Border Patrol that just couldn't go home and sleep at night if some son of a cabron bitch had beaten us. It's that kind of competition that makes a good tracker. They had other good trackers in other sectors of the Border Patrol, but those were men who had done it for years. We were producing some good trackers in a short period of time, men who could track over terrain where most people couldn't see anything. In a normal walking pace, they were seeing a clue or evidence with every step they took."

During the early fifties, Ab Taylor and his group of elite sign cutters tracked illegal aliens all over Southern California. In one case, they employed their skills to apprehend a group of Mexican Indians who were heading north to find work. "They were country people, and had walked all of their lives," remembered Taylor. "They stuck to the brush and took the time to wipe away their tracks. They were also traveling by the stars, and so they didn't stay on a straight path. They were a tough bunch—we didn't try to stay on them at night. We'd hop back on their trail in the morning, but they were traveling at such a clip we had a hard time overtaking them during the day. When we finally caught up with them on the third day, they had traveled more than seventy miles. We honked our horns when we found them, to celebrate and out of respect. Believe it or not, it was the first time they had rode in a vehicle."

Taylor also came across the occasional guide, leading groups of paying customers north. "They would go to jail if they got caught, and they knew it," said Taylor. "There was a pretty good penalty for smuggling then. We had room to hold them, and we had courts and judges who would put them in prison, so they didn't smuggle, get caught, and then get right back to it like they do today."

Although Taylor usually caught his man, he didn't always find his targets alive. Those who were unfamiliar with the desert often got lost, and then shortly thereafter fell victim to the harsh climate. As they neared the end of their physical rope, their steps grew erratic, they began falling over, and oftentimes they began stripping off their clothes. "We found a lot of dead Mexicans in the desert, and other times we found those who wouldn't have lived another day," said Taylor. "As we tracked people, we could tell when they didn't have much longer to live. Sometimes we would find them that day, and other times we would have to come back and find their bodies the next."

Taylor and his sign-cutting abilities became so renowned, in fact, that soon he was recruited by agencies outside the Border Patrol, including various search and rescue teams. The majority of these cases involved children, who often hid in bushes or ran from rescue teams as they approached out of fear. Finding people who didn't want to be found, however, was Taylor's bread and butter—he rounded up dozens of them every night along the border. In less than a year, Taylor had helped San Diego Search and Rescue locate over a dozen children lost in the mountains and desert. He gained national recognition for the art of tracking, which at the time was rarely utilized by rescue teams, and before long he was being called all over the country to assist on difficult cases.

The most gratifying case he worked on involved a little girl who was kidnapped. The FBI was brought in, but after exhausting all leads they called in Taylor and his crew to see if they could help. One of the Border Patrol agents found a heel print directly beneath the girl's window, but because the FBI had already trampled the scene they had no connecting evidence for six days. On the seventh day, however, one of Taylor's trackers spotted similar prints on a sign-cutting road, heading south. The entire sign-cutting crew was called to the scene to began tracking on it. "We found the son of a bitch within one mile of Mexico," recalled Taylor. "He was taking that little seven-year-old girl back with him . . . to marry her."

Another agency that benefited from the Border Patrol's tracking ability was a North Carolina sheriff's department. After learning basic tracking skills from Taylor, the sheriff went home and made thirty-eight felony arrests with his new man-tracking knowledge. A year later, he sent all of his officers to attend the course, and they too put their sign-cutting skills to use when a local felon killed a young state police officer and then retreated into the hills. The state police took control of the manhunt, but because temperatures were well into the nineties, the bloodhounds they brought out soon ran out of steam. The local officers continued to track the killer, who now had a twelve-hour lead, up into the dense, deciduous woods, with Taylor's step-by-step method.

Soon the officers came across one of the killer's accomplices. He had been shot in the leg and tied to a tree because he wanted to turn himself in. Next, they came across a camping area that the state troopers had evacuated. The area was littered with a hundred different tracks, but the officers managed to pick up the killer's trail and slowly gain ground. By nightfall they were only thirty minutes behind him, but by this time the killer had positioned himself on a ridge overlooking a freeway the state troopers had blocked off. When the killer saw that the coast was clear, he bolted across the road. A couple taking a walk in the nearby woods happened to see him, and shortly thereafter the state police closed in and took him into custody.

A few minutes after the arrest the two officers tracking him showed up on the scene. "If that couple wouldn't have seen him, he would have slipped passed the state troopers," remembered Taylor. "But the officers I had trained were right on him, and they would have caught him within the hour."

Despite the success of Ab Taylor and other experienced sign cutters, the Border Patrol was far from stopping the flow of illegal immigrants. By 1954, more than a million workers had crossed the Rio Grande illegally. They moved across the border in record numbers in Texas, New Mexico, and California's Imperial Valley. The massive pool of cheap labor continued to displace native workers and create other economic problems in border towns, but still the Border Patrol was not supplied with the equipment or manpower to stop the mass invasion.

"When I came on duty in '49, there was a clique in Washington running the Border Patrol that for all practical purposes had no interest *in* the Border Patrol," said Taylor. "They were highly thought of by Congress, because year after year they would make the budget statement and say, 'We wouldn't dream of asking for an increase in the budget this year because we know how difficult things are for Congress.' So they got accommodation after accommodation. It was a ridiculous thing, because what good does it do to keep the budget down if you're not meeting your obligations. We didn't have enough bodies, we didn't have enough cars, we didn't have enough gasoline. We didn't have enough of anything but talk. By keeping the damn budget down they made themselves glisten, look ever-so important, but nobody bothered to see that the wheels had fallen off the wagon two or three years before."

During these years when the budget was tight, the Border Patrol also lost many good men to other federal agencies. The younger, smarter men Taylor trained would usually leave the Border Patrol in two or three years and join the Secret Service or the FBI. The scant Border Patrol salary was a part of it, but then so was the budget. "Our superiors didn't have the balls to increase the budget and say that we were being overrun—that the country was being taken over," said Taylor. "During my time, I had crews sitting around in the office waiting for the shift ahead of them to come in so they could go to work, because I didn't have enough patrol cars. When they came in, the same damn car might have had its motor running for the last week or two non-stop. I never had enough equipment or men. For years, twenty two agents were the most I ever had, and I had over a thousand square miles to cover."

Help finally arrived in 1953 when President Dwight D. Eisenhower made his old war buddy, General Joseph M. Swing, commissioner of the Immigration and Naturalization Service. That same year the American G.I. Forum and the Texas State Federation of Labor conducted a study entitled *What Price Wetbacks?* to get the federal government to pay more attention to the negative impact of illegal immigrants working in the United States. The study concluded that illegal aliens in the United States not only displaced American workers, but also posed a serious threat to national security.[4]

General Swing took this study to heart and set out to build the U.S. Border Patrol. One of the first things he did was try to improve their appearance by making everything uniform. "He painted everything green," said Taylor. "The buildings, the god dang cars, the uniforms. Everything. Before that, you'd go to a Border Patrol station and they would have whatever color car came off the assembly line. It would be the same quality of vehicle, but there would be black ones, red ones, whatever colors they made during those days. Then Old Swing painted everything green." Not long after this, patrolmen across the nation subsequently became known as "the Men in Green."

But changing the Border Patrol's color wasn't the only thing Swing managed to achieve; he also introduced the agency to the wonderful world of military surplus. Within a matter of months, the Border Patrol had old C47 and C46 warplanes buzzing through the air, hauling aliens to Brownsville, Texas, for deportation. On the ground, he had patrolmen load all the illegal aliens they caught onto trains headed for the interior of Mexico. "That didn't work very well," said Taylor, "because every time the train stopped they would bribe the

Mexican guards and bail out. The objective was to get them back close to their homes, hoping they would stay." To keep them from escaping, Swing changed his tactics—instead of loading them onto trains, he began loading them onto the C47s and flying them home.

During his first year at the helm of the INS, Swing used every connection he had in government to strengthen the Border Patrol. "He got us some equipment, money, and some people," said Taylor. "And he got us some firm dealing with the law. He dispensed with a lot of the damn mockery that had been going on for the last twenty-five years in the Border Patrol. He really, seriously, undertook to enforce the law, and he did a damn good job of it."

One way General Swing enforced the law was by initiating Operation Wetback, a repatriation project to remove illegal Mexican immigrants from the southwest, which began in July 1954. For the project, the United States Border Patrol aided municipal, county, state, and federal authorities in a search and seizure of all illegal immigrants.[5] "He took all of us away from the border and made us up into teams. I was on a twenty-man team," remembered Taylor. "We went from Bakersfield right down to the L.A. area, and they had already started from the L.A. border down into Mexico. We had enough publicity in the paper, both good and bad, that the smart Mexicans got up and went home. The rest of them we tracked down on farms and ranches, rounding up hundreds and shipping them back to Mexico any way and every way we could."

The same sweep was conducted in other border towns such as El Paso, where thousands of illegal aliens were rounded up every day and brought back to Mexico. Although trucks and buses were often used, in the later part of the operation, General Swing began transporting the illegal workers on ships, taking them farther into the Mexican interior. "That's one of the great things he did," remembered Taylor. "He hauled them down to Brownsville and then put them on boats—Mexican boats. Any Mexican who made that trip, it would be a long time before he jumped again."

During this roundup, U.S. border communities that depended on the cheap labor made the patrolman's job even more difficult by barring gates and ordering their illegal workers to run and hide when patrolmen came around. Local media also began portraying patrolmen as savages, claiming that they were trying to devastate local farming practices by eliminating their inexpensive labor force. "During that time," admitted Taylor, "I had death threats and every-

----

thing else. We had a saying at the Border Patrol, 'You are damned if you do, and you're dammed if you don't.' We had a pretty tough hide, though, and so we learned to live with that."

Despite the negative repercussions, General Swing considered the operation a success, as did many border patrolmen. In just a few months, the Immigration and Naturalization Service reported that almost 1,300,000 Mexicans who were working and living in the United States illegally had been deported. "It cut illegal immigration down to a manageable level," said Taylor. "We got them all out and not as many were trying to come back in. And we had enough people down there that we were catching 90 to 95 percent of those entering. As long as we had the equipment and the manpower, we could keep that border pretty secure."

When the operation came to an end in the fall of 1954, General Swing changed the Border Patrol's plan of operation to ensure that the process didn't start all over again. He rounded up all the agents working at stations in the interior and placed them along the immediate border. "'Hold them at the line,' was his philosophy," said Taylor. "He didn't see it, but his successor saw the folly of that situation. All of those interior stations were there for a reason—they were backing up the line. It's like trying to play football without any linebackers. With everyone on the line, you could do a pretty good job down there, but when they found a hole they came in by the army, and then you had no way of going to get them because you had to stay on the damn line."

But those armies didn't find their way to the United States for another decade. General Swing's operation managed to considerably reduce the amount of illegal immigrants crossing the border, and, as a result, the majority of Mexican workers coming north were doing so legally through the Bracero Program, which had been extended since World War II to appease agriculture's addiction to cheap labor. For the first time in history, patrolmen had their guard pretty much under control, but by no means did their daily duties prove to be dull.

OLE MISS

On a summer afternoon in 1962, Ab Taylor and the rest of his sign-cutting crew were called into headquarters. Their patrol agent in charge had something important to tell them—the first black student was being integrated into the University of Mississippi, and President Kennedy had personally asked the Border Patrol to help escort him onto campus for registration. With retaliation being expected, they needed all the volunteers they could get.

Like most Americans, Taylor had been hearing about James Meredith in the news, and he was willing to do whatever he could to help the young man receive an education. He told the patrol agent in charge to sign him up, and an hour later he loaded onto one of Swing's old C47s with twenty other agents and was flown to a military airbase outside of Memphis, Tennessee. Once the plane touched down, Taylor was ushered into a hangar where three hundred other border patrolmen were receiving basic instruction on how to control a crowd and wield a nightstick. Thirty minutes later, they were all deputized as U.S. Marshals.

It was Sunday afternoon, a day before Meredith's registration, and those in charge of the operation had a serious dilemma on their hands—how to get three hundred federal agents onto the campus in the next few hours. Mississippi State Troopers, hundreds of students, and even the governor of Mississippi had taken positions around the perimeter of the school, fully prepared to stop either Meredith or Federal agents from impeding their segregated way of life. "They kept us under wraps while they dillydallied back and forth over how they would let us in," said Taylor. "One of the ideas that had come up was to have us dress in civilian clothes without our guns and force our way onto campus. That was an absolutely lunatic proposition. We're facing Mississippi State Troopers who are well armed—and had Doberman pinschers—in their own state, and we're going to tell them to get out of the way? Our bosses said no way, our men won't go—they weren't going to sacrifice us. So they negotiated some more, and they decided that we could go in with our guns, but they wouldn't be loaded. Well, bullshit. Try pointing an empty gun at a Mississippi trooper and you're going to get killed. So then they finally decided that we would go aboard our own way—we had some damn good bosses back then, fighting for us every step of the way. We were to drive onto campus, but that didn't work out and so they flew us in again on the old border patrol plane to an airstrip somewhere close to the university. Fortunately for us, the rednecks were all at a football game in some other town, so we didn't have a whole lot of resistance." But they still had over fifteen hours to go.

Taylor and his twenty-four-man crew, all dressed in civilian clothes, used the relatively calm atmosphere to prepare themselves. Responsible for protecting the last building on campus, they parked four military trucks in front of them to serve as a blockade. It wasn't until an hour later that Taylor realized what they were up against—the crowd started coming back from the ball game in the late afternoon, cursing and throwing bottles. A few fights broke out, and someone lit a garbage can on fire. By five o'clock in the afternoon the street in front of the university had filled with an angry mob. "Guys were coming up from Texas, Alabama, Georgia, all those places," said Taylor. "There were thousands of them rioting, and they would work themselves up into a frenzy. It's the [most] awful sound you've ever heard. I'd been a lot of places during World War II, but that sound of humans hysterically screaming, yelling, and working up into a frenzy gets inside your skull. And then here they come running, and they sound like a herd of cattle coming at you."

Patrolmen held their ground. "The only thing we had was tear gas, and we soon ran out of that. They had a construction project on campus, and they were throwing bricks and knocking us down right and left. And the worst part about it was they were smart. They would take those bricks and break them in half, and then boy they could really zing you with those. A full brick is pretty unwieldy, and so you see it coming and have a chance to dodge it a little. But those half-bricks are something else. And my crew didn't even have gas masks or helmets, because the Kennedys didn't want us to look like the military. Back in the hangar they had been painting all these olive green military helmets white, but the ones for my crew hadn't been finished before we left. But we were soon taken care of, because every time someone would get knocked down or couldn't fight we'd take his helmet and gas mask. I remember helping carry this guy away from the riot—he was so thankful—and then I start stripping off his gasmask and helmet. He looked at me like, 'What the hell are you doing?' He wasn't going back out, but I knew that I was. For the first forty-five minutes to an hour we fought with wet handkerchiefs over our noses because the tear gas we were putting out was so bad."

An hour after the riots had begun, the street in front of the school looked like a war zone. Cars had been overturned and set on fire. And still they kept coming. As more and more patrolmen were injured, it became critical to get them to a hospital, but the mob had blocked all escape routes. "I don't know who thought of this, but they were smart," said Taylor. "They brought a hearse in from the back entry, and the crowd didn't even mess or fool with them, and so they hauled out the wounded that way. Somebody was doing some thinking—I was too busy fighting."

And that fight was growing more dangerous with every passing hour. Taylor was forced to rush out into the mob when somebody hotwired a bulldozer and aimed it directly at the military vehicles they had set up for a blockade. But when he knocked the guy out, someone else hopped in. Eventually one patrolman managed to drive it into the safety of their compound, but by then the mob had gotten ahold of a fire truck. "They were running it right at us. We knocked them out of that a couple of times and broke all of the sparkplugs with our nightsticks, but somehow they got the thing jury-rigged and started driving it at us a third time. And then they started getting the fire hoses down toward us. That would have wiped us out, because they had it coming from a fireplug up in the grove. When it got to the point that they only needed one more link to wipe us out, we went in a herd and drove them back with tear gas and our nightsticks. The marshals had told us not to raise our night-sticks above our heads—they said it infuriated the crowd and looked bad. Well, five minutes after we got out there it looked like the wood-choppers ball—we were whacking and chopping, doing whatever we could. In the midst of all that, we were able to run them back and get them away from the hose. I tried to cut it with a pocketknife when it was full charged, but there is no way in hell you can cut it with a pocketknife. We were told not to discharge our weapons, not to even consider it, but something had to be done, and so I just walked over and emptied my gun into the hose. Everyone that followed me emptied their gun, and so it made like a giant sprinkler—we had water going about fifty feet in the air, turning everything into a fog, which actually helped us out a lot."

With the crowd confused by the mist, one of the Border Patrol agents dressed in civilian clothes sneaked away from the madness and came back with a rental truck full of tear gas, but by then the mob had resorted to arming themselves with more than just bricks. "Some shooting started," said Taylor. "I had a guy shoot maybe a foot or two above my head. I was leaning up against this big pillar, like the kind they have in Rome, worn out and sick from the damn tear gas. My guys were yelling at me to get out of there, but when the bullet hit above my head it didn't hardly register; it didn't get any more adrenaline out of me, because my adrenaline had flowed out by then. So I just got up and walked into the building—it wasn't courage, but just total exhaustion. As it turned out, the shooter was in the second story of one of the buildings to the left of me. They finally took him down out of there; he had a couple rifles and a whole lot of shells. I found out later who he was, some vice president of a major company. So it wasn't all just idiots and crazy kids—there were some strong feelings in the south.

"We literally fought for our lives until four o'clock in the morning, and then the Kennedys finally got smart and sent the paratroopers in. They came in about four o'clock in the morning, and they came in strong. They had their bayonets locked and their guns loaded. They meant business, while we were in there trying to save the political face of the dipshits in Washington. We really had our lives on the line—we didn't know it at the time, we were just in the fight."

As the paratroopers pushed the crowd back, Taylor and his men got their first break in over thirty-six hours. The tear gas had taken its toll on all of them, and as Taylor leaned into the bushes to vomit, a photographer snapped a picture that would turn up in the October 12, 1962 issue of *Life* magazine.

While Meredith joined his fellow students later that day in the university's cafeteria, Taylor and his men were heading back to San Diego, sleeping soundly on the C47. "It was a thing that we did that we were proud of, even though it made us a lot of enemies," said Taylor. "What it illustrates is when they wanted some good men in good shape with fighting ability and courage, they tapped the Border Patrol. You know, Bobby Kennedy called my boss a few days after that and asked how many patrolmen had resigned. My boss said, 'Not a one.' Kennedy couldn't believe it, because quite a few of the U.S. Marshals had."

Taylor had his hands full when he stepped back onto the line the following morning in San Diego. It was the early sixties, and Mexico was catching up with the times. A large portion of their labor force was now skilled in a number of trades. Many of them hoped to work legally in the United States under the Bracero Program, but it wasn't meant to be. Feeling that the Braceros displaced native workers, Mexican-American citizens' groups began to influence Washington; in 1964, the Kennedy Administration put an end to the Bracero Program.

With the lawful mechanism to find jobs in the United States shut down, many Mexican immigrants decided to jump the line and fend for themselves. "The increase came about when the ones who hadn't been caught went back to Mexico in a car, showing how prosperous they were," said Taylor. "Every one of them was an ambassador to ten or twenty or thirty more of a working age. Mexico's unemployment never went below forty or fifty percent—but you couldn't call it real employment. If a Mexican had a job one or two days a week, he was employed according to government statistics, but he wasn't necessarily making enough to feed his family. Their birthrate never decreased. So they were just manufacturing more people to feed that had no place to work except the United States."

A NEW WAVE

In the fifties, California opened up with farming, business, and industry. Along with booming opportunities, the Golden State also paid its workers better wages by and large, so while the illegal crossings in El Paso virtually stopped, Arizona, New Mexico, and California found their borders under siege.

The government had invested little money into solving the problem of illegal immigration, so along the majority of the southwest border, the only thing separating Mexico from the United States were intermittent stretches of barbed wire fencing, which was erected by U.S. farmers in an attempt to keep their cattle from being infected by the hoof and mouth disease common in Mexican livestock. With little standing in the way, the borders in the western states became a virtual freeway for migrant workers.

Joel Hardin, who joined the Border Patrol in 1965, was among the first wave of recruits hired to guard the California border against this new invasion. Although he wasn't scheduled to graduate from the Border Patrol Academy until September, by August 1, the influx of aliens had risen to the point that Southern California was being overrun. In dire need of agents, supervisors from the San Diego sector urged the chief of the academy to cut the cadets' training short so they could be brought on duty. Three weeks before he was to graduate, Hardin was sent to California to reinforce the line. "I entered the Border Patrol during the last months of the Bracero Program," Hardin remembered. "One of the provisions in the terminating of the agreement was that all persons here on contract had to be back in their own country. By the middle of July, the normal wages that were paid to these individuals were running out. In the last ten years of the program, an entire generation had become accustomed to coming to the U.S. on contract, and within two weeks people were going hungry down there. But because there were no more contracts, they were coming back into the states illegally."

Once on the line, Hardin realized just how much pressure the Border Patrol was under. In the years following Operation Wetback, the agency boasted that it caught every illegal alien that came across the border. Now that the numbers were increasing, they were faced with upholding the reputation they had already established. Although there was little structure as to how Hardin spent his day, the more aliens he caught, the more he was respected—and the more he was respected, the more responsibility he was given. On average, he worked twelve to fifteen hours a day, and like all trainees he put in a six-day workweek.

As it had been in the forties, sign cutting was the primary tool for apprehending illegal immigrants, and Hardin became adept at it. To learn this ancient art, he joined Ab Taylor's group of sign cutters. "They were a very small elite group that pretty much did their own thing," said Hardin. "They pretty much came and went, and nobody told them what to do. I wanted to be a part of that, and I managed to get assigned as a trainee. This meant that they were willing to take me for a two-week period of time, and in that two weeks, if they believed I had potential to be a tracker, then I could stay on the unit until I learned something. It was an old cowboy thing—if you could keep your mouth shut, didn't ask too many questions, always managed to stay one step ahead, cleaned the rattlesnakes they wanted to eat, and washed their jeeps, you got to learn from them. Not too many Border Patrol agents made the grade to join the sign cutters. But there was great pressure on Ab Taylor and the others to train more trackers because more and more immigrants were slipping past the line. The border had a barrel full of fish, and we could hardly go wrong."

To make the most of their limited manpower, the San Diego sector of the Border Patrol created an intelligence unit to combat illegal alien smuggling. "As the aliens found a way to be successful," said Taylor, "the Border Patrol had to find a way to plug it. That was what Special Detail did. If you were part of the detail, you would

During winter months in the 1920s, Border Patrolmen guarded the most frequently traveled routes along the U.S.–Canada border by snowshoe.

In search of illegal activity, two Mounted Patrolmen roam the U.S.–Canada border in the 1920s.

Border Patrolmen searching a random vehicle for illicit alcohol during the early years of Prohibition.

Appointed "Mounted Chinese Inspector" for the Immigration service in 1904, Jefferson Milton traveled the U.S.–Mexico border from Texas to California on horseback, searching for the trails smugglers used to bring Chinese immigrants to meeting points, known as Chinese Farms, located on U.S. soil. He is regarded as the first Border Patrolman.

A 1925 flow of traffic through San Ysidro, the port of entry that links San Diego and its Mexican sister city, Tijuana.

The agents of El Paso in the 1930s, responsible for guarding the most violent stretch of land during the bloodiest years in Border Patrol history.

During the 1930s, not all immigrants could be apprehended along the immediate border. Patrolmen frequently checked boxcars farther into the interior.

Border Patrolmen laying an ambush for smugglers along the U.S.–Mexico border in the 1940s.

spend your time over in Mexico. Most of the agents dressed up in nice suits and clothes, and hovered around in the bars of Mexico, getting what information they could."

Through this intelligence unit, Hardin learned which trails illegal immigrants were planning to use in upcoming months and then focused his energy on the hot spots. But as the months went on, there were more hot spots than San Diego–based agents could adequately cover. While in the past it had been primarily agricultural workers jumping the line, now entire families were heading north, looking to build a new life in the United States. Among them were not just Mexicans living in neighboring Tijuana, tempted by the fruits of San Diego, but also entire families from as far south as Panama.

A good portion of them were born and bred in the city and had no idea how to maneuver over the rugged border terrain. Once they reached the international border, they needed someone who could lead them across the rattlesnake-infested, cactus-spotted terrain and into San Diego.

This was where human smugglers came into play. Patrolmen called them *coyotes,* because they stealthily pushed their groups over the mountains and through the ravines under the cover of night. A single guide could make multiple runs a week, bringing hundreds of aliens into the United States every month. And with thousands of Latin Americans arriving on the streets of Tijuana every night, more and more Mexican boys were being trained to lead groups of country-naive immigrants north.

Hardin was well aware of these "schools," and many nights he would make reconnaissance trips to the border. After snaking over a series of mountains and working his way down through the canyons, he'd hide in the brush just north of the border and observe what went on in Mexico. More than once he saw groups of seventeen- to nineteen-year-old boys being taught by their elders how to walk, where to walk, and how to cross trails and roads without being seen. An army of coyotes was being bred to lead an even greater army of workers north, and Hardin knew that shortly the border was going to be overrun.

During these trying times, the Border Patrol got some help from the Navy SEALs who were preparing for Vietnam. "They used to come and work with us in the evenings because it was on-the-job training," said Hardin. "They got fantastic training out there catch-

ing aliens at night. One of the trade-offs was that they brought
equipment that they were testing. Once this exchange became unofficially acknowledged, the manufacturers of military equipment
began bringing all their equipment to the Border Patrol for testing.
We got night-vision scopes, infrared scopes, and sensor equipment.
They would give it to us and say, 'Try this out and tell me how it
works.' We would tell them what the problems were, they would
take it back, refine it, and then give it back to us. We were testing
state-of-the-art security and sensor equipment, because the border
was a ready-made testing ground."

Despite the added help, Hardin's prediction came true by 1973.
On any given night, an agent could apprehend fifty or more illegal
immigrants at the Chula Vista bus terminal just north of the border.
The detention centers were overcrowded, and there were not
enough buses to transport them all back south. "Near our station in
San Diego they had one of the old barracks where they held
Japanese prisoners during World War II," said Taylor. "It had coiled
prison wire around the top of it, and there were barracks inside with
iron bunks. When we became overrun with aliens, we began keeping
some of the aliens in there instead of hauling them all to jail. It was
a tough job trying to keep them sorted out, because we needed to
keep the aliens in one section and the smugglers in another. We had
to keep track of who was going to testify against whom."

But when the old military barracks filled up, patrolmen had
nowhere to turn. "Every day our superiors would say, 'you can get
fifty today, or seventy-five today,' but usually we'd catch them in less
than an hour," said Hardin. "Some days we were told we could catch
sixty-five, but we would catch eighty-five, and then there was
nowhere to put them. Pretty soon they said 'don't catch them, we
can't handle them.' " This was only the beginning of the great revolving door. Because Congress was unwilling to delegate the funds
to build additional detention centers, eventually INS implemented
a system known as Voluntary Departure. This allowed non-criminal
illegal aliens who had been apprehended by the Border Patrol to
waive their rights to a hearing and immediately get sent back across
the line. It was the perfect system for them, because only a few
hours later they could once again be hiking north.

Trying to apprehend the masses of illegal workers, however, wasn't
the patrol's only job—in many instances, patrolmen were now protecting immigrants along their journey. Although coyote guides

were experienced outdoorsmen, they did not promise to keep their paying customers out of harm's way while crossing the border. Many aliens were under the false assumption that once they reached the U.S. side of the border the only threat they had to worry about was getting deported. Naively, they carried their life savings in their socks and the valuables they could not part with on their backs.

Word of their ignorance spread quickly, and soon hordes of Mexican bandits swarmed to the no-man's-land that separated Tijuana's teeming residential sprawl from the desolate canyons of southern San Diego. Some were heroin junkies, and others were ten-year-old boys from youth gangs. Just like in the old west they formed gangs, laying ambushes alongside frequently traveled trails leading to San Diego. When along came a group of unsuspecting immigrants, they sprang from cover, their faces covered by handkerchiefs or ski masks. Brandishing knives and rusted guns, they used violence to intimidate the group. Once they had their submissive victims on their hands and knees, they stripped them of all valuables. Then the abuse began— torture, murder for pleasure. With no one around to stop them, sometimes they controlled a group for eight hours or more, having their way with the women and forcing the men and children to watch.

The majority of these crimes did not happen on the Mexican side of the border; they occurred on U.S. soil. Each group of bandits formed their territories, and some were operating as far as twelve miles north of the U.S.-Mexico border. "That was the beginning of a bad era," Hardin remembered. "Every night along the border there were killings and rapings and stabbings of aliens by other aliens. Gunfights every night between Border Patrol agents and smugglers. High-speed chases. Tracking as I had known it was fading rapidly." Hardin left the southern border in 1973 to get away from the madness, but in the coming years things only got worse.

Although the Border Patrol toiled to find a way to end border violence, they were undermanned and couldn't possibly patrol the thousands of desolate square miles of southern San Diego. Bandits were well aware of this fact, as were many corrupt Mexican police officers. After driving up to the border in their patrol cars, they'd slip through one of the many holes in the fence and go hunting for a group of aliens. The money they earned through strong-armed robbery more than made up for the poor wages they received as officers of the law.

There was no way to tell just how bad things had gotten on the southern edge of San Diego, one of the richest cities in the world, because aliens feared U.S. officials and seldom reported the crimes committed upon them. If a woman was raped, it often went untold; if people were killed, their bodies were most likely dragged back to Mexico by the surviving family members.

Border violence continued to escalate during the early seventies, but the majority of the American public was not concerned. The war in Vietnam was coming to a close, and there were seemingly larger and more important issues to deal with. But that changed in the fall of 1976 when San Diego reporters began covering more stories about border violence. One day the *Union Tribune* would run an article on an alien boy who had been murdered while in his mother's arms. That evening, the local television news would air a tragic story of an alien woman who had been gang-raped. And then the next morning there would be yet another article written about a group of aliens that had been robbed and slaughtered in the night. The press never got tired of telling these heartbreaking tales.

The president of Mexico, Luis Echeverria Alvarez, petitioned the U.S. government to address the issue of border violence in the summer of 1976.

The Border Patrol was under tremendous pressure—not only from American citizens concerned about what they were learning in the news, but also from people in Washington who wanted to maintain a good relationship with Mexico, which was now producing vast quantities of oil. The Border Patrol was expected to come up with a solution, despite severe budget restraints.

This was not an easy task. If agents approached suspects in their vehicles, the bandits would slip back over the border. And if an agent on foot wandered too close to the border fence, which in many places was nothing more than posts stripped of wire, criminals on the other side routinely shot at him. And so they had to sit back and watch the bandits move back and forth after a night of ruthless activity. Many agents began to loathe the bandits. Some agents even began to dream of ways to get revenge.

By mid-summer of 1976, the San Diego-Mexico border had become like an old west town without a marshal. Something had to be done.

Chapter Three
THE BANDIT TEAM

DICK SNIDER, a lieutenant in the San Diego Police Department and a former U.S. Border Patrol agent, thought he had a way to seriously cut down on the violent crimes occurring on the San Diego-Mexico border. His idea was to create a special task force comprised of both police officers and Border Patrol agents. Together they would roam the canyons and ravines at night, acting as a visible deterrent for bandits who were raping, robbing, and murdering illegal immigrants in the canyons of southern San Diego. The police officers would be responsible for arresting criminals, filing charges, and leading the prosecution. The Border Patrol agents would be responsible for navigating through the backcountry and enforcing immigration laws. Nothing like this had ever been done, and although Snider's superiors realized that sending San Diego's Finest out into a lawless realm of cutthroats without backup could go terribly wrong, they agreed to the experiment out of desperation.

In the summer of 1976, the Border Alien Robbery Force, which would come to be known as the Bandit Team, was well on its way to getting off the ground. Because of the dangerous nature of the job—and the fact that the stretch of land they would be patrolling could best be described as a war zone—officials wanted agents who had previous combat experience.

David Krohn, who had been a U.S. Border Patrol agent for four years, was a perfect candidate. Before joining the Patrol, he served his country for eight years as a marine, spent four years fighting in the jungles of Vietnam, and worked as a police officer on the east coast. "It was an application process," said Krohn. "They chose us on the basis of past experience. First off, you had to want to be a part of the team. It was the most dangerous, most risky detail on the Border Patrol. I was picked because I had former military experience and prior combat experience." But even though Krohn had served in the armed forces during Vietnam, he would shortly learn that the battle he was entering on the desolate border was an entirely different kind of war.

"I knew it was going to be dangerous, but it was a way to finally be able to do something," explained Krohn. "As a Border Patrol agent, you sit back and watch the bandits go back and forth across the border. Because we patrolled in marked vehicles, we couldn't sneak up on them—we couldn't catch them in action. I knew the kind of things that were going on out there. I knew exactly where the bad guys were, and I knew how they operated. But the only time there was any justice along the border was if a group of aliens was large enough, and brave enough, to take action on the bandits—and that seldom happened. It might sound kind of crude, but a part of the reason I wanted on the team was for revenge. Many times I had come across aliens who had been robbed and women who had been raped. I wanted to be able to do something."

Training the task force proved difficult. Because nothing like this had ever been done, they didn't know what to expect. And because they didn't know what to expect, it was hard to prepare the agents. But one thing was certain—working the canyons at night was going to be dangerous. With the Bandit Team patrolling the border's darkest and most inaccessible regions without backup, confrontations were guaranteed to occur up close and personal.

The team was given additional firearms training at Camp Matthews, located on the outskirts of San Diego. It was decided that each member should carry at least two firearms, and most agents went with a semi-automatic pistol and a revolver. In addition, one team member would also carry a sawed-off shotgun, something that would come in handy for close-quarter battle.

"We brought in a hand-to-hand combat expert to teach us takedowns and different techniques," said Krohn. Each member learned how to sweep the feet out from under a suspect, apply submission holds, and disarm a suspect without using excessive force. Although the training focused little on punching and kicking, these natural defenses would soon be necessary in the canyons.

As the training progressed, it became evident that the police officers on the team knew very little about patrolling in the backcountry. "Working along the border was quite different from working downtown," explained Krohn. "The police officers were used to having their radios up and calling in. They're used to high visibility. The Bandit Team detail was very low visibility." Many of the police officers also couldn't tell the difference between a cactus and sagebrush. They didn't know how to navigate outdoors, and if they somehow got separated from the group they wouldn't have the slightest clue how to find safety.

The Border Patrol agents, on the other hand, understood what they were up against. They had spent 90 percent of their time alone in the backcountry, with very little radio communication. On a nightly basis, they single-handedly approached vehicles loaded with a dozen or more illegal aliens. They chased suspects for miles in the darkness. They knew how to walk over rocky terrain, how to pull cactus needles out of their skin, and where the many dangerous critters of the canyon lurked.

So it was the Border Patrol agents who taught the police officers the tricks of the trade and the lay of the land. This, however, went far beyond instructing them how to track, navigate, and apprehend large groups of suspects. Although the objective of the Bandit Team was to be a highly visible deterrent, many of the Border Patrol agents knew that in order to catch the bandits, they would have to lay ambushes, hide in the darkness, and even go so far as to pose as illegal aliens, which would mean actually communicating with the bad guys. To pull that off effectively, the cops needed to learn the necessary Spanish slang. They also had to learn how to act like illegal immigrants, who generally crouched submissively when threatened to avoid confrontation. But even with this new knowledge, none of the cops, or the Border Patrol agents for that matter, were prepared for what they encountered on the border after dark.

UNDERCOVER

When the Bandit Team set out into the canyons on an October evening in 1976 to rid the border of violence, they looked like a unit from the Navy SEALs. Weighted down with binoculars, flashlights, and an arsenal of weapons, the Bandit Team was highly visible—the bandits could not only see them coming from a mile away, but they could also hear them.

On their first night, they encountered nothing out of the ordinary, at least for the Border Patrol agents. Trudging down muddy trails, over mountains, and across ravines, they heard the waves of illegal aliens making their way north, led by coyote guides. In the darkness it was nearly impossible to tell who was who. Who were guides and who were aliens? Who were kids and who were bandits? Who posed a threat and who didn't?

"The politically correct job of the bandit detail was to be a high-visibility deterrent," said Krohn. "But that was very hard to do in the dark in uniform without flashing your lights around. You go out there flashing your lights around in uniform, the chances are you're going to get shot."

The police officers quickly realized what the Border Patrol agents already knew—that being a highly visible deterrent wasn't going to cut it out here, not if they wanted to remain alive and make arrests. So the Bandit Team went from wearing boots and goggles and a uniform to wearing the rattiest clothes they could find. "We unofficially dressed down in an undercover capacity in order to make arrests," said Krohn. The team's new plan of attack was to blend in with the migration of aliens trekking north.

When someone approached the team, they would play the part of illegal aliens. When asked where they were going, they would say they were heading north, or searching for a guide, or that they were lost. And if that someone went on their way, the agents would wait for another group to come along. But if that someone asked for their money, or their shoes, or pointed a gun at their faces, they would take them down hard and fast and make arrests. Their new plan of attack was to get up close and personal—to put themselves in a position where they would get threatened, robbed, or beaten. Their new plan of attack was to use themselves as bait.

Five nights a week, Krohn and his fellow team members arrived at the station in Chula Vista just before dark. After greeting their fellow agents, they all sat down and disassembled their firearms. Hiking through bushes and over mountains meant that their weapons filled with grit, sand, and mud. A properly functioning gun could mean life or death in the field, so every night before heading out, they tore them apart, cleaned them, lubricated them, and then reassembled them. They had all become experts at this process, but before concealing their weapons under their worn flannel shirts, or securing them in the back of their ragged jeans, they would first be passed around the table for inspection. Knowing their partners were carrying functioning weapons cut down the stress considerably.

Then they would head out—Krohn, two fellow Border Patrol agents, and three police officers. Many nights there was nothing. They could go an entire shift without encountering a single criminal, which for Krohn was sometimes worse than having to confront five or six armed bandits. When the border was eerily quiet and still, shadows transformed into robbers holding guns. The wind became voices whispering in the dark. A rabbit scurrying in the distance could cause a man to pull his revolver, or his semi-automatic pistol—or sometimes both. With every night that passed without incident, the inescapable feeling that something terrible lurked just ahead grew more intense. "While we were waiting for something to happen," said Krohn, "I'd have this nervous apprehension, just as I did in the jungles. Out there it was different, though. In Vietnam there was anonymity to it, but along the border I knew just who and what we were up against. It wasn't a matter of *if* a gun-toting bandit would creep up on us with a knife or gun, but rather a matter of *when.*"

Of course there were the nights where the buildup did have release, and a lot of it. In the winter of 1977, Krohn and his fellow bandit hunters were patrolling a canyon on the border when three men approached them, one of whom carried a brown paper sack. Playing the part of illegal immigrants, or *pollos,* all team members crouched.

This was normal in the canyons: They could be coyote guides searching for paying customers to take north; they could be a lost group of *pollos,* stopping to ask for directions; they could be a group of friendly aliens wanting to share a cigarette on their journey north; or they could be a group of criminals, looking for victims.

Because he was not Mexican-American, Krohn squatted in back, out of sight. His ears and eyes, however, were focused directly upon the advancing men, waiting to hear a threat or see a weapon so arrests could be made. With his hand on his revolver, he could feel the apprehension growing in the pit of his stomach, eager for release.

"Where are you going?" asked one of the strange men.

"Waiting for our guide," said one of the Spanish-speaking agents.

"We could take you north."

The agent declined, and then a moment later the three strange men turned and headed north, up a winding trail that led to the Promised Land. "As they started to walk away," said Krohn, "I saw a paper bag in one of the alien's hands and knew he was packing."

Because no threat had been made, the men were allowed to go on their way. The Bandit Team was not in the canyons at this time of night to arrest illegal aliens—they were there to protect them. Normally what they would do after such an uneventful encounter was remain seated and wait for another group of men to approach them. But not this night. Krohn couldn't get that paper bag out of his mind. He was sure a gun was inside. Perhaps the bandits hadn't pulled it because they suspected something was amiss. Word traveled through the canyons quickly, and all bandits were on the lookout for hard-hitting American agents dressed in ragged clothes. Perhaps the bandits were looking for an easier group to rob.

While he was standing amidst the cactus with his fellow team members, listening to the strange men's footfalls growing ever more distant, another thought occurred to Krohn. Perhaps they hadn't pulled the gun because there were no women among them. Perhaps these bandits were not on the prowl to earn their next fix of heroin, but rather to satisfy an entirely different desire.

"I think we should follow them," Krohn said to the other five members of the team. "I think that one with the bag had a gun."

One of them had a hunch, and nothing more was needed. Risking their lives out there together for months and months had made them brothers. They trusted one another.

They headed down the path after their suspects and spotted them a hundred yards up ahead, standing by the side of the trail. The bandit who had been carrying the paper sack was now pointing a gun at a group of aliens cowering before them. The other two were slapping and kicking their victims, trying to single out a woman hiding in the back of the group.

The team continued down the trail with their guns drawn, but the bandits were so consumed with their current project—whether it was raping the woman they had singled out, Krohn will never know—that they didn't hear the team creeping up on them. "We came in behind them," remembered Krohn, "and they had no idea. We took them down hard."

But not all their arrests went so smoothly. Later that year, Krohn and the other members of the Bandit Team were conducting their search along the border, seeing if they could entice criminals with their alien disguises. For the first several hours there was nothing out of the ordinary, just groups of aliens being led by coyote guides. Slowly they worked closer and closer to the border, seeing what they could stir up.

Just when it seemed as if the night would pass without incident, two Mexican men emerged from under the border fence and approached them. As usual, the team cowered as if docile immigrants, waiting to see what would come next. One of the agents in front was asked for a cigarette, which he handed over without reluctance. As the two foreigners smoked, there was the normal small talk: *Where are you heading? The border is dangerous these days. You need a guide to take you north?*

Although it seemed that the two Mexicans were doing nothing more than taking a smoke break before a night of hiking, Krohn did not let his defenses down. As he studied the strangers' faces, his hand squeezed tighter around the handle of his revolver. Krohn didn't need to look at his fellow team members to know they were also holding their weapons. They were all waiting for a threat, for a hand to disappear behind a back.

And when the Mexican in front dropped the cigarette to the earth and replaced it with a handgun, every member of the Bandit Team was ready. "So many shots were fired at the same time it was like the Fourth of July," explained Krohn.

Most of the bullets went flying into the night sky. Three of the bullets, however, punctured the bandit holding the gun, sending him flat to his back. The other bandit ran, but Krohn and his fellow mates were hot on his trail. They chased him through cactus patches and over jagged rocks. Jacked up on adrenaline, they stopped him before he could reach the Mexican side of the border.

The glow of gunplay had faded from their eyes when they returned to the man dying on the ground. Despite his agonizing moans, this was a moment of celebration. All the team members were alive and accounted for. "If a bandit went down in a shootout, there were always a lot of high fives," explained Krohn. "But if one of our guys went down, there was a lot of anger."

It wasn't until ten minutes later, when the agents assigned to the mobile unit arrived with the first-aid kit and extra ammunition, that the reality of what just happened began to set in. One or more of them could very well have been shot and killed. They all began searching for the gun the dying bandit had brandished, just to be sure they hadn't imagined it.

The bandit didn't die, however, and according to the Mexican government he wasn't a bandit at all, but rather an ex-police officer from Mexico City. His accomplice, the one who was stopped just short of the border, was his brother.

"The officer came up with his brother to join the Tijuana Police Force," said Krohn, "and was out robbing aliens to get enough money together to buy a police uniform. The officer drew a gun on us, and so we had to shoot him."

Encounters such as these were not unusual for the Bandit Team. In fact, they were a common occurrence. The world of aliens, robbers, rapists, and killers opened up to them: They had knives pressed to their throats; they had groups of bandits surround them and demand that they hand over all their valuables; they were threatened and punched and stoned; they were shot at. But the arrests were coming in. They took down teenagers from youth gangs, heroin addicts, and corrupt Mexican police officers who had strolled over the border to make a little extra money.

Almost every week, the Bandit Team members found themselves in the press after a shootout or a major arrest, and their nightly excursions became a serious debate. Many San Diego citizens were outraged, believing that the Bandit Team was only making it easier for aliens to cross illegally into the United States. Other citizens sympathized with the aliens, and believed that, although they were entering the country illegally, they deserved a safe passage—at least from rapists and murderers. Then there were the Latin-American civil rights groups that considered the members of the Bandit Team to be cold-blooded killers, and the Bandit Team groupies who simply wanted to hear every last detail about the heroic shootouts.

But despite the team's critics, Krohn knew that every knife-wielding, gun-toting, rock-throwing bandit he either shot or arrested made the border that much safer—not just for illegal aliens, but also for his fellow agents. "It was a very meaningful time in my career," said Krohn, "because we were allowed to make a change and there were no policies getting in our way. Now there are so many restrictions on what you do it is impossible to get the job done. We were the law, and there were no 'ifs, ands, or buts' about it. We were like marshals in an old west town—I carried two firearms and a sawed-off shotgun."

THE KILLING CONTINUES

The Bandit Team was officially disbanded in April of 1978. In the eighteen months they patrolled the canyons, they made a dramatic impact along the San Diego-Mexico border. "When we started, bandits were robbing aliens as much as twelve miles north of the border," said Krohn, "but after only a few months we had pushed the bandits back into Mexico." The criminals who had for so long ruled the desolate no-man's-land between the two countries now feared the U.S. authorities who dressed as *pollos*.

But despite the reduction in crime, the Bandit Team had become a liability to both the San Diego Police Department and the U.S. Border Patrol. The hundreds of arrests pleased them. They could even deal with the gunplay, in which criminals, corrupt Mexican police, and U.S. agents were wounded. The one thing they couldn't deal with, however, was all the political pressure. In April 1978, administrators of the San Diego Police Department and the U.S. Border Patrol decided to shut down the experiment to satisfy local and national Latin-American civil rights groups, who felt that the Bandit Team members were ruthless killers murdering innocent immigrants.

But the day the team pulled out of the canyons, the bandits moved back in.

Between 1978 and 1984, the bandits in the canyons became braver, and their crimes more violent. Groups of immigrants were ambushed and held hostage for eight hours or more, during which time they were beaten, tortured, and the women repeatedly raped. The canyons just north of the border had been stripped of vegetation and trash covered the earth. Agents patrolling this area during the day would frequently come across a pair of shoes, then a pair of pants, then a bra, then a pair of women's underwear, and then a plot of soil covered with blood and patches of hair. At dusk bandits could be seen perched on the mountaintops, drinking beer and smoking dope, waiting for the hordes to begin their journey. In certain areas, U.S. authorities were pulling at least two bodies out of the canyons every week.

By 1984, the San Diego side of the international border was harboring some of the worst criminals operating on U.S. soil. Once again, something had to be done.

Another joint task force was created, only this time it was called the San Diego Border Crime Prevention Unit (BCPU). Captain Sing of the San Diego Police Department was put in charge of the unit, and working with the Border Patrol he began searching for agents and officers who were both qualified and willing to be a part of this dangerous unit.

One of the first police officers recruited was Manny Garcia. "I volunteered for it," said Garcia. "I served in the army, but that didn't give me any idea of what it would be like out there. It was very different. We were police officers *and* Border Patrol agents, and we were not supposed to be fighting a war—but in many ways we were. It had just gotten to the point where the laws of California *had* to be enforced. So administrators said, 'Let's go back there, but this time let's be more organized.' In order to do this, we relied more heavily upon the Border Patrol. The area was pretty treacherous out there, and the Border Patrol knew where all the trails and dangers were. Once the Border Patrol had scoped out the entire area, they brought in the officers and trained them. The Bandit Team had been a kind of a rag-tag team that went undercover. We were more formalized and highly supervised."

The twelve-member unit was broken into two teams, each with three officers from the San Diego Police Department and three agents from the San Diego Border Patrol. Five members from each team would head out on patrol, while the sixth was stationed in a 4x4 vehicle nearby, serving as backup.

Because Manny Garcia was a Mexican-American, it was decided that he would serve as "point man" for one of the teams. "I was born and raised in Mexico, so I had the ability to engage Spanish-speaking people," said Garcia. "I would talk to aliens heading north and get information as to where the bandit activity was the heaviest. I was the intelligence officer at the time. I was in charge of gathering the crime analysis for that particular area, and so I was always out in front, with my guys behind me serving as backup. It was the most dangerous position, but it was the most fun as well. It had its pay-offs."

Once again America's finest set foot onto the rugged border terrain. But to avoid the same fate as the Bandit Team, the rules of engagement were changed. Instead of wearing normal street clothes, which many Latin-American civil rights groups felt was a form of entrapment, BCPU agents wore uniforms and badges, adding even more danger to the assignment.

This, however, did not keep the BCPU from making arrests. Because of the overwhelming darkness in the canyons at night, and the increasing boldness of bandits, criminals approached them despite the uniforms they wore. Sometimes bandits would demand their money, and then catch sight of their badges. Other times, bandits would simply fire on them from a distance, thinking they were intimidating a group of *pollos*, only to wander close and find an arsenal of weapons aimed in their direction. "Even in uniforms we were accosted," said Garcia. "In one situation, two bandits attempted to rob me. They just came up on me in the darkness. One pulled a knife, and the other had his hand in his jacket, simulating a weapon. I yelled *police*, but there was no time. The guy with the knife was within four feet, moving toward me, telling me that he needed money. I had my partner with me, but the rest of the team was farther north. I had to shoot them, and ended up killing them both."

This was not an uncommon occurrence. Two days after this incident, the BCPU was involved in yet another shooting. "One of my fellow agents was squatting down, looking for bandits through his night-vision goggles," said Garcia. "He didn't see anything, and so he took them off—but it takes a few minutes for your eyes to adjust. When his vision finally focused, there was a guy standing right beside him with a rifle, pointing it at him. Because the agent was squatting down, he drew his gun, fell to his back, and started shooting. I think he hit the bandit twice in the leg before the guy took off running toward Tijuana. I was in the mobile unit, and so I started driving through the area, looking for the guy. I found him lying a few hundred yards away, and after we put him in the ambulance, I took his mask off. I recognized him from earlier that day. I had seen him mingling with a group of aliens, and I realized he had only been scouting out the victims he was going to rob that night. That was kind of a scary thing for me—knowing that I had walked right

past the guy during the day and that that night he could have become a cop killer."

Despite serious gunplay on a weekly basis, the BCPU was not producing the same kind of arrests as the Bandit Team had, and in the
first twelve months two team members were wounded in the line of
duty. "On many occasions, we had to walk with our guns drawn,
ready to pull the trigger," said Garcia. "There was this one canyon just
north of the border called the 2/11 Draw. Every single time I walked
through that place, my skin began to crawl because it was so dangerous. The area was filled with so much vegetation that the branches
of trees would brush your skin as you walked by. At any moment,
anyone could just lunge out of hiding and stick you with a knife. It
was an unconventional patrol method—it was like we were doing
recon patrol, Vietnam style."

Captain Sing began to worry about his agents' safety, and he
could no longer sleep at night. To make sure his men were getting
proper training to combat the border criminals, he brought in
George Williams, a tactical specialist who had developed training
programs for SWAT, K9, and police administrators.

"Although the Border Crime Prevention Unit was in no way an
undercover operation, you have to understand the area in which
they worked," said Williams. "They were working in rugged terrain,
and it was dark. It was so dark that the bad guys were coming up and
robbing the team. Half the shootings started when the bad guys
would just start shooting into the team to intimidate them. The
team wouldn't even know they were there."

Williams reviewed the tactics the team used in the field, and immediately saw ways to make their nightly encounters more effective
and safe. With the Border Patrol agents, the first thing he did was
break their habit of leaving the group and chasing down suspects
alone. In the academy, Border Patrol agents had been trained to
pursue a fleeing suspect, but out in the canyons it would only get
them killed. With the police officers, Williams had to keep them from
using their flashlights. Although the lights helped them on the hunt,
they also made them a target.

Once their bad habits were broken, Williams brought them to
the firing range. "Every team member was trying to shoot as fast as
he could," said Williams. "This was not good. In conditions where
there is low light or no light, they have mussel flashes. When you
have that, it doesn't take very long until you are night blind. Before

I came in, each team was expending over a hundred rounds per shooting, and many times they didn't hit anything. When you fire as fast as you can, after two or three rounds you are blind. Then it is pure luck."

Williams slowed down their shooting to no more than one round per second. "I knew the adrenaline was going to catch up and push them faster in the field. But once they slowed down the shooting, they had guys who were able to fire fifteen or sixteen rounds and not go night blind because they were firing slowly enough so their eyes could catch up. They began shooting with dead-on accuracy in the worst of conditions."

BCPU agents also learned hand-to-hand combat. Williams was an expert in the martial arts, and he taught them how to punch, kick, and take suspects to the ground. "The team used constant force," explained Williams. "When someone was trying to do strong-armed robbery on them, they would just use their hands. When someone was trying to do armed robbery on them, they used their weapons."

With just a few months of this improved training, the entire attitude of the unit changed. "The main thing was to immediately overcome the bandits," said Garcia. "That meant getting them down fast, cuffing them, and then asking the questions. We did the job more efficiently than normal law enforcement officers. You just don't see the cops taking down suspects in a 7-Eleven store like we did out in the canyons. We did that on the border because of the extreme dangers involved. We didn't kick them down, but we took them down immediately and then asked the necessary questions. I truly believe that kind of contact saved lives. Not only ours but also theirs."

The team also made use of their new firearms training. In a two-week period, there were three gun battles with bandits, and on each occasion two or three suspects were shot and killed. "The team was constantly involved in shootings, so it wasn't as strange a situation as it was for most police officers and Border Patrol agents," said Williams. "And because it was such a dangerous operation and assignment, each of the team members were high quality. People who didn't have personal discipline didn't last on the team. Pretty soon they were keeping such a cool head in firefights that they just couldn't pull the trigger without hitting someone." With the advanced training and the weekly gunplay, the BCPU unit was beginning to seem invincible.

"We didn't feel pressure to make arrests, because we always made arrests," said Garcia. "We were very successful in curtailing robberies. The crowning glory was to shoot and kill a bandit. Deep down inside every officer, they all wanted to have the right circumstances—one where they got to kill an armed robber. Our object was to say, 'Look, if someone is going to come after us with a gun, we have enough firepower to blast them off and still say we had a righteous shooting.' 'Righteous Shooting' was always a good thing to hear from the homicide detectives."

Just as with the Bandit Team, the border criminals began to fear the BCPU. "We constantly changed our tactics," explained Garcia. "Sometimes we would walk in groups of six, other times groups of ten, and then sometimes in groups of two. We'd go out scouting during the day in full brigade, and let the bandits see how we were dressed so they knew how to spot us. Then when we went out into the canyons at night, we'd change our attire. We'd wear different boots and combat uniforms to throw them off. We did whatever we could to stop them. The chief of police would say that the bandits used 'pre-demand' violence, meaning they would use violence before demanding any money. When BCPU was not around, the bandits would run rampant, killing people for the sheer sake of killing. But when we were around, they thought twice. We changed our tactics so much we had them tiptoeing around, not sure who were U.S. authorities. Because of this, they let more and more potential victims past."

There were many bandits, however, who chose to fight rather than flee. The hardened criminals refused to be pushed back into Mexico, as they had been by the Bandit Team in the late 1970s. The desolate canyons of southern San Diego had become *their* stomping ground.

One group of bandits that constantly taunted the BCPU consisted of five particularly ruthless criminals from Tijuana. Three weeks before their fatal encounter with the BCPU, they held a family of three brothers and three sisters hostage for seven hours. "The bandits stopped them, forcibly raped the females, had the brothers rape their sisters at gunpoint. And then, as the brothers were kneeling and the sisters were orally copulating, they shot the brothers in the back of the head," said Williams.

The women were spared. The bandits pointed them in the direction of San Diego and sent them off into the night, telling them to relay a message to the agents of the Border Crime Prevention Unit.

When the team stumbled upon the bleeding, hysterical young sisters, all the girls could say was, "They're coming to kill you!"

The showdown occurred less than a month later. After a brief exchange of gunfire in an isolated canyon, all the agents of the BCPU walked away unscathed. Not so much could be said, however, for the bandits, all of whom were shot multiple times. Three of them died on the spot, and the other two spent months in the hospital. "In the thirty-six months the team patrolled the canyons, they averaged a shooting every three and a half weeks," said Williams. "You just won't see any other team, regardless of who they are, that can fire with that kind of discipline and accuracy in those types of conditions."

Despite their effectiveness, Latin-American civil rights groups were very concerned with the team's presence along the border and the methods they were using to control crime. "There were many people opposed to what we were doing," said Garcia, "including administrators in the police department and the Border Patrol. There were a lot of mixed emotions running around, even amongst the team members. Every night the Border Patrol agents would see groups of three hundred illegal aliens making their way across the border, but had to let them go. Catching those guys was the Border Patrol's bread and butter, and here we were protecting them.

"The city cops didn't so much care about the illegal aliens, they just wanted to catch the crooks. Because I was a Mexican national, I was somewhere between them both. I understood who the aliens were—they were poor people trying to find a job, and here they were being victimized by their own race. I went through a lot of mixed emotions, but every time I shot and killed someone, I hoped that I had saved a group of aliens from being robbed and raped. Maybe the guy I shot was going to kill someone that night."

Although many Latin-American civil rights groups were bashing the BCPU in the press, the illegal aliens who were routinely victimized appreciated the hard-hitting American Border Patrol agents and police officers who wandered the canyons. One night, when the BCPU was involved in a shooting near the border with a group of bandits, thousands of illegal aliens preparing for their journey north heard the gunfire and came running toward the fence. "Kill them," they shouted to the agents in Spanish. "Kill them!" And when the bandits were lying there, bleeding on the ground, the masses that had pooled on the Mexican side of the fence began to cheer.

"It was really crazy, the politics involved," said Williams. "The Latin-American civil rights groups were convinced that the agents were murdering poor, innocent people, but the illegals were rooting for the team. They knew they were there to protect them."

The critics' concerns were ignored for the time being, and the BCPU continued to improve its statistics in the canyons. "The last shooting the team was involved in was with three suspects, all heavily armed," remembered Williams. "One bandit was twelve feet away, another was eighteen feet away, and the last was thirty-two feet away. The bandits produced firearms and the team fired upon them. They were now limiting their shots. In conditions from near to total darkness, they had eighteen rounds fired with seventeen torso hits." All three bandits were killed.

"The Bandit Team was more romantic, but the BCPU was very professional, highly supervised, better selected, and the guys were better taken care of," said Williams. "But eventually they got so lethal, the president of Mexico petitioned Ronald Reagan to end the team. First the Border Patrol withdrew, and then the San Diego Police Department withdrew."

The Border Crime Prevention Unit was disbanded in May 1987. It had lasted almost twice as long as the Bandit Team, and once again U.S. authorities had succeeded in pushing a majority of the bandits back over the border. But when the BCPU's presence was no longer felt in the canyons, the bandits immediately returned, leaving the aliens to fend for themselves on the verge of the Promised Land. "Everyone who was on the Border Crime Prevention Unit had been dedicated twenty-four hours a day," remembered Garcia. "It's an honor to say that we never had any of our own killed, and that only two were wounded."

The controversy continued. Two years later, San Diego SWAT attempted to tackle the problem of border violence. They sent teams out into the canyons during the day to make arrests, but would return to their station before dark, which was when the true criminals emerged.

Thousands more were victimized before the U.S. Border Patrol came up with a labor-intensive and controversial solution in 1994, called Operation Gatekeeper. Hundreds of new agents were hired, but instead of patrolling the border on foot, they were stationed for hours at a set location, acting as a deterrent for bandits and aliens alike. New technology was also put to use, and instead of creeping though the dark, agents could now spot suspects miles away using infrared devices.

Although the U.S. Border Patrol reinforced and lengthened thousands of miles of fence-line in order to separate the two nations, the age of the gun-toting bandit was far from over. They too had gone high-tech, but instead of robbing aliens in the night, they were now smuggling mass quantities of drugs.

Chapter Four

THE ART OF SMUGGLING

O N THE morning of June 17, 1967, San Diego border patrolmen George Azrak and Theodore Newton failed to return to the Temecula Station at the end of their graveyard shift. This was out of the ordinary for these two outstanding agents. Just a year prior, Newton had graduated first in his class at the Border Patrol Academy in Port Isabel, Texas. Azrak, although still a trainee, was pursuing his lifelong ambition of following in the footsteps of his father, who was an INS detention officer in Miami. Both of them took their jobs very seriously, eager to move up the ranks. Never before had they failed to arrive on time.

By nine a.m. they still hadn't reported in. The morning shift was backed up in the office—they needed Newton's sedan and Azrak's Jeep Carryall to head out on patrol. Perhaps one of the cars had broken down; it was certainly plausible, considering that many of the Border Patrol vehicles dated back to the end of World War II. Or maybe they had simply lost track of time. Both of the agents were young, in their mid-twenties. With the weather warming and the air fresh with the scent of summer, time had an easy way of slipping by while patrolling north of the border, especially for the new guys.

Another fifteen minutes passed. Frustration filled the station, but underneath the grunts and moans was mounting concern. The patrol agent in charge picked up a microphone and attempted to contact the missing agents by radio. Static hissed back at him. He set the mike back in its cradle, and then snatched it back up fifteen minutes later. Static once again.

Where the hell are they?

Not here.

How about the night before?

They were seventy-five miles north of the Mexican border on Highway 79, setting up a portable traffic-checkpoint outside the high desert community of Oak Grove. Stopping cars and checking for illegal immigrants, contraband, narcotics. Routine stuff.

They should have been back by now—but they weren't. Another fifteen minutes passed and still static hissed over the radio. The patrol agent in charge began thinking the worst. He plucked up a set of keys and slipped into a Sedan, determined to sort this mess out. But when he arrived at the checkpoint location on Highway 79, the agents and their two Border Patrol vehicles were nowhere in sight. All he found were random tire tracks along the shoulder of the road and rugged country stretching out to the four corners of the earth.

A decision had to be made—the patrol agent in charge didn't hesitate. Thinking about his agents' welfare—and the wife and two children Newton had at home—he contacted Special Agent Robert Evans, who was in charge of the local FBI office in San Diego. Shortly thereafter, an official manhunt began.

A command post was established at the U.S. Forestry Building in Oak Grove. Border Patrol agents from all surrounding stations flooded to the area, as did Coast Guard helicopters. Within hours they had located Azrak's Jeep Carryall less than a mile from the checkpoint location. It had been driven through two fences and then abandoned under a tree in an open field. The radio was torn out, the gearshift knob broken. All other equipment had been stripped. Things did not look good—the two agents and Newton's Border Patrol Sedan were nowhere in sight.

The little evidence they had to go on pointed toward abduction. Knowing time was a crucial factor, they needed the best of the best to try and track down the agents. Ab Taylor and twelve other master sign cutters were called to the scene. While they scoured the site looking for clues, the search took on a life of its own. Marine helicopters and the Border Patrol's C47s took to the air. On the ground, four hundred men from a variety of law enforcement agencies moved through Oak Grove. And then came the media, broadcasting news of the missing agents. Local civilian clubs and organizations banded together, and soon four thousand men, women, and children joined the search. A map of the area was divided into grids. Teams were formed, walking shoulder to shoulder down trails, country roads, and across farmers' fields. But despite the massive efforts to locate the missing agents, forty-eight hours passed without a serious lead. In the mind of Special Agent Evans, the fate of the two youthful patrolmen was looking ever more grim.

Then, on the morning of June 19, a retired fireman searching the countryside for the missing agents discovered Newton's Border Patrol Sedan covered with brush on an obscure back road approximately eight miles northeast of Oak Grove. "The car was up a little box canyon at the end of this wide, sandy wash that was six or eight feet deep," said Ab Taylor. "They had gone up there and cut brush and covered it over, and that's the reason it was four days before we found it. Normally a Border Patrol pilot would have found it the first or second day, but we didn't have a clue where to begin looking."

Not far from the vehicle, the fireman noticed a dilapidated, one-room shack on a hillside. By this time, rumors had already begun circulating about who could have abducted Newton and Azrak. It had been mentioned that in recent years Highway 79 was not only a choice route for illegal immigrants attempting to sneak inland, but also for narcotics smugglers. The fireman didn't want to take any chances, so instead of inspecting the shack he raced back to the command post and informed authorities.

Hundreds of law enforcement officers soon arrived at the location, but the FBI held everyone at bay until Ab Taylor arrived. "Nobody approached the car," said Taylor. "They gave me first shot. When I got there, I began walking the car tracks, because I wanted to be damn sure I didn't miss anything. By doing this, I came up with the tracks of four people, two close together and two outboard. Later, I realized that that was two of the kidnappers leading the agents up to a little cabin not far from the car. There was a dirt bank there about shoulder high, and so they had walked up that and left some good impressions. While I was checking those tracks, my boss shouted at me to check the trunk of the car. If I had been thinking, I would have realized that there should have been an aroma or smell after four days. So I went through a lot of hell with a tire iron trying to get that trunk open. While I was doing that, my boss and an FBI agent came around the other side so as to not to disturb the tracks. They walked up to the cabin, and a few moments later they said, 'They're here, Ab!' "

When Taylor stepped into the shack, he was not prepared for the horrible scene that awaited him. Among the trash and debris of this forgotten retreat, the two agents were lying facedown on the floor. They were handcuffed together, Newton's right arm to Azrak's left, under an old Victorian wood-burning stove bolted to the floor. "The killers had stood on the porch when they executed them," said Taylor. "Newton had been shot first, and you can imagine what Azrak was thinking and trying to do when that was going on. They went to shoot him next, but missed him two or three times. Finally one of them went over and put a plug in his ear. I can't imagine what it was like to be handcuffed there, flailing around as those sons of bitches shot them with their own guns. That was their final hour."

Every Border Patrol agent who arrived at this remote location was given a chance to stand on the porch and see the bodies of their fallen brothers. Tears began to spill, and then anger surfaced. Not for fifteen years had a patrolman died in the line of duty. Those who had committed this unthinkable act were going to pay.

News of the double murder made headline news across the nation. Special Agent Evans was under tremendous pressure, both from the Border Patrol and superiors in Washington, to solve the case. He was not without leads, however. Using Taylor's analysis of the prints left at the crime scene, authorities began looking for a suspect wearing a pair of Redwing boots that had come on the market just a few years prior and were still relatively rare. The recovery of those boots could link the killer to the crime scene and prove invaluable in a court of law. News of this discovery, however, was somehow leaked to the media. The four killers—Harold and Alfred Montoya, Victor Bono, and Florencino Mationg—who were now holed up in the Wagon Wheel Hotel in Oxnard less than eighty miles away, got word of what was going on from the nightly news. "They apparently liked to tease Bono, because he thought he was in charge of the operation," said Taylor. "They teased him that the FBI was going to get him now because a Border Patrol tracker had gotten his boot print, and so he cut those boots up and dumped them in the trash. At one point, they had FBI agents searching the dump."

But it would take more than the disposing of incriminating evidence for the killers to dodge Special Agent Evans and Ab Taylor, both of whom were now pounding the streets of southern California looking for leads. Although these two Federal law enforcers were from different sides of the spectrum—one from an agency that tended to hoard all the glory, and the other from an organization that would rather slip past the cameras unnoticed—they worked side by side, sharing information. Taylor was invaluable when it came to tracking and identifying prints, and Evans returned favors by slipping Taylor into official briefings that were closed to all but the FBI. Together they explored every avenue. "With all the heat coming down, the killers got spooked," said Taylor. "Some of their friends who previously saw them as heroes now wanted nothing to do with them. Bono was shacking up with this girl, and she had a boyfriend who told her that she needed to get to the cops. So she ratted him out."

It was the break they had been waiting for. Approximately thirty miles from the checkpoint location, the FBI surrounded Bono's house in Riverside County on June 29. Once everyone was in place, Robert Evans approached the door alone with a search warrant and a shotgun. "When Evans used to work up in Alaska, he was called Rack-Rack," said Taylor. "He loved to go into those sorry hotels and chase after felons all by himself. Like I do, he preferred the pump shotgun. That's how he got the nickname Rack-Rack. He would go up to a door and say, 'Joe Bloe!' When no one answered, he would go "Rack-Rack" with his shotgun. He never had to call their names a second time. So when he went up to Bono's door alone, I believe he was planning to draw and return fire. That's the kind of man he was. Unfortunately, Bono and his crew had fled twelve hours before. It would have ended that day if left up to Bob Evans."

Shortly after FBI agents secured the residence, Ab Taylor, who had been waiting patiently at the Temecula Border Patrol station, was called in out of courtesy. When he stepped into the garage, he saw more marijuana than he had ever seen before. "It was in big burlap bags, huge bags," said Taylor. "They also took two trunk loads of weapons out of that house, the most I had ever seen in one place."

Victor Bono's wife, who was present at the time of the raid, was arrested on suspicion of concealing marijuana. A day after she went in for questioning, arrest warrants were issued for Victor Bono, Florencino Mationg, and the Montoya brothers. Due to the discovery in Bono's house, the four men were now wanted for smuggling one of the largest-known shipments of marijuana over the U.S.-Mexico border, in addition to the double homicide.

An all-points bulletin spread to police stations throughout California. Information began trickling in. Following a lead in San Francisco, authorities learned that the outlaws had recently sold 440 pounds of marijuana and purchased a truck with a camper shell. This meant one thing to Special Agent Evans—they were planning to run.

The manhunt expanded to Mexico. The Montoya brothers were spotted on the outskirts of San Diego, and then just across the border in Rosorito, Mexico. By this time Mexican authorities were working in conjunction with the FBI, and after receiving a tip that the brothers were hiding out on a mountain ranch in the state of Sonora, Mexican police moved into position around the residence. They watched the brothers through binoculars for several hours, and when they stepped out to get a bite to eat both of them were arrested at gunpoint.

Subjected to the Mexican version of interrogation, it did not take long for the Montoya brothers to talk. They confessed to smuggling a large shipment of marijuana across the border, and even to running into Newton and Azrak's checkpoint. But they denied all responsibility for the agents' deaths. If authorities wanted to know more about what happened after the agents' abduction, the Montoya brothers suggested they should talk to Bono and Mationg, both of whom were probably still hiding out in East Los Angeles.

The FBI intensified their efforts, and, despite an intricate network of friends shuffling Mationg and Bono from one safe house to the next in the Los Angeles area, the FBI closed in and brought them into custody. Shortly after they were questioned, Border Patrol agents across the nation finally learned just what had transpired on Highway 79 in the middle of the night. "These clowns had been bringing an 880-pound load of marijuana across the border in an old military ambulance," said Taylor. "They brought it in right through the desert, and then cut across on Highway 79 to avoid our checkpoints. By this time, they thought they were home free. Normally the way they did it was to have a scout car go through an area first, and if it was clear they'd call back to the load vehicle with a two-way radio to let them know. The scout car, however, had gotten behind the load when they were out on 79 because they thought they were safe. Then they came across Newton and Azrak's checkpoint.

"While the agents were checking the back doors, the scout car came up behind them. That's when Bono and Mationg drew their guns. They got the drop on the patrolmen, but Bono convinced them that they were going to take them somewhere and leave them instead of killing them. Apparently the agents went along with them rather willingly." While the Montoya brothers stashed Azrak's Jeep Carryall in a nearby field, tearing out the radio and stripping everything of value, Mationg and Bono drove the agents eight miles from the checkpoint in Newton's Border Patrol Sedan and then escorted them up to the cabin. They were told to lie down. Their hands were cuffed. Then, while locked in an indefensible position around an old wood stove, they were savagely executed.

Mationg and Bono, who both confessed to the murder, received life sentences. The Montoya brothers, charged with second-degree murder, each received a thirty-year sentence. The conviction of the four killers brought peace of mind to Border Patrol agents all across the country, but their lost brothers were not forgotten. Thirty years after their abduction and murder, George Azrak and Theodore Newton were honored at a dedication ceremony near the checkpoint location on Highway 79. As officials unveiled a stone pillar that recounted the tragic tale more than a quarter of a century before, Ab Taylor stood quietly in the background. For him, that long-ago day at the cabin was the beginning of the Border Patrol's war on drugs, a war that got more dangerous and bloody with each passing year.

Not long after these two agents were laid in the ground, San Diego became a hotbed for narcotics smugglers. Granted there were drug runners who crept over the line in El Paso and various locations in Arizona, but by and large California became the epicenter for the drug trade, the one place in the nation where large quantities of dope did not draw hordes of attention.

To meet the demand, small-time Tijuana drug smugglers began hiring coyote guides to haul shipments of marijuana over the border to predetermined drop spots on the outskirts of San Diego. To complete the mission, the guide would usually recruit starving boys off the streets of Tijuana to serve as his mules; each would carry a burlap backpack filled with marijuana. Together, they would creep across the desert or mountains into San Diego, dump their shipment in the bushes for American drug dealers to pick up at a later date, and then head back. The entire journey could take less than ten hours.

This put a new demand on San Diego sign cutters. By this time, however, Ab Taylor and his crew had become more skillful at reading sign. By analyzing the impressions left by sign makers, they could determine how fast a group was traveling, what kind of gear they were carrying, their familiarity with the terrain, and whether or not they had a definitive purpose or objective in mind. "The way smugglers walked showed in their sign," said Taylor. "Some of them tried to carry sixty or eighty pounds of weed, but the smart ones would only carry thirty or forty pounds. We could still spot them relatively easy, though. Their steps were close together due to the added weight, and they staggered a lot. Even if we didn't catch them on their first load through, we would follow them and find out where they had been picked up. So the next time they came through, we had someone sitting down there waiting. And then we would try to get the guide or the mules on their way back to Mexico. That was the backup, trying to catch them as they came back to Mexico. And usually we succeeded. It was a chess game that went back and forth; you beat me now, but I'll get you later."

During the early sixties, sign cutting became a handy tool for hunting down drug smugglers traveling on foot, but just as it had been during Prohibition, the border jumpers carrying illicit cargo had more to lose than just a few days of their time if they were caught. Many of them began carrying weapons, forcing agents to protect themselves with firepower of their own. Few of the hostile encounters that resulted made headline news like the slaying of Newton and Azrak, but they often ended just as tragically. "The Border Patrol pretty much had a manner of handling things which nobody outside the Border Patrol knew about," admitted Joel Hardin, who patrolled the San Diego-Mexico border throughout the sixties. "The less other people knew, the better. The Border Patrol took care of itself, and handled things as low key as possible. I remember one time a partner of mine encountered a Mexican backpacker with a load of drugs in a train tunnel over toward the desert. He tried to apprehend him and they had a wrestling match. He finally got his revolver out and put it against the Mexican's chest. He shot him five times, but the guy was still fighting, trying to get the gun away from him. Finally he had to cave the guy's skull in with his gun to kill him. Things like that happened often enough that it wasn't a really unusual situation. It wasn't covered up, but it wasn't dramatized, it wasn't advertised, and seldom did it make its way into the media. The only time confrontations made the media was when something happened away from the border and the media arrived before the Border Patrol could get the blood cleaned up and were gone."

While the Border Patrol had its hands full tracking down armed bandits toting backpacks full of drugs, a less likely group of smugglers entered the picture to meet the increasing demand for marijuana in the United States. Included in this lot were middle-class American families and hundreds of American college students who traveled south of the border on a little "vacation," and then came back with pounds of dope that they could distribute throughout university towns for a hefty profit. As the months went on, and the amount of drugs reaching U.S. soil increased dramatically, it became evident that the Border Patrol was not equipped to handle this new and expanding problem. "The government was typically always way, way, way behind," said Hardin. "The guy on the ground knows when things need to change, but change always comes very slowly in the organization. The need takes time to be verified, identified, and then there is always the need for funding and manpower, as well as equipment. The Border Patrol was always strapped. Before I left, many times we only had gas enough for one vehicle. We'd go out and stop a smuggling rig on the road, and sometimes we had to siphon gas out of it so we could get another vehicle running. We were always short of money. Barely enough money to operate. In those days, you could have been driving truckloads of dope through, and there was no way we could stop them because we didn't have any vehicles."

Eventually the patrolmen's concerns reached the ears of officials. They looked into the matter and were shocked by what they found. With drug smugglers clearly having the upper hand, the U.S. government attempted to regain control of the border on the afternoon of September 21, 1969 by launching Operation Intercept. Two thousand Border Patrol agents were lifted from various stations and sent to thirty-one points of entry along the southern border to conduct surprise inspections. The Federal Aviation Administration monitored their radar systems, notifying the Border Patrol anytime unauthorized or suspicious aircraft neared the line. And to cut off those who smuggled drugs by sea, coast guard and navy ships were set in strategic locations, prowling the coastal waters for alien craft. The massive campaign to shut down the U.S.-Mexico border to drug smuggling was timed to detour Mexico's September marijuana harvest.

Being the nation's largest peacetime search-and-seizure operation conducted by civil authorities, Operation Intercept garnered a fair amount of attention even before the government released the official plans to the public. *New York Times* journalist Felix Belair Jr. broke the story two weeks early, and shortly thereafter it became a heated topic of discussion.[1] With the details of the operation making headlines, even the most ignorant smugglers north and south of the line learned of the crackdown that was coming their way. This, in turn, led to very few apprehensions once Intercept was set into motion. Smugglers stayed at home. Shipments rotted in warehouses. Although the goal of the operation was to focus on deterrence rather than apprehension, as the days ticked by many reporters began deeming Intercept a failure. Where were the photos of agents standing beside mountains of confiscated dope? Where were the staggering statistics? There was the word of local pot consumers who testified that it was virtually impossible to find dope on the streets after the operation went into effect, but who wanted to listen to them?

Without being able to prove the operation's efficiency, the militant-style intervention fell under attack. At the ports of entry, commuter traffic was backed up in places for six miles. American citizens coming home from vacation were subjected to strip searches, and local border businesses, which thrived on the back and forth traffic, suffered a devastating blow. There were also critics saying that stopping marijuana from entering the country only turned many college students to harder, more dangerous drugs. And then there was the Mexican viewpoint—many officials south of the border thought the operation was in direct violation of the Good Neighbor policy, in which the United States had agreed not to meddle in Latin America's affairs. In no time at all, large protests were organized and congressmen and senators alike were notified of the negative impact of this drug interdiction program.

Three weeks after this massive effort to curtail drug traffickers began, the operation fell apart. As U.S. forces along the southern border thinned, smugglers picked up right where they had left off,

Cadets at the Border Patrol Academy learning how to read topographic maps in the 1950s.

Many of the illegal workers rounded up on ranches and farms by the Border Patrol during Operation Wetback were transported back to Mexico by plane.

As the Border Patrol increased its efforts to shut down the U.S.–
Mexico border to illegal immigrants, workers became desperate,
often endangering their lives to cross the line.

A California Border Patrolman keeps a watchful eye on the Mexican side of the border, in the early 1970s.

During the 1970s, Border Patrolmen discovered forty-six illegal immigrants hidden in this rental truck shortly after it crossed the U.S.–Mexico border.

Along with bales of hay, over thirty illegal workers were packed into this horse trailer that crossed the U.S.–Mexico border in 1975.

pushing north by air, land, and sea. But some good did come out of the operation in the long run. Due to all the attention focused on the line, the Border Patrol was sitting in the spotlight for the first time in decades. They received equipment—binoculars that used starlight to illuminate the countryside, video monitors, and electronic sensors that could guard sections of the border with the highest concentration of traffic. "But one of the ridiculous things about electronic sensors and video monitors is they don't catch anybody," said Hardin. "You can see the person on the monitor, but if you don't have an agent out there it doesn't do any good. If you didn't have the manpower to go out there and man all those things, then it was useless."

Drug smugglers kept close tabs on the men in green during the years to come. When the Border Patrol increased their defenses in one location, smugglers simply spent a portion of their profits to move around the blockade. This was never truer than when the Mexican cartels began to emerge in the mid-seventies. "It was like any other business that needed to generate funds and money," said Hardin. "It took a little bit before organized crime actually got involved. First, they had to get the money to finance marijuana-growing operations: the harvesting, the packaging, and the transportation. Then they had to set up distribution points in the United States. In the beginning, drug smuggling was very much an isolated incident. Primarily, you would catch someone that wasn't from the border area, and they might have five kilos of weed. But we later learned that while we were catching those small-timers, syndicated and organized crime was planning and conniving. During those years they were trying to figure out how to make a business out of drug smuggling."

By 1975, Mexican crime families had taken over the drug trade. They began much as the small-timers had—shipping drugs over the border on the backs of mules. But each of these couriers could carry only forty or fifty pounds of weed, depending on how far they had to go to reach their destination. With five or six mules to a group, they brought in three hundred pounds of marijuana. This was fine for those who wanted to make thousands, but Mexico's criminal elite had millions in mind. The amount of drugs six mules could carry on their backs could easily be thrown in the truck of a car and driven across the border. So that's what they began doing. They made secret compartments in the floorboards of cars, under

----

the hoods, in the roofs. They also began flying the drugs across. Marijuana, however, wasn't their only cargo. With a growing demand for all illicit drugs in the United States, their main product shifted from weed to heroin. Shortly thereafter, methamphetamines were lumped into the shipments. "Everything grew every day—alien smuggling, drug smuggling, and, slowly, the Border Patrol," admitted Hardin. "But the Border Patrol was always one step behind."

Just how far the Border Patrol was behind, however, wasn't discovered for another decade.

BLOOD ON THE BORDER

While Mexican drug traffickers were learning the art of smuggling in the late seventies and early eighties by pushing marijuana and heroin over the California, Texas, and Arizona borders, seasoned Colombian drug lords laid an artery into south Florida and began pumping the United States full of cocaine. Across the Caribbean they brought it by the ton, by air and sea, turning the streets of Miami into a battleground. To crack down on this isolated hotbed of smuggling, Ronald Reagan created a joint task force involving agents from the Border Patrol, DEA, FBI, Customs, and several other federal law enforcement agencies. Millions of dollars in shipments were seized by interdiction forces, and with the U.S. government only promising to intensify their efforts in Florida, Colombian cartels were forced to search for an alternate smuggling route.

"We call it displacement traffic," said Lynne Underdown, the patrol agent in charge for the Miami sector. "It doesn't matter if it is aliens or drugs. If they are using a certain corridor and we intensify our efforts on that one, that traffic is going to pop up somewhere else."

Mexico quickly became a viable alternative. The halfway point between producer and consumer, it was in a prime location to serve as a rest stop for Colombian cocaine bound for the United States. Airplanes carrying shipments could fly over the Central American isthmus and then land on one of the thousands of obscure Mexican airstrips for refueling before continuing the journey. And if flying the drugs across proved too risky, shipments could be dropped in Mexico, loaded into vehicles, and then driven across the two-thousand-mile U.S-Mexico border, which in places was virtually unguarded or unobstructed by either man-made or natural barricades. Although this method of transportation was entirely new for the Colombian cartels, there were dozens of Mexican drug traffickers eager to lend a helping hand. They knew the tricks of the land-smuggling trade, and had already established staging areas for cargo on the U.S. side of the border. They felt more than ready to handle this new responsibility, and once the Colombians were convinced of their efficiency, deals were quickly struck between the two drug factions.

At first Mexican traffickers were only used for transportation. Once they successfully maneuvered a shipment around border patrolmen and onto U.S. soil, they would then hand it back over to the Colombians for distribution. But when it came time to be compensated for their services, many Mexican traffickers chose to accept cocaine as payment. Using this merchandise they established independent operations, instantly making them major players in the drug game. This new arrangement worked out so well that by 1985 it was estimated that the Mexican drug cartels were supplying the United States with 70 percent of its cocaine.[2]

Miguel Felix-Gallardo, Ernesto Fonseca-Carrillo, and Rafael Caro-Quintero were among the first Mexican "Marijuaneros" to make a firm connection with the Colombian cocaine exporters. Based primarily out of Guadalajara, they took advantage of the U.S. Border Patrol's lack of equipment and manpower and began pushing cocaine over the border in trucks, planes, and on the backs of immigrants heading north. Each year they grew in power. They bought mansions, restaurants, and hotels. They bribed politicians, police commissioners, and generals in the Mexican Army. Swimming in wealth and guarded by the law, they seemed invincible. But then, on February 7, 1985, they took things too far when they ordered the kidnapping of DEA Agent Enrique Camarena, who had been working in Guadalajara to identify drug traffickers.

Camarena's disappearance stirred up anger both north and south of the border. While DEA agents stationed throughout Latin America pried their informants for any information concerning the abduction, an additional twenty-five DEA agents were flown to Guadalajara to organize an investigation. Mexican police were also pressured to use all available resources to track down the missing agent, but despite the massive efforts to locate Camarena, his mutilated body was discovered less than a month later in a farmer's field, triggering the largest and most intricate homicide investigation the DEA had ever conducted.

U.S. authorities were relentless in their quest to bring the three drug kingpins to justice. Along the way, when it came to light that a smaller drug trafficker by the name of René Martin Verdugo-Uriqdez aided in the kidnapping, the DEA enlisted the help of the Mexican police to take him into custody, then secretly smuggled him over the U.S.-Mexico border. Once they had Verdugo-Uriqdez safely across the line, U.S. border patrolmen rushed him to the Border Patrol station in Calexico, California, where he was officially arrested by U.S. Marshals.[3] The Mexican government considered this kidnapping, but the DEA shot back with complaints of its own. For years officials in the Mexican government and military had claimed to be doing everything in their power to fight America's war on drugs, and now the DEA was beginning to learn that many of them were major players in the game.

Despite mounting tensions between the two governments, justice was eventually served when Miguel Felix-Gallardo, Ernesto Fonseca-Carrillo, and Rafael Caro-Quintero were arrested and prosecuted in Mexico for their involvement in the abduction and murder of Camarena. With the three underworld kingpins off the street, many suspected that the Mexican drug trade had been dealt a devastating blow. That, however, was not the case. Close family members stepped up to assume leadership roles, and the cartels lived on, splitting Mexico up into massive zones to manage the transportation of Colombian cocaine to the United States.[4]

Benjamin and Ramon Arellano Felix, nephews to Miguel Felix-Gallardo, soon ruled the West Coast. Benjamin was the brain behind the organization, and his brother Ramon was the executioner. They began by ousting all the rival drug lords from the Tijuana region, primarily by murder. Fear was the way they gained control, and so their use of violence was not dished out with discretion. Along with seeing to the elimination of their competitors, they also saw to the murder of prosecutors, judges, and journalists—basically anyone who stood in their way. And when the number of executions became too great for Ramon to handle himself, the two brothers began recruiting San Diego gang members, as well as starry-eyed rich boys from wealthy Tijuana families who wanted nothing more than to live the gangster life-style. These ruthless teenagers were known as "narco juniors," and after learning various torture techniques from Ramon, their means of eliminating enemies were oftentimes as brutal as those of their creator.

In April 2000, a group of narco juniors supposedly working for the Arellano family got ahold of a Mexican prosecutor and his two aides. Their mutilated bodies were found a few days later, their heads caved in after being crushed in an industrial vice. In another incident in 1993, a group of ten San Diego gang members were tasked with eliminating one of the Arellano family's rivals at the Guadalajara airport. The group completed their mission hailing with bullets what they thought to be the drug lord's limousine when it came to a stop. It wasn't until after the fact that the gang members realized that instead of murdering Arellano's drug rival, they had murdered Juan Jesus Posadas Ocampo—a Roman Catholic cardinal—by mistake. Despite this rather serious blunder, the Arellano brothers continued their killing spree. And if Ramon or his youthful assassins were too busy to take care of a needed task, there were always plenty of Mexican ex-military personnel willing to get their hands bloody.

While the Arellanos turned the streets of Tijuana into a bloodbath, Amado Carillo Fuentes, nephew to the infamous Ernesto Fonseca-Carrillo, was doing much the same in Ciudad Juarez. Ruthless and shrewd, Fuentes possessed all the necessary traits to get ahead in the world of drug trafficking. Using his uncle's connections, he developed personal relationships with the top-ranking members of the Colombian cartels. Shortly thereafter came the Boeing 747s, transporting unthinkable amounts of cocaine from the jungles of South America into Ciudad Juarez. Before long, Fuentes had earned the title, "Lord of the Skies."

The new leaders of both the Tijuana and Juarez cartels picked up right where their benefactors left off, smuggling hundreds of tons of cocaine, marijuana, and heroin into the United States. Although they often utilized ships and small aircraft, almost 80 percent of their shipments were toted by land over the U.S.-Mexico border. To keep an eye on their arch-nemesis, the U.S. Border Patrol, a healthy portion of their profits was spent on counter-surveillance. Informants supplied with night-vision goggles hunkered in bushes and alongside roads on the U.S. side of the border, monitoring the activity of agents and using encrypted two-way radios to inform their counterparts when it was safe to bring a load across. When these informants were discovered or apprehended, the cartels planted others. In Nogales, Arizona, a drug cartel disguised an informant as a local gardener and placed him on the downtown streets. While trimming weeds and mowing lawns, he was secretly communicating with smugglers, navigating them across the line and through the maze of law enforcement officers.

The U.S. government responded to the cartels' increased efforts by recruiting thousands of law enforcers from a variety of federal agencies, including the Border Patrol, DEA, and Customs, and forming anti-narcotics task forces to intercept shipments and break up money-laundering schemes. In turn, the Juarez retaliated by beginning a campaign of narco-terrorism. This involved fishing for the names of Border Patrol agents who had seized loads of their narcotics, and then offering upwards of ten thousand dollars for their home addresses.[5] Soon after, they placed a two-hundred-thousand-dollar bounty on the heads of all law enforcement officers working along the southwest border. With the Juarez cartel generating an estimated ten billion dollars a year in profits from the sale of cocaine, the FBI acknowledged that the threat could be quite real and contacted the INS, whose Border Patrol agents were prime targets. This news, however, was not surprising or new for the men in green. Since the beginning of the drug war, at least twice a year they received word that someone was willing to pay for executions of their members.

Both sides continued to turn up the heat. The U.S. government launched operations with flashy titles like Impunity, Green Air, and Tar Pit to crack down on the southwest border. The Mexican cartels fought back by buying guns and body armor and giving them to ruthless smugglers who were more than willing to let the bullets fly when confronted with arrest. Assaults on Border Patrol agents stationed on the southwest border skyrocketed 45 percent between 1995 and 1996, and it became evident who was winning the battle. Unlike in years past, human mules pushing dope over the border were no longer willing to abandon their merchandise at the first sight of U.S. authorities. They had been ordered by their cartel bosses to fight—with knives, with rocks, with automatic weapons.

When Kevin Oaks took charge of the Border Patrol station in Naco, Arizona, in March 1997, smugglers had completely given up on the game of cat-and-mouse traditionally played with patrolmen. Armed to the teeth, they were now making highly visible midnight runs across the border in 4X4 vehicles. Customs officials had videotaped several of these smugglers in action, and upon viewing the tapes, Oaks was surprised to learn that the drug runners were using small-unit military tactics to ensure that their shipments reached the United States. They began by sending recon scouts over the border twenty-four hours prior to the shipment. After hunting down the sensor locations, the scouts then concealed themselves in bushes to monitor the patterns of patrolmen through night-vision goggles. Once they had figured out the exact time of the Border Patrol's shift change, they relayed the information to smugglers south of the border via two-way radio. Next came the security element—usually two or three heavily armed drug runners who positioned themselves on the U.S. side of the border in such a way that they could provide cover fire for the load. And, finally, when everything was in place, a convoy of 4X4 vehicles smashed down the border fence and bolted toward Highway 90, which ran parallel to the border only a few miles away. More often than not, they reached the pavement without being detected, traveled to their destination, dropped their shipment, and then raced back across the line. But on the occasions when patrolmen happened to be in the general vicinity, all hell broke loose.

During Oaks's first few months in Naco, such high-intensity confrontations occurred several times. On one occasion, an agent roaming the border spotted a vehicle cross the line and hop onto Highway 90. As the agent gave chase in his Border Patrol sedan, a passenger in the smuggler's vehicle extended an AR-15 assault rifle out the window and began cranking off rounds. Instead of backing off, the agent slammed his foot on the gas until he was bumper to bumper with the smuggler's rig, keeping to the right to avoid the hail of bullets. The smugglers, knowing it was only a matter of time until they were forced off the road, grew desperate. They swerved into the opposite lane, playing chicken with oncoming traffic. The agent backed off, but once the smuggler's rig jumped the shoulder of the road and made a break for the safety of the border, he immediately resumed pursuit. Less than a hundred yards from the line, he found the smuggler's vehicle belly-up in a ditch. The suspects were gone, but they had left behind eight hundred pounds of marijuana, an assortment of weapons, and several pairs of night-vision goggles.

With such showdowns becoming nightly occurrences along the border, the death toll began to mount. On June 3, 1998, agent Alexander Kirpnick and his partner were roaming the canyons outside of Nogales, Arizona, searching for anyone illegally crossing the line. Shortly after midnight, they spotted five men carrying backpacks who were heading north. Suspecting they were hauling narcotics, the two agents separated to make the apprehensions. Kirpnick approached two of the suspects and ordered them to lie on the ground. Instead of obeying his command, however, one of the smugglers produced a handgun and shot Kirpnick at point-blank range in the head. Only four days after this tragedy, two more Border Patrol agents were killed outside of McAllen, Texas, by heroin traffickers.[6]

With smugglers growing ever bolder, Oaks knew it was only a matter of time until one of his agents was killed in the line of duty. In an attempt to restore some order to his stretch of the border, he called BORTAC, the Border Patrol's national tactical unit. Three members from the elite task force, who specialized in counter-narcotics operations, arrived less than a week later and were teamed up with six agents from a Customs interdiction force. Together they dug in along the border, gathering intelligence and learning the exact locations where smugglers were making the incursions. Then, on the night of September 3, 1998, they blew out the tires of a Ford Bronco and two pickup trucks shortly after they blazed over the border fence. All three vehicles crashed. Smugglers spilled out with automatic rifles, opening fire as they desperately retreated back across the line. Within minutes, the Border Patrol's Black Hawk helicopter was circling overhead, but by then the smugglers were mocking them from across the international border. The agents involved weren't too disappointed, though; the smugglers had abandoned 2.3 tons of a drug lord's marijuana. Their days were numbered.

It was a victory, but a small one. For every load that they confiscated, two more made it across, giving the Juarez and Tijuana cartels unlimited funds to take the fight to the next level. And, as it turned out, that next level was bribing Mexican military personnel who were in control of the troops stationed along the U.S.-Mexico border. "Publicly, the Mexican military always claims they're stationed along the border to help us in the drug war," said Kevin Oaks, "but the real fact of the matter is their military and law enforcement is heavily involved in supporting all those illegal activities—not just narcotics, but also alien smuggling. They had a unit camped out on the main drive-through near Naco for eight or ten months. Just about five feet on the other side they had a little base camp set up, probably about a platoon size. We used to go there every day and track them. We tracked their military boots all over, all the way up to the road where we had lost loads of narcotics."

But it wasn't just footprints they were coming across. During the early nineties, border patrolmen often found themselves face to face with heavily armed soldiers from the Mexican Army on the American side of the line. Although over a hundred such encounters had been recorded in just a few years' time, the Mexican government continued to spit out the same excuses—they were anti-narcotics task forces that had somehow got lost and wound up miles north of the border. If that was true, why then was a major in the Mexican Army, who had been stopped by patrolmen at a port of entry near Naco, found to possess a detailed drug-smuggling map that marked not only the various trails smugglers used to bring their narcotic shipments into the United States, but also the exact locations of the drop zones?

Such answers were never given, and the U.S. government never demanded them. Rather than create an international incident, it was much easier to accept the Mexican government's explanation. But that didn't help border patrolmen, who were putting their lives on the line each time they stepped out onto the line. As expected, the problem only got worse.

On March 14 2000, two Mexican military Humvees smashed down the barbed-wire fence marking the international border near Santa Teresa, New Mexico, and drove onto U.S. soil shortly after ten p.m. A U.S. Border Patrol agent roaming in a marked sedan happened to be nearby when the incursion happened. Between the barbed-wire fence and the massive Border Patrol decals on the side of the agent's sedan, the Mexican soldiers should have been well aware that they were no longer in Mexico. To eliminate any remaining confusion, the agent flipped on his emergency overhead lights, casting bright red and blue rays through the clear night air. But instead of surrendering or turning around, the nine soldiers in the lead Humvee—who were armed with two .45-caliber pistols, seven automatic assault rifles, and one submachine gun—advanced on the agent in his sedan. The agent was uncertain as to their motives—but their actions clearly indicated that they were either transporting a load of narcotics, or clearing a path for a load vehicle.

Realizing he was outmanned and outgunned, the agent did the only thing he could; he took off down a dirt road used for sign cutting, hoping if he got deeper into the United States the soldiers would back off. This, however, was not the case. Sticking to him like glue, they chased him all the way to the U.S. Border Patrol's horse barn, located more than a mile into the United States. Unwilling to retreat any further, the agent slammed on his brakes. When both vehicles came to a stop and the soldiers pulled their weapons, the agent pulled his, leading to the first standoff of the evening.

The agent shouted at the soldiers, trying to remind them of their current location. The soldiers returned shouts of their own, demanding surrender. Border Patrol agents in the horse barn called the city police and requested backup. Just as the confrontation was getting heated, three police vehicles entered the scene, lights blaring and sirens flashing. With the odds growing ever bleaker for the Mexican soldiers, their captain claimed to suddenly realize that he was in the United States and ordered his men to throw down their weapons.[7]

While this rather bizarre showdown was transpiring, an agent on horseback was having his own set of problems closer to the border. Shortly after the incursion, he had drawn the attention of the second Humvee, which was also packed with nine heavily armed Mexican soldiers. When they were within shouting range, the agent demanded that they stop and turn themselves over. Apparently, the soldiers didn't take this command too well, because they swung their vehicle around and headed directly for him. Like the agent in the sedan, he realized the odds were not in his favor and began galloping across the brushy knolls that pocked the landscape. Over the beating of his horse's hooves, he could hear the soldiers' angry voices behind him, demanding that he stop. When he did not, the soldiers retaliated with gunfire.

In grave danger, the agent made use of his horse's mobility and managed to shake his followers and hide in a nearby gully. The soldiers, however, were far from retreat. Upon spotting another mounted agent, who had come to investigate the commotion, they turned their attention to him. The agent identified himself, but it did no good. Moments later he too found himself being chased through the night, a Mexican military vehicle packed with armed soldiers hot on his trail. Using his knowledge of the landscape to his advantage, the agent maneuvered over difficult terrain, and before his aggressors could catch up with him, they found their high-tech 4X4 vehicle stuck in the sand half a mile between the international border and the Border Patrol's horse barn.

As the soldiers were trying to figure out how to get out of the mess, two more Border Patrol agents arrived for backup. They confronted the stranded Mexican soldiers, and a second standoff occurred. While agents and soldiers were demanding that the other side throw down their weapons, two of the younger Mexican soldiers got spooked and attempted to head back to Mexico on foot. Once they were separated from their comrades, one of the agents blocked their path and cast the beam of his flashlight into their eyes, hoping for an easy apprehension. A few seconds later, Mexican soldiers opened fire on a United States federal agent for the second time that night.

Although the agents had all the right in the world to return fire, they backed off, allowing the soldiers to free their vehicle from the sand and head back to Mexico.

Once the high-stress confrontations were over, the Mexican soldiers captured at the Border Patrol's horse barn were brought to the Santa Teresa Border Patrol station for processing. Mexican officials claimed that the soldiers were a part of a Federal anti-narcotics unit that had recently been transferred to the area and were unfamiliar with the international border markings. The soldiers claimed that they didn't know they were in the United States, despite the fence they smashed down, the Border Patrol decals on the side of the sedan, the flashing lights, and the agents' constant shouting that they were U.S. federal officers.

Others, including many Border Patrol agents, didn't buy the "I didn't know" theory. They suspected a much darker reason for the incursion—that the soldiers were in fact coming to collect on the two-hundred-thousand-dollar bounty offered by the Juarez cartel. And still others suspected that the reason for the incursion was drug related. Even though the apprehended Humvee carried no narcotics, the second Humvee very well could have, giving them even more incentive to use firepower to escape back to Mexico. Perhaps such questions could have been answered during an investigation; after all, the Mexican soldiers had violated several laws and racked up numerous felony charges. But shortly after Border Patrol Chief Luis Barker met with the soldiers' commander at the Paso Del Borte Station in Mexico, the detained soldiers were released back to their country with their Humvee and weapons, to avoid an international confrontation.

It was the same song and dance—catch them, let them go. Although most patrolmen didn't agree with it, the majority of them got used to it. Local border town communities, however, did not. With their backyards being overrun by illegal immigrants and drug runners, they began contacting their congressmen and telling them the cold, hard truth—that the U.S.-Mexico border had turned into a battlefield. Congressmen contacted the INS; in turn, the INS contacted the individual stations. Bring the border under control, they were told. But without additional funding or equipment, the majority of patrolmen stationed along the southwest border didn't know what else they could do. How were they supposed to win the battle if their superiors weren't willing to adequately support them? And so most of them changed little. They stepped out onto the line night after night and put their lives at risk by making apprehensions.

One patrolman, however, decided the cycle had to stop, and he set out to change the way the Border Patrol had conducted business since its inception.

Chapter Five

- - - - - - -

A PARTIAL SOLUTION

O<small>N THE</small> morning of September 18, 1993, border patrolman Silvestre Reyes stood just south of downtown El Paso on the muddy bank of the Rio Grande, gazing across the river at ten thousand immigrants preparing to make the final leg of their illegal journey into the United States. Those from Central American countries were heading north to pick cotton or wash dishes, while the majority of Mexicans from neighboring Ciudad Juarez were only coming for the day, to work in the fields near El Paso for ten or twelve hours before returning home. Despite their varying intentions, once they had crossed the river and massed on the U.S. shore, they would work as a team, making one great rush into the downtown area. That's when the chaos would begin; patrolmen chasing immigrants through the streets, demanding papers; immigrants filing charges of abuse; crimes being committed in various neighborhoods; citizens complaining about people hiding out in their backyards.

"Chaos," Reyes mumbled under his breath. In his mind, there was no other word to describe it.

Times had definitely changed, as had his perception of the border. As a child growing up on a farm not a stone's throw from this very spot, he had believed El Paso and Ciudad Juarez were one community, separated by a line that existed only on paper. People in both cities spoke Spanish, they ate the same food, and they had the same traditions. They were alike in every way; the only difference between them was that they lived on opposite sides of the imaginary line.

At ten years of age, Reyes began to understand the realities of the line when his father placed him on the edge of their property as a lookout. Every time he sounded the air horn when patrolmen were near, the illegal Mexicans working in their cotton and alfalfa fields would run and hide. It was a game back then to elude the men in green, a thrilling adventure, but as he got older he began to realize the importance of immigration laws, and how illegal workers affected their community as a whole. Every year, that imaginary line grew more tangible, until he could almost see it lurking at the bottom of the Rio Grande.

A lifetime had passed since the innocence of his youth. In 1966 Reyes was drafted to Vietnam. When he came home, a profession was in order, and so he applied to all the federal agencies, taking one Civil Service exam after another. Ironically, the Border Patrol was the first one to offer him a position. He had never resented patrolmen while growing up; in fact, there was always a certain mystique about what they did. Reyes hoped that with his understanding of both sides of the equation, he would make a positive impact in his community. And so he began by patrolling the line in the Del Rio sector, located in south-central Texas. Two decades later, he had been promoted to chief and placed in charge of the McAllen sector along the Gulf of Mexico. Then, just recently, he was reassigned to El Paso. After a quarter of a century in the patrol, he had come home.

It's what he had come home to that bothered him. The Border Patrol had become the scourge of the community. There were seventy investigations pending against patrolmen—everything from violations of civil rights to abuse of authority. The Border Patrol was also being sued for supposedly roughing up an illegal immigrant on the campus of a local high school, which was located right along the immediate border. Agents were so disliked that people were openly advocating moving the patrol and its jurisdiction twenty-five miles outside the city limits just so they could get rid of them.

In an attempt to make peace, Reyes had spent his first few months as chief of the El Paso sector visiting the American families living right along the border, and speaking at different organizations and clubs around town. He quickly learned that Mexican-American citizens were sick and tired of being harassed by patrolmen on the streets because of the color of their skin. In their minds, the men in green served little purpose; despite their presence, ten thousand illegal immigrants moved through El Paso each day. Reyes could have blamed the persisting problem on a lack of manpower and equipment, both of which would have been truthful explanations, but in his mind the root of the problem was deeper than that: it was the Border Patrol's long-standing strategy of "catch them once they cross the line." It made no sense to chase people through the streets, harassing citizens, and so instead of making excuses he told the communities of El Paso that he would see what he could do.

Reyes thought he had another strategy that might work. Over a decade earlier, the McAllen sector had experienced a dramatic increase in the number of Central American immigrants skirting up the east coast of Mexico, over the Rio Grande, and then up through Texas. As chief of the sector, Reyes had asked the Mexican government to tighten security along their southern border with Guatemala to alleviate some of the pressure. The Mexican government, however, was under the assumption that it wasn't their problem. The immigrants from countries such as Guatemala spent their hard-earned dollars in Mexico while traveling north, and then they exited the country before the Mexican economy suffered the negative impacts of mass migration. Reyes was told, "These people are just passing through our country on their way to the United States, so you'll have to solve the problem yourself."

Not willing to absorb the entire burden, Reyes set out to enlist the support of the Mexican government through coercion. To do this, he wrote up a plan to have several hundred Border Patrol agents detailed in McAllen. When the reinforcements arrived, he placed them right on the Rio Grande, guarding every trail day and night. Within a matter of days, immigrants realized it was futile to cross. They began to back up on the Mexican side of the border, which in turn created problems for the Mexican border cities. Just as Reyes had expected, this changed the thinking of the Mexican government, and soon they were setting up checkpoints on their southern border to prohibit Central Americans from illegally entering their country.

Although the strategy had originally been designed to pressure Mexico, Reyes thought it might do wonders for El Paso. If he could create a virtual wall of agents along the most frequently used corridor between Ciudad Juarez and El Paso, one that could remain standing twenty-four hours a day, seven days a week, the illegal immigrants would have no way of crossing the river. Every time they tried, they would be standing face-to-face with patrolmen. And with the border shut down to all illegal crossers, agents would no longer have to chase immigrants through the streets of downtown El Paso. The complaints would cease, the community would revitalize, and the Border Patrol would once again be respected. The tricky part wouldn't be implementing the operation, but rather convincing headquarters to allow him to abandon the traditional method of apprehension. By mid-August 1993, Reyes charged his staff with putting together a plan to be submitted to headquarters.

It was a tough sell. The operation called for overtime money, and headquarters was quick to inform Reyes that there was no overtime money. Not to be defeated, he went to a friend in the budget department, who subsequently made $325,000 available to him. But when Reyes went back to headquarters and notified them that the overtime problem was solved, they then said that they were concerned about the strategy itself. So Reyes rewrote and changed the plan several times. He even identified what the Border Patrol could expect by listing three critical time frames.

The first time frame was seventy-two hours after the operation was launched. Because they planned to implement it by surprise, it would take approximately three days for the immigrants who routinely crossed the border to realize that the relocation of agents along the immediate border wasn't temporary. So, Reyes figured, seventy-two hours into the operation, people in Mexico would react. They might try to block the bridge between downtown El Paso and Ciudad by rioting or burning tires so American businessmen and tourists wouldn't be able to reach their destinations in Mexico. Once that failed, and the Border Patrol's troops still remained along the river, they might try to cross the river in force and rush the wall of agents. To handle any such emergency, Reyes had a one-hundred-man unit standing by.

The next time frame he identified was seven days. By then, pressure would have built up on both sides of the border. People in the United States would no longer be able to get their maids, their gardeners, or their day laborers, while workers on the Mexican side would be growing desperate for work. The Border Patrol would receive hundreds of complaints from American employers, perhaps even the Mexican government, but this would only be proof that the operation was working.

The last time frame he identified was thirty days, which was when the overtime money ran out. At that point, depending upon the operation's success, they would have to decide if they should support the operation or break down the wall of law enforcement agents standing guard along the Rio Grande.

Between the time frames Reyes had identified and the detailed plan his staff had written up, headquarters ran out of objections. They gave Reyes the go-ahead to launch Operation Blockade, and now, as he stood on the muddy bank of the Rio Grande a day before it went into effect, any doubts he'd experienced in the last few weeks were gone. Watching the masses come across the river on life preservers and homemade rafts, he could envision the chaos that would shortly be triggered downtown. He wanted patrolmen to be respected, and although El Paso would always experience the ebb and flow of a good economy/bad economy with its sister city in Mexico, he knew from experience that chaos didn't have to be the end result.

Now all he could do was wait.

On Saturday at midnight, September 19, 1993, four hundred patrolmen convened on the northern shore of the Rio Grande. Under Reyes's command, the agents spread out, making sure they could still see the patrolmen to their left and right. Once everyone was in place, the view from above looked menacing—a wall of law enforcement officers twenty-five-miles long.

Mexican workers confronted that wall the following morning. Thinking they had just picked a bad spot, they retreated, moved a few miles to the east or west, and then paddled across the Rio Grande a second time. But there it was once again, a line of agents standing tall. They tried this three or four times, and then began to gather in groups on the southern shore. They whispered to one another and pointed north. They even sent out scouts to find a gap, a way to sneak past, but patrolmen were everywhere. If workers wanted to cross the border that morning, they were looking at a twenty-five mile hike on the Mexican side of the Rio Grande, and then another hike of equal distance once they crossed the river. The majority of them eventually gave up and headed home, hoping that the next day illegal traffic into the U.S. would resume as usual.

That wasn't the case. Although some of the agents were now

seated in lawn chairs, iceboxes parked by their sides, they were still
there—hundreds of them, all stationed along the immediate border. Instead of heading home, many workers camped out on the
southern shore, waiting for agents to get tired and head back to the
shady streets of downtown El Paso. But at all hours of the day and
night, there the patrolmen were, nabbing the crossers who decided
they just couldn't wait any longer.

After seventy-two hours of the blockade, Mexican migrants began
to fear the impossible: the border had been shut down. Just as Reyes
expected, riots broke out on the bridges connecting the two cities.
Rocks and fruit aimed at stationary agents sailed across the river.
And still patrolmen held their ground. Within a week, everyone,
both north and south of the border, began to wonder just how long
the Border Patrol planned to hang around. When the complaints
began pouring in from American employers who needed their workers, Reyes couldn't help but smile. Everything was working according to plan. "It sealed off a lot of the corridors that had traditionally
been used," said Douglas Moisure, spokesman for the El Paso sector. "We made repairs to the fences, and were serious about being
out there twenty-four hours a day. That strategy, essentially, reduced
apprehensions by over 70 percent almost overnight. The police department later told us that it helped cut the crime rate across the
border by about 15 percent. It just gave us much more manageabil-
ity, and it gave us control that we hadn't had in a long time."

That control garnered the attention of the El Paso community
and of reporters nationwide. Could Reyes have actually found an
immediate solution to the persisting problem of illegal immigration? Judging by the streets of El Paso, he might have. Patrolmen
were no longer chasing illegal aliens downtown; there were no illegal aliens to chase. They were all backed up on the south side of the
river. This was true a week into the operation, then two weeks into
the operation. But when this was still the case three weeks into
Operation Blockade, and just as Reyes had anticipated, the pres-
sures from above started to build despite all the positive press.

The government of Mexico considered Blockade a hostile operation against a friendly nation, and they wanted it removed. In addition to this, officials at INS were also suggesting that Reyes break
the wall down. They were worried not so much about repercussions,
but rather about how it made them look to have a local initiative be-

come so successful. Reyes ignored them and listened to the people of El Paso instead.

"Those people who I had walked through their neighborhoods now felt safe sitting out there after dark," said Reyes. "They could leave their lawn chairs, water hoses, and sprinklers outside without the fear of them being stolen." When INS continued to pressure him about bringing down the operation, Reyes told them very frankly, "It's working. El Paso likes it. The city has taken on a new feel and look to it, and I think if we stop the operation we're going to have some serious problems and backlash from the community. We literally went from being the scourge of the community to being the heroes of the community."

Reyes knew headquarters wouldn't give him a direct order to terminate the operation, and so he kept Blockade up and running until the thirty-day mark, at which point the governor of Texas, Ann Richards, came down to see what all the media hype was about. She embraced the operation, embraced the chief for turning El Paso around overnight. In one bold, experimental move, Reyes had changed the way the Border Patrol conducted business, and the results were immediate. Apprehensions dropped. Tension between citizens and patrolmen dropped. Chief Reyes had worked a miracle, and he was treated as such. Known as the man responsible for restoring order to the El Paso-Mexico border, he was thrust into the spotlight.

With all the attention the operation was receiving, somebody at INS headquarters said, "Well, maybe we ought to embrace it and say it is something that has worked, and something that we support." Reyes got the funding needed to keep the operation running for the long term. To appease the Mexican government, he changed the name of the operation from Blockade to Hold the Line to sound less offensive. But the strategy was still the same. "We went from a strategy of arrest and chaos to a strategy of high visibility and deterrence. Amazingly enough, nobody had ever come up with that concept before."

Because of his revolutionary thinking, when Reyes retired a year later he was elected to congress. His operation, now backed by INS, continued to shine and gain notoriety in his absence. In fact, INS decided to adopt his strategy for the entire U.S.-Mexico border. They planned to crack down on illegal immigration by reinforcing the most frequently used corridors from California to Texas, starting with the most troublesome spots. As the hot spots came under control through deterrence, the strategy would then be expanded to other areas, until the entire southern border was once again manageable. Although it was well known that a "prevention through deterrence" strategy would never reduce the attraction of the United States for immigrants seeking better economic conditions, if Operation Hold the Line was any sort of barometer it would certainly produce statistics. In the fiscal year of 1993, El Paso had about 285,000 apprehensions for the sector. The year after Hold the Line was put into place, the number dropped to seventy-nine thousand.

Appearances were everything, especially during election years. With a majority of the public supporting anti-immigration and tighter security along the borders, soon politicians jumped on the bandwagon. While the Clinton Administration had been in favor of relaxing immigration laws in the past, it was now standing behind the men in green. A race even began between Republicans in Congress and the Clinton Administration to see who could get credit for bringing the U.S.-Mexico border under control first. INS funding nearly doubled in 1996, up to $2.5 billion. Within just a few years, the Border Patrol Academy was packed with new recruits. Patrolmen were issued night-vision goggles, electronic sensors, and sparkling new sedans. Their stations also received PC workstations, equipped with digital cameras and fingerprint scanners that could keep track of the thousands of illegal immigrants they processed each week. From that point on, all patrolmen had to do was roll a suspect's finger across the scanner to determine if he was a felon, a smuggler, a terrorist, or just an illegal immigrant who had been previously deported while trying to find work. For the first time since General Swing sat at the helm of the INS, it looked as if border patrolmen were being encouraged to do their job.[1]

The question of where to implement Reyes's strategy next was answered relatively easily. Although the San Diego sector was only responsible for sixty-six-miles of the two-thousand-mile U.S.-Mexico border, it accounted for over 40 percent of all illegal immigrants apprehended on the line each year. Officials from the San Diego sector had done everything they could think of to regain control over their border, including building a wall that began at a point on the Pacific and ran east. The wall hindered those who tried to drive around the designated points of entry, but it did little to stop immigrants who traveled on foot. When it was realized that immigrants were scaling the wall, massive lights were installed so agents could monitor anyone coming over. This worked well, in theory, but with many agents working independently, these illuminated portions were often left unmanned. Despite all their efforts, problems that had existed for decades were only getting worse.

Gustavo De La Vina, chief of the San Diego sector, realized it was time to try something new, and the Imperial Beach Station, responsible for the westernmost portion of the sector, was the place to do it. Along that one stretch of land, immigrants came at all hours of the day—individuals, families, and groups numbering into the hundreds. During certain times of the year, border jumpers could outnumber Imperial Beach patrolmen two hundred to one.

Despite Operation Hold the Line being the foundation of INS's new border strategy, De La Vina resisted creating an exact replica. He grew alarmed at the thought of creating a virtual wall of patrolmen in San Diego. Many of the immigrants crossing the line in California were coming for the long haul rather than just day jobs, so they tended to be more determined than those in Texas. If a large group of line jumpers found themselves nose-to-nose with a long line of agents, there was no telling what might happen. And besides, the terrain wouldn't allow it. San Diego was not flat like El Paso; there were canyons and hills and mounds of rocks covered with brush. To create an impenetrable line, agents would have to be positioned two feet apart.[2]

Instead of a human wall, De La Vina chose a three-tier deployment. The first tier consisted of agents on highly visible, fixed positions along the border. Their job was to serve as watchdogs—to observe what went on and make their presence known. Behind them, the second and third tier would round up anyone who had made it past the front lines. Although it wasn't quite as menacing as a strand of agents twenty-five miles long, De La Vina had great expectations for his operation—he hoped it would push immigrants farther east into the rugged mountains. Due to the length and difficulty of such a journey, immigrants would not only be forced to pay smugglers steep fees to lead them across, but they would also be left out in the wilderness for a much longer period of time, increasing the Border Patrol's odds of apprehending them.

Shortly after Operation Gatekeeper was launched at the Imperial Beach Station on October 1, 1994, Border Patrol officials were calling it a resounding success. Just as in El Paso, apprehensions soon dropped. There were fewer confrontations, less violence, and fewer crossings in the immediate area. But despite the impressive numbers, many reporters, congressmen, and even Border Patrol agents stationed on the front line were not so convinced. "All it did was dim the tide in one small area and pushed them elsewhere," said Border Patrol agent Joel Hardin. "One way of thinking about it is like a flow of water on a flat surface. You can hold it in one area with your hand, but it's only going to go around in another area."

The Border Patrol had expected a shift in migration patterns; they hadn't, however, expected the overwhelming number of immigrants who were willing to make treacherous journeys to reach the United States. So while the numbers of apprehensions dropped in places like El Paso and Imperial Beach, due to the added policing, apprehensions skyrocketed along more desolate portions of the border. Those who made it to the United States often stayed when their jobs were finished instead of returning home.

Did the "prevention through deterrence" strategy reduce immigration as a whole? That depended entirely upon who was interpreting the data. The only real certainty was that the Border Patrol's strategic efforts had made it more difficult and dangerous to enter the United States. A greater number of immigrants now had to rely on human smugglers, but with the chances of apprehension having increased so dramatically, many of the old-school coyote guides began to retire their walking sticks, allowing Mexican drug traffickers to take over the human smuggling venture across the U.S.-Mexico border. They changed the way business was done, and made it so that the guides were only responsible for leading a group of immigrants over the line. From there, a group of transporters picked them up and maneuvered them past inland Border Patrol Checkpoints and dropped them at safe houses, where they would later be picked up by another group that took them to prearranged job sites. As could be expected with the new system, smuggling rates soared from three hundred dollars to fifteen hundred dollars almost overnight. "It doesn't matter who you are or where you're from—if you touch Mexico, you're going to be moved by the Mexicans," said Juan Estrada, a member of the San Diego sector's anti-smuggling unit. "It's all kind of a Scarface thing—'It's my area, and you don't mess with my area without paying me some money.' " Instead of doing away with human smuggling rings, Operation Gatekeeper only made them more elaborate and powerful.

The most serious repercussion of the beefed up border zones, however, were the deaths of immigrants. Prior to Operation Gatekeeper, it was estimated that between thirty and forty illegal immigrants died each year in the San Diego sector while attempting to cross the border. Once Operation Gatekeeper was in full effect, that number jumped to well over a hundred. Ruthless coyote guides were heavily to blame. In the name of profits, they often lied to immigrants, telling them it would only be a few hours' walk, when in actuality it was a four-day walk. Not knowing what to expect, immigrants were often unprepared for the journey. In the desert, they became severely dehydrated after drinking all their water the first day. In the mountains, they were paralyzed by hypothermia when trapped in snowstorms without gloves, boots, or jackets. And when they were too sick or exhausted to take another step, instead of stopping to help them, their coyote guides left them to die. Some immigrants tried to find their way to safety and ended up wandering deeper into the desert or mountains. Others sat down and waited to be rescued, but because the whole purpose of taking these remote routes was to avoid the Border Patrol, seldom were agents around to help them.

In response to the increasing numbers of immigrant deaths, the INS created the Border Safety Initiative in June 1998. Within months ads were being run on Mexican radio and television, warning immigrants about the dangers of crossing the border. Warning signs were posted on fences and posts near frequently traveled routes. But still it was not enough. With many immigrants willing to cross the border despite the dangers involved, the Border Patrol needed to take a more drastic, lifesaving measure.

BORSTAR

During a surprise storm that struck Southern California on the weekend of April 1, 2001, Border Patrol agents traveling along Interstate 8 spotted five individuals by the side of the road shortly past midnight. When the agents stopped to investigate, the Mexican immigrants were more than happy to see them—for two days they had been in the mountains to the east, thinking they were going to die as they pushed forward through the biting rain and snow. As they guzzled water and covered their bodies with blankets in the warm confines of the Border Patrol sedan, they informed the agents that several members of their group were still stranded a quarter of a mile down the trail.

Under normal circumstances, additional Border Patrol agents would be called to the scene to round them up. But on this particular night, the conditions were far from normal. The storm was picking up, pounding the mountainside and adding to the two feet of snow already on the ground. If agents went looking for them, they were likely to get lost, and then the Border Patrol would have an even graver situation on their hands. The information about the missing individuals was relayed to headquarters, and a few minutes later BORSTAR, the Border Patrol's elite search-and-rescue team, was notified.

Agent Keith Jones, who had been around since the team's inception and was now in charge of this unique group of lifesavers, took the call. Even in this early morning hour, his agents were ready to deploy on a moment's notice. They had begun preparing even before the storm began—organizing their gear, monitoring weather patterns, studying maps. In less than half an hour, a small group of BORSTAR agents dressed in Gortex suits deployed to the mountains, where they located five more individuals not far from Interstate 8. All of the immigrants were borderline hypothermic and needed immediate medical attention. While in the process of assisting them, however, the agents learned that there were still others farther down the trail. In light of this discovery, BORSTAR agents delivered the current group to safety and then redeployed in the now blinding snow. Trained to work under such conditions, they managed to locate three more immigrants huddled together in an attempt to keep warm. Although the immigrants were pleased to see the agents, they were also frantic, speaking incoherently between chattering teeth. When the agents managed to calm them, they received some more bad news—there were still others lost in the storm.

About this time BORSTAR agents realized that this wasn't a small group of aliens making a break north, but rather a mass migration executed at exactly the wrong time. Some of the immigrants were dressed in T-shirts and sneakers, their arms and faces exposed. The nighttime temperatures were dropping rapidly, and if they were all to be saved, additional forces would be needed.

In addition to bringing in BORSTAR's Huey helicopter, both San Diego County Search and Rescue and the Coast Guard were asked to help locate the missing members of the group. Under the guidance of BORSTAR agents on the ground, a Coast Guard helicopter arrived at the scene and managed to locate the few individuals who had been reported by the previous rescued group. The pilot landed, loaded them into the chopper, and then took off. While en route to a local hospital, however, he spotted thirteen more immigrants clustered together on top of a rock, all in advanced stages of hypothermia.

BORSTAR members immediately deployed to the location, but when they arrived one immigrant had already died due to exposure. As they attempted to revive him, San Diego County Search and Rescue arrived in their Astria helicopter. Thinking on their feet, BORSTAR members identified the areas where they thought additional immigrants might be stranded and sent them to investigate. It did not take long for San Diego County Search and Rescue to locate an elderly man who had a core temperature of eighty-two degrees and was close to death.

While the elderly man was being airlifted out by San Diego County Search and Rescue, things got more difficult for BORSTAR. Still evacuating the thirteen men and women located on top of the rocks, they were notified about another group of immigrants stranded two miles away. They sent a portion of their team to investigate, and soon they were overwhelmed with immigrants in distress, many of them grieving over family members who had already died.

"We started at two o'clock in the morning, and I don't think we pulled out of there until late in the evening the following day," said Keith Jones. "There was one guy—his feet were so frostbitten that they started a fire sometime during the night, and he had put his feet up against the fire and actually melted his shoes to his feet. You just do what you have to do—it's no different than firefighters and police officers. When you have a crisis, you've just got to suck it up and do it. All in all, it was about thirty-one people, plus or minus, that we ended up pulling out. And I believe there were nine dead."

It was nights like April 1 that had prompted the San Diego sector to create a unit specifically designed for search and rescue. Originally this responsibility was going to be delegated to San Diego's Regional

----

Emergency and Crisis Team (REACT), a highly trained group of Border Patrol agents who handled everything from riot control to serving high-risk warrants. But once it was realized just how specialized this border search-and-rescue team was going to have to be to achieve their goal—which was not only to rescue immigrants, but also to provide the best possible medical treatment during evacuations that could last up to fifteen hours—it was decided that adding such curriculum to REACT's already demanding training regimen would be too much. So a separate team, which came to be known as BORSTAR, was created—one that could maintain the integrity of the search-and-rescue discipline.

Jones jumped at the chance to be a part of it. During the five years he had been a member of Team REACT, he had rescued countless immigrants along the border and decided that saving lives was right up his alley. "Definitely when you get out there and you make the rescue, knowing that if you had not been there that that person would have died, is extremely rewarding," said Jones. "It's rewarding to train and maintain a high skill level, and to be able to put that into practice in a real-world environment. There's no better feeling than when you pull a four-year-old boy out of the desert and hand him over to his parents. It just doesn't get any better than that."

But earning these gratifying moments requires years of dedicated training. Right from the beginning, the founders of the team realized that not every Border Patrol agent would make the grade to join BORSTAR. They started by requiring a minimum of two years in the Border Patrol, and then, in order to weed out the applicants who couldn't handle the demand, they implemented a three-phase selection process.

As in most elite units, the first phase is a stringent physical-fitness test. Throughout the course of a day, hopefuls drop to do push-ups and sit-ups before running and swimming long distances. With physically unqualified agents eliminated from the picture, the selection process truly begins as it moves into the second phase, a field test where agents can prove that they have what it takes to cope with rough terrain and teamwork—the bread and butter of this border search-and-rescue outfit.

During the field test, applicants are separated into teams of five, and each team is tasked with carrying a person on a medical litter for five miles over arduous terrain. How to accomplish this task is left entirely up to each team, and requires cool heads and sound judgment, especially when instructors complicate matters by having the mock patient resist all help or feign a medical emergency that requires attention. "It gives us an opportunity to see if they can think on their feet and adjust to changes in the situation," said Jones. "The strength of the team originates from our ability to work together, and we need to select individuals who can work as a team, especially when they get tired. When things get a little difficult, their true personalities tend to come out."

The few teams that accomplish this difficult task then move on to the final phase of the selection process, an oral interview. The interview not only gives officials an opportunity to get to know the applicants, but it also allows them to warn agents about what they're getting into: twenty-four-hour calls; freezing temperatures one day, blistering heat the next; and, above all else, constant training that can only be described as rigorous. Those who still want to join this elite force are then shipped off to Camp Pendleton Marine Corps base for a four-week basic-training academy.

Their day begins at 0500 (five a.m.) with three hours of physical training. The first hour and a half consists of running though obstacle courses and over various types of terrain. Because many of their rescue operations will take place in the water, at the end of this exhausting routine, they are then dumped into the pool for another hour and a half to swim laps, practice drown-proofing techniques, and engage in mock rescues. Then it is off to either the classroom or the field, depending upon the curriculum for the day.

In the classroom they are taught search-and-rescue fundamentals, as well as basic EMT skills. Out in the field, where the majority of their training takes place, they learn how to read maps and a compass as well as GPS computer-navigation systems. They practice technical rope rescues, patient packaging, and litter rigging. Then they move on to air operations, infilling and exfilling out of the UH1 Huey helicopter. They learn basic aircraft safety, landing zone management, aircraft marshaling—the list goes on and on.

Throughout the duration of training, agents not only have to meet the increasing physical requirements, but they also have to receive at least an 80-percent grade on all tests. Failure to do so results in immediate disqualification. And for those who continually make par, there is still one final test—a twelve-mile run carrying a person on a medical litter.

Less than 50 percent of those who attend the basic-training acad-emy make it to graduation, and then even more are lost during the training to come. Before agents are assigned to a BORSTAR team, they must first become EMT certified and master one of BORSTAR's five specialties, which include Technical Rescue, Medical, Navigation, Communications, and Operations.

"When we get them back from the academy, we say, 'Okay, you did particularly well on the land navigation portion, so I think I'm going to send you to my land navigation team,'" said Jones. "From there they are given a reasonable amount of time to complete the training and testing required to become a specialist/instructor in that particular discipline. To write the criteria for each specialty we looked at a lot of different sources and teams from all over the country, and we took what we felt was the most applicable, the best from each team, and incorporated it into our own program. And we drew upon a lot of personal experience. We send our guys to a lot of different training, from the private sector to the military. We're con-stantly training. Our technical rescue team, for example, will go though the Marine Corps helicopter rope suspension training class. Every time we send someone to training, they will bring that knowl-edge back, share it with the team, and we'll decide if we want to in-corporate it into our program."

Once agents have mastered their specialties, their busy schedules only get busier—six weeks of active duty, where they will be on call twenty-four hours a day, seven days a week. A large portion of their time will be spent patrolling high-threat areas along the border to locate immigrants before they can get in trouble. When storms pass over, they're out in the sleet and rain looking for anyone in distress. Their fingers and toes begin to freeze. Rain works down into their jackets as they hump over mountains, through ravines, and along trails. They follow tracks for miles—tracks of lost immigrants that lead away from civilization and into the danger zones. Sometimes they find these suspects alive; sometimes they find them dead. But they are always out there, trying to save lives.

And just when they think their day is over, when they finally re-turn to the station and get to take off their boots and warm their feet, they often receive a call from headquarters—another coyote guide has abandoned his group, and they are all in bad shape. Some are elderly, and others are children as young as five. They are suffering from dehydration, or hypothermia, or an injury that no longer allows them to keep walking. Now they are sitting down and praying for someone to save them.

Such was the case with a seventy-year-old man who had paid a guide to lead him to the United States to find work. A day into the trip he was overcome by dehydration, and could no longer keep up. Every hour, the rest of his group slipped farther ahead, until he could no longer see them. Then the trail disappeared. He got lost. Soon he found himself searching for footing on the side of a steep slope in Windmill Canyon, located in eastern San Diego. The rocky soil beneath his feet gave way and he plummeted thirty feet down into a gorge inaccessible by foot. His ankle was sprained. The sun was out, and, plagued by dehydration, he couldn't so much as muster a scream.

He spent three days at the bottom of that gorge, his skin slowly burning under the blaze of the sun. The only thing that saved him was an unlikely circumstance. While tracking a separate group of illegal aliens, agent Jason Rissman happened to come across his tracks and immediately recognized the erratic footprints as those of a man in need. He followed them, and a few hours later he arrived at the gorge. Upon peering over the edge, he saw an elderly man on the verge of death, curling up like a dying animal in the wild. "He had been there for four or five days and was drinking his own urine to stay hydrated," said Jason Rissman. "He had nothing to eat and thought he was going to die. He was cold and in shock, real beat up and bloody."

For the next forty-five minutes Rissman slowly worked his way down into the canyon, breaking though the brush that stood in his way. Once at the bottom, however, he realized that the old man could not walk on his own. Carrying 140 pounds of dead weight out of the canyon was not feasible for a lone agent. He notified headquarters, and BORSTAR was called in. "They dropped down in from the mountains in their chopper," said Rissman. "They got him stabilized, and then they dropped a basket and got him out." Less than an hour later the elderly man arrived at a local hospital, where he fully recovered from his injuries.

Situations such as these were not uncommon. But in an attempt to find immigrants who might be stranded on remote paths, more and more patrolmen were finding themselves in need of a helping hand from BORSTAR. "A lot of the time our agents will experience heat exhaustion," said Kevin Jones. "They're wearing all the equipment, they are tracking, it gets hot, and before you know it they run out of water and they're in an area that's not very accessible. We've long-lined agents using our Huey. We assisted an agent who had an anaphylactic reaction to some of the plant life out in the east county. We've had broken ankles, you name it."

BORSTAR does not discriminate—they've saved the lives of all who've found themselves either lost or injured along the U.S.-Mexico border. In February 2002, they helped rescue a four-year-old boy who was part of a park-sponsored tour of Anzo-Borrego Desert. Sometime during the tour, the boy had gotten separated from the group and wandered off on his own. By the time they realized he was missing, he was nowhere to be found. Immediately, San Diego County Search and Rescue was called in, but because it was wintertime and the nighttime temperatures were dropping rapidly, they needed all the help they could get. BORSTAR was asked to assist, and using their man-tracking abilities, they immediately located the boy's footprints. They tracked them for as long as they could, but when the prints disappeared, BORSTAR brought in their canine unit.

"We began with five different specialties," said Kevin Jones, "but we've actually expanded. We now have our canine program here in San Diego, one of only two Search-and-Rescue-specific canines in the Border Patrol. Two Labrador retrievers—they're certified through the National Police Working Dogs Association for search and rescue, tracking and trailing, and area search." The dogs picked up the scent, and in less than half a mile the prints reappeared, leading agents right to the boy. Less than two hours after the hunt began, he was reunited with his parents.

Because BORSTAR's main objective is to save lives, BORSTAR has also begun teaching Mexican border officials how to rescue immigrants who may be stranded or abandoned south of the border.

"We conducted a basic two-week search-and-rescue academy and taught search-and-rescue fundamentals, first aid, introduction to technical rescue, and land-navigation to a total of thirty-seven Mexican officials," said Jones.

The San Diego sector didn't stop there, however. To rescue the growing number of aliens drowning in the eighty-mile-long All American Canal, which runs through Imperial Valley in Southern California, they added another specialty to their operation—swift-water rescue. And to deal with an increasing number of deaths occurring during storms, they also created the First Alert Snow Team (FAST).

"Those are agents out of the Campo Border Patrol station that were selected because of their knowledge of the Campo area, which happened to be one of our threat areas, especially during the winter months," said Jones. "Their job is to actively go out twenty-four to forty-eight hours prior to a storm. They clean up all the cut roads that they use for sign cutting and make sure there isn't anybody out there before the storm hits. We're usually out there in conjunction with them, and so if they have a problem or it turns into a rescue situation, we're right there and respond. It's always better to be proactive rather than reactive. We would much rather get to these people before they get themselves into trouble than afterward."

With the successes of the Border Patrol's search-and-rescue team in San Diego, other sectors that were also experiencing an ever-increasing rate of fatalities created BORSTAR teams of their own. But despite each team being supplied with state-of-the-art equipment, such as helicopters and an assortment of 4X4 vehicles, there were still an alarming number of deaths along the border each year.

Since the INS adopted the new deterrence strategy, the Mexican government estimated that more than two thousand migrants have died trying to cross the line. On March 14, 2002, four bloated bodies were found floating in the All American Canal. In July, fourteen illegal immigrants trying to traverse the Arizona desert were found dead from dehydration and exposure to heat. Such tragedies were being acknowledged on both sides of the border, and when Presidents Vicente Fox and George W. Bush met in Guadalajara in 2001, they not only characterized migration as one of the major ties that bound the United States and Mexico, but they also recognized the importance of cooperating to increase border safety.

But agreeing to increase public safety campaigns and search-and-rescue efforts was not enough. With the guarantee of jobs in the United States, immigrants continued to shift their patterns to avoid apprehension, making it nearly impossible to determine exactly where to deploy search-and-rescue efforts. One month the masses moved across the line in Arizona, and the next, California was overwhelmed. New routes and trails were constantly being blazed, each proposing new elements of dangers.

This was never truer than for those who made the mistake of trying to cross the line in Cochise County, Arizona. Along with the threat of apprehension and dehydration, waiting for them on the American side of the line was a new kind of border guard, one who took their passage through the area very personally.

Having tracked down a lost family trying to cross a desolate stretch of the U.S.–Mexico border, two Border Patrolmen lead them to safety.

A portable bridge, built by smugglers to transport their vehicles over the guardrail running along the U.S.–Mexico border.

Border Patrolmen getting a handle on the ATVs used on patrol.

Border Patrolmen prowling the waters off the coast of San Diego.

Just as the Mounted Guards did in 1904, these three Border Patrolmen guard the U.S.–Mexico border on horseback.

Cadets at BORTAC's Basic Selection Course perform the "spider drop," during tactical team-building exercises.

Illegal immigrants frequently made use of hidden compartments in vehicles. This time, they made a compartment out of a person.

While searching this cargo train near the U.S.–Mexico border, two Border Patrol agents discover a group of illegal immigrants hiding in this boxcar, and radio for a transport vehicle.

Agents practice rappelling from a helicopter.

At a Border Patrol checkpoint, two agents use a K-9 to search for narcotics.

Chapter Six

GROWING SENTIMENT

Aᶠᵗᵉʳ finishing his Saturday morning cup of coffee, Rodger Barnett slung his M-16 automatic rifle over his shoulder and headed out the door with his cunning sheepdog, Mikey. The sun had barely risen above the horizon, and already it was 92 degrees. The day was going to be painstakingly long, hiking along the network of trails that wound between the mesquite-soaked hills of his twenty-two-thousand-acre ranch, located just four miles north of the U.S.-Mexico border in Cochise County, Arizona. He didn't want to be out there, taking the law into his own hands, but he knew that if he didn't protect his property, no one would.

While he was walking the fence line, the damage became apparent. A cattle gate had been left open. One portion of the fence had been cut, another portion smashed down. A water pipe, most likely cracked by someone wielding a rock, sent a geyser twelve feet into the air. His No Trespassing signs had been torn down, ripped up, and thrown around. And still there was more. Hesitantly he looked through his binoculars to the north, at the three-thousand-foot mountain that sat at the apex of his property. Abandoned backpacks made of burlap sacks hung in the trees. Water bottles littered the ground. Tortilla wrappers swirled in rising thermals like a flock of birds. It seemed impossible—he had just been out there seven days ago, cleaning up the mess. How could all of this have happened in one week?

Barnett closed the gate, fixed a fence, and then began his true work—tracking down as many of the three hundred to five hundred illegal immigrants who trespassed on his property every day. After years of doing this, he knew every inch of his land. He knew the trails coyote guides favored, and where they stopped to rest. He knew what they ate for lunch, what they talked about, how much they paid to make the journey, and where they were planning to work. In his mind, he knew all too much about illegal immigration.

Not far from the fence line on a narrow trail leading north, he spotted a cluster of tracks. Fresh tracks. With his eyes focused on the earth, he began following them, letting Mikey's nose lead the way when they vanished on harder ground. After coming across a pile of excrement and a discarded water bottle, he heard voices up ahead, whispering in Spanish. Without hesitation, Barnett approached the voices and found nine immigrants sitting in the shade under a tree, eating lunch. Their food wrappers had already been discarded in the bushes.

"Don't move," Barnett demanded in Spanish, his M-16 held firmly in his hands.

The majority of the group froze; they knew Barnett, either from past encounters or from the stories that circulated south of the border. A younger man in black, however, appeared unfazed. He studied Barnett's attire—flannel shirt and jeans. "You're not immigration," he said, and then lumbered to his feet and attempted to walk away.

Anger surfaced on Barnett's face. He acted instantaneously, gripping the immigrant by the collar of his shirt and forcing him back to the ground. There were gasps from other members of the group, but no one made a move as Barnett pulled out his cell phone and dialed the number of the local U.S. Border Patrol station. It was better not to resist. In a few hours they would be back in Mexico, but come the next day, they would be sitting in this very same spot.

While waiting for the men in green to arrive, Barnett took a moment to relax. He was tired—had been growing ever more tired for the past five years, fighting a war which was not his to fight. By the end of the day, he'd have rounded up more than a hundred immigrants on his property and turned them over to the Border Patrol. In 2002, he apprehended twenty-two hundred illegal immigrants. It wouldn't be so bad if there were an end in sight, but in recent months things had only gotten worse.

"The people are coming across the line at will, whenever they feel like it," said Barnett. "If they get caught, they get put back across and they make it again. . . . Ten years ago there was no problem down here. Six years ago there was no problem—you didn't see it. But in the last five years it has gotten totally out of control. The Border Patrol said they could get it handled, but I saw something the other day that said it was going to be ten years. Ten years! I mean, I have to put up with it for another ten years? It's already five years out of my life. It shouldn't be that way."

When migration patterns shifted to the area shortly after the implementation of Gatekeeper and Hold the Line, Barnett had attempted to solve the matter by spending twenty-five thousand dollars on electronic sensors to monitor the most frequently traveled routes on his property. But the harder he tried to keep illegal immigrants off his land, the more desperate they became. "They stole one of my trucks before," claimed Barnett. "And one of the neighbors was telling me that another time they put a bunch of rocks in the road trying to force a car coming over the hill to hit their brakes and stop so they could commandeer the car. But instead of stopping the car, the woman's grandson slid out of control and turned the thing over. It hurt him up pretty good, and the guys took off running. . . . This guy that I know who lives down there in Douglas found a prayer rug the other day that Muslims use. And he found a pair of prayer shoes. So it's not only people from Mexico coming across. The other day I caught a guy from Portugal. So it's every nationality that is coming across."

Desperate times called for desperate measures, and so when the No Trespassing signs and electronic sensors didn't do the trick, Barnett began patrolling his property with his dog and an M-16. It didn't take long for rumors to spread south of the border. Stories were exaggerated, and Barnett became a modern-day bogeyman, one who cast fear in the minds of immigrants preparing to illegally cross the line in Cochise County. In fact, some were so fearful of crossing Barnett's path that they began to jump the line farther to the east or west. Smuggling syndicates responsible for this corridor did not take the loss of business well, and soon Barnett found a price tag on his head.

"They tried to retaliate at one time," said Barnett. "I've heard several times that they put threats on my life. It kind of makes me mad. I'm an American citizen, and my government is supposed to protect me, but they don't. . . . A lot of people think we shouldn't have guns because we don't need guns. Boy, let me tell you, down there you better not go out without one."

In addition to smuggling organizations, many Mexican civil rights groups are also growing frustrated with Barnett's actions. Some have even chosen to fight back. In June 2000, Carlos Ibarra Perez, a Mexican civil rights activist concerned about the increased acts of violence committed against illegal immigrants along the border, publicly announced a ten-thousand-dollar reward for anyone who killed a U.S. Border Patrol agent. He believed that since American citizens were arming themselves with intent to kill immigrants, then why shouldn't immigrants arm themselves and kill patrolmen?

As would be expected, this caught the attention of law enforcers throughout Arizona, many of whom felt Barnett's vigilante antics were stirring up a hornet's nest. But despite their concerns, Barnett refused to abandon his patrol. He had gotten involved in this war to protect his property, but now he was fighting for a greater cause—his community.

The closest hospital to Barnett is in Douglas, Arizona, but according to him they are preparing to close their doors due to the financial problems caused by offering free services to illegal immigrants. Similar situations are occurring in other border towns—their hospitals are going belly-up as illegal immigrants abuse the 1996 Federal Law that grants them the right to emergency medical care. "When I get sick or get into a major accident," said Barnett, "they're going to have to ship me to El Paso or into Phoenix. A person isn't going to live that long. I'm fed up with it. My neighbors are fed up with it. Even the citizens around this area are getting fed up with it."

Barnett's solution to illegal immigration is simple—militarize the border. This, however, had been tried once before, and it met with disaster. In 1989, the Border Patrol teamed up with Joint Task Force 6 (JTF-6), a military unit involving personnel and equipment from the marines, air force, and army. Although the military was prohibited from engaging in domestic law enforcement under the Posse Comitatus Act of 1878, the law had been temporarily relaxed due to the violence spurred by the booming drug trade. But because the very nature of JTF-6 was skating on thin ice, they had clear orders along the border. They were to serve as backup for the Border Patrol by gathering intelligence, conducting ground surveillance, and observing the border through night-vision goggles. If they spotted any illegal activity, they were to inform the Border Patrol so arrests could be made. Even though members of the task force were armed to the teeth, prepared for the worst-case scenario, under no circumstances were they to confront civilians.[1]

This, however, was harder than it seemed, especially in American border towns, where rural homes pressed up against the line. On May 20, 1997, four marines from JTF-6 were conducting a roaming patrol along the Rio Grande when they spotted a young man carrying a .22-caliber rifle outside the town of Redford, Texas. With their suspicions aroused, the team began tracking him from a distance. It was their job to monitor the border and observe any irregular activity. But things suddenly got complicated when the young man supposedly started shooting at them. The marines were trained soldiers, and they gave a soldier's response. A moment later, eighteen-year-old high school student Esequiel Hernandez was lying on the ground, fatally wounded by an M-16 bullet that had pierced his chest. He had been shot two hundred yards from his home while rounding up his family's herd of goats.

As a result of this tragic and confusing incident, the military withdrew its armed ground forces along the border and began supporting the Border Patrol in other ways. "Now the military does primarily engineering missions," said Robert Coleman, a member of BOR-TAC, the Border Patrol's national tactical team that worked in conjunction with JTF-6. "They use technology, they are sensor help, there is some aircraft help, and there is a lot of engineering help. They have done a lot with roads, fences, and lights. And that is what the military is really good at, the engineering missions, particularly in San Diego, Tucson, and places like that—helping to ensure there is a better infrastructure."

But if left up to frustrated ranchers like Barnett, the military would once again be stationed along the border, armed to the teeth and ready for action. Although this seems like a very inviting solution to those who routinely suffer the negative impacts of mass migration, the problem can't be solved so easily. As operations such as Gatekeeper and Hold the Line have proved, immigrants are overwhelmingly resilient and always manage to find a way around increased security. As it stands, they are willing to run the risk of getting robbed and raped in the no-man's-land that lies between the two nations. They are willing to risk apprehension, dehydration, and death. As long as U.S. employers continue to offer jobs that can better their economic condition, they will find a way to come. And why

shouldn't they? Once they make it past all the forces along the immediate border trying to keep them at bay, they're welcomed with
open arms by thousands of employers.

The U.S. government's attempt to hinder employers from hiring
illegal workers has been limp-wristed at best. In 1986, when apprehensions along the southwest border had reached an all-time high
of 1,615,844, Congress passed the Immigration and Reform Control
Act, which aimed to hinder the flow of illegal workers by increasing
law enforcement efforts, granting amnesty for illegal immigrants
living in the United States, and introducing employer sanctions.
Many had high hopes, especially about the employer sanctions; if
there were no jobs, there would be no reason for immigrants to illegally cross the line. Almost immediately, Border Patrol stations across
the U.S.-Mexico border experienced a drop in apprehensions because, at the time, it was imagined that the Immigration Service
would have the resources to enforce the employer sanctions. It did
not take long, however, for employers and illegal workers to realize
otherwise, leading to a massive upsurge in illegal crossings during
the early nineties and creating the need for operations such as Hold
the Line and Gatekeeper.

"That has been a colossal failure," said Congressman Silvestre
Reyes, "not because of the law itself, but because of the unwilling-
ness of Congress to fund the necessary positions that would enforce
employer sanctions. Those first three years that the law was in place,
the assumption was that there would be no jobs because employers
would comply with it. They would make sure that people had their
documentation. If they had a doubt, they would call the INS and get
that issue resolved. That never happened, because INS was never
given the resources. . . . So we had a situation where we had dispar-
aged enforcement of employer sanctions, not through any fault of
INS or the strategy, but because where you had the resources you
could enforce the law—where you didn't, you couldn't."

The reason Congress didn't delegate the funds to enforce employer sanctions is because few politicians truly want to solve the
problem of illegal immigration. Democrats are constantly pushing
for amnesty because many illegal immigrants depend upon social
services, and when they earn the right to vote, they tend to vote
Democratic. Republicans want illegal immigrants in the United
States because they supply cheap labor for big business. So instead
of actually trying to solve the problem by supplying the INS with the

proper funding to crack down on employers, it better serves their purpose to focus the spotlight on the immediate border. Beefing up security in metropolitan areas close to the line creates the illusion that things are under control, satisfying anti-immigration voters. Meanwhile, the thousands of immigrants pouring north along more desolate portions of the border please industrialists and agriculturalists. Everyone is happy—except civilians like Rodger Barnett. "The sad part about it is that our government knows all about it," said Barnett. "Bush knows about it. Ashcroft knows about it. This whole mass security thing they've got going is just a big old joke. It's just a feel-good deal. They're trying to make everyone feel good except me and the people who know about this mass invasion."

While Barnett wants the military stationed on the border to protect his home, others argue that the U.S.-Mexico border needs to be militarized to combat drug smuggling and terrorism. But history has proven that drug traffickers are just as resilient as illegal immigrants—and terrorists even more so. When the government made a major effort to crack down on drug smuggling in Florida during the eighties, Colombian cartels shifted their trafficking routes into Mexico. When the government managed to bring notorious Mexican smugglers like the Arellano brothers to justice, others popped up in their place. In 2002, police followed a tip-off and raided a pig farm just north of the U.S.-Mexico border near Tierra Del Sol, California. Upon searching the premises, they discovered a large safe located in a closet of the residence. When they opened the safe, they found a shaft descending to a twelve-hundred-foot tunnel that led to another shack located on the Mexican side of the border. The tunnel was complete with electronic lights, ventilation ducts, and a rail system that moved carts filled with drugs from one country to the other.[2] In November 1999, El Paso authorities learned that smugglers were ferrying narcotics along an intricate network of sewer drains that connected their city with Ciudad Juarez. Over the last ten years, sixteen tunnels have been discovered skirting underneath the U.S.-Mexico border, and the Border Patrol's anti-smuggling units are constantly hearing reports that there are dozens more out there.

Even if the government spent billions of dollars every year to create a wall of troops from Texas to California, smugglers would still find a way in. Meanwhile, a whole new set of problems would arise from having the military stationed on the border. "First of all, you can not unfairly penalize one part of our country because of geography and put them under martial law," said Congressman Reyes. "It does not make good public policy sense to use the military when we ought to be hiring and making sure there are well-trained federal officers able to monitor the borders, especially under today's circumstances with terrorism.

"It also affects us negatively with the military. You can't take a soldier that is trained to kill in combat and put him in a situation where he or she might react under those rules of engagement in a civilian function. It just doesn't work. And then it's even worse if you have them enforcing the law on the border and then six months later you put them in a situation in Bosnia or Korea or Afghanistan, and that soldier who was trained for combat now has to decide, 'Am I in a combat situation, or am I in a civilian law enforcement situation?' Either way, it's a prescription for disaster and we shouldn't do it."

The solution is to go to the heart of these two problems—both of which lie far from the imaginary line that stretches from California to Texas. The Border Patrol was never designed to attack employment practices or drug habits in the United States, but until politicians take the necessary steps to confront these problems head on, the men in green will be expected to find temporary solutions. Under these conditions, men like Silvestre Reyes and Gustavo De La Vina have worked miracles, as have all the men and women who guard the line twenty-four hours a day, seven days a week, saving lives and deporting smugglers and violent criminals.

"We have a lot of dedicated, committed, professional federal officers out there that are working very hard trying to do the best they can under difficult circumstances," said Congressman Reyes. "We need to fund them, we need to support them, we need to deploy technology, and understand that in today's world, with the spectre of terrorism threatening the country, it becomes even more urgent that we rely on those professionals. That's been my position since I've been in congress. I'm the only member of congress who has this background, so it's helpful on one hand, but also frustrating on the other because I think I've got a good understanding of what's needed out there, and sometimes we can't get the support needed at this level. It's very frustrating. . . . You're never going to seal the border. I think we learned that through experience in the iron-curtain countries. Berlin and the infamous wall showed that people who are desperate enough are going to try and go across it. So we can't ever

seal the border, but we can sure manage it to a level that is accept-
able, and that is about 85 percent [sealed]."

But attempting to reach that number has grown ever more dangerous in recent years. Because of this, the Border Patrol turns out
the most highly trained agents of any federal law enforcement
agency in the country. "The strength of the Border Patrol has always
been in the individual agent—always," said Lynne Underdown, the
first female patrol agent in charge in Border Patrol history. "The
training that they get, their professionalism, their esprit de corps—
our people are trained like no others in the federal government.
We're trained not only to deal with the worst-case scenario, but to
excel dealing with it. I think that is what sets our people apart from
many of the other government entities that say, 'Okay, if things go
bad, this is how we will deal with it.' Well, the Border Patrol takes
that one step further. It's not enough for us to just deal with it—
we're expected to do something with it. That comes across with
every single agent in the patrol, and that's why you hear about the
strength of the Border Patrol being the training that we put into
every single individual. And then you take ten or twenty of those
people and put them on a unit, you have a pretty formidable re-
source. We have cameras, we have technology, we have sensors—but
without our individual agents that has no value. Since 9/11 the entire country is getting a better exposure and appreciation for what
the Border Patrol is capable of doing. We are not a publicity-driven
organization. Tell us what we need to do, and we will get the job
done because of a pride of mission, a pride of accomplishment—not
because we are going to make the newspapers."

In order to find the people who have what it takes to patrol the
line, the Border Patrol has altered their recruiting practices in recent years. Previously they had set up booths in shopping malls and
visited career seminars around the country, but the ultimate result
was a high dropout rate from the Border Patrol Academy, which in-
volves long hours in the classroom and in the field. Underdown,
who volunteered as a Border Patrol recruiting officer during her
twenty-year career decided to take a different approach.

"It seemed very natural to me to share my experiences along the
border with people," said Underdown. "It's really a wonderful feeling when you get to be honest with people and know you're not
reading from a script. You can be honest with them, and tell them,
'Look, the academy is going to be very difficult. But the day they

hand you that badge on stage will be overwhelming. That sense of accomplishment no one can ever take away from you. The Border Patrol Academy is recognized government wide as a very demanding, arduous course, and people will have automatic respect for you when they know that you have completed the academy.'"

That goes for women, as well as for men. When Underdown first joined in 1980, she knew all the women in the Border Patrol, which totaled twenty nationwide. But in recent years there has been a dramatic increase, a large part of it having to do with the success of women already in the patrol. "In 2003, the National Individual Female Pistol Champion was a Border Patrol agent," said Underdown. "She was just one of many women who have decided that this is my life, this is my career, and I'm going to give it 110 percent. I don't consider male and female Border Patrol agents as two different things. I have never yet spoken to a woman in the Border Patrol who wanted that for even a moment. We all wear the same uniform and the same badge. They told us that from day one, and if anyone had a problem with that, they were free to leave."

Along with more women joining the patrol in recent years, the Border Patrol also gets a large portion of their recruits from the military. "We get some of our very best people out of the military," said Underdown. "We get them from the air force, army, marines, and navy. Most of them are exactly what we are looking for, because they are mission driven. That's something we teach very well at the Academy, but the individuals from the military have a little bit of a head start. And their patriotism drives them to a huge extent, and, of course, we are always looking for that. The commonality that everyone along the border has, no matter where they came from, is that they're patriots. You couldn't do this kind of work unless you felt strongly about that.

"The Border Patrol is a family, and I have increasingly seen children of agents join the patrol. Seeing second- and third-generation Border Patrol agents is not uncommon. That tradition is alive and well in the Patrol, and I think it says a lot about the values that agents bring home for both their sons and daughters. Those children choose to live the life knowing that it is going to be difficult and a challenge, but I also think that they know by watching their parents that the reward far outweighs any difficulties that they are going to face over their careers. A patrolman might be in a vehicle and drive out of the parking lot alone, but they know they are never alone out there."

But even though the Border Patrol is stronger and better trained than it has been at anytime in its history, in many cases it's still not enough to hold the line. In order to deal with any problem that should arise, they have also created a number of tactical units. The anti-smuggling unit was designed to infiltrate and destroy notorious smuggling rings based around the world, and BORTAC was created to respond to national emergencies and clandestine operations overseas. Although these elite forces follow the code of the old school, keeping their missions out of the public eye, they are the brains and brawn behind more high-profile operations than one could ever imagine.

Chapter Seven

TRAINING THE ELITE

ALLAN BOOTH stepped into one of the many cramped offices at BORTAC headquarters and stood at attention. In front of him, behind a small desk, sat a thick-shouldered field operations supervisor who had spent the last decade breaking up riots, serving high-risk warrants, and conducting clandestine operations overseas.

"Sit down," said the supervisor.

"Thank you, sir."

"Would you like a glass of water?"

"No, thank you."

"All right then. Tell me why you've decided to apply for BORTAC training?"

Booth cleared his throat. "One of the supervisors at my station, Ruben Miranda, is a BORTAC agent. I've always admired how he carries himself, the consummate professional. A great leader. And I credited the way he works in the field to his BORTAC experience. It inspired me."

The supervisor nodded absently as he shuffled through some papers. "I see that you aced the Physical Fitness Battery you took this morning. You find it difficult?"

"No, sir," said Booth, and it was the truth. Push-ups, sit-ups, and a mile-and-a-half run in less than eleven minutes—it had all been a cakewalk compared to his daily duty. For the past three years he had been stationed in Lordsburg, New Mexico, one of the few Border Patrol stations that hadn't fallen under INS's new deterrence strategy. Because they were located seventy miles north of the border,

119

agents weren't required to establish checkpoints or sit in their patrol cars in fixed positions for eight-hour stretches. Everything was roving patrol, horse patrol, and ATV patrol. On average, he spent ten hours a day on his feet, hiking through canyons, sign cutting, and chasing down smugglers.

"That's good. But you do understand that the actual training is much, much harder than today's Physical Fitness Battery?"

"Yes, sir," Booth said, trying not to crack a nervous smile. "I've heard stories."

"Are you afraid of heights?"

"No, sir."

"So you have no problem rappelling from helicopters."

"No."

"Are you willing to be detailed away from your home, wife, and family for up to a hundred and twenty days?"

"Yes."

"And you know we have no overtime here at BORTAC. Long hours, tough missions, dangerous jobs. You'll probably be asked to work hours that, quite frankly, you might not get paid for."

Booth nodded his head adamantly. "I understand, sir."

"All right, then," the supervisor said. "You have any questions for me?"

"Yes. What are some of the missions BORTAC agents are detailed to?"

The supervisor smiled. "Breaking up riots in INS detention centers, as well as on the street. You'll do a lot of drug interdiction missions along the southwest border—camping out on remote trails for days on end, monitoring smuggling activity, then making arrests. You'll serve some high-risk warrants. And there's always the possibility that you'll be called to go to countries like Guatemala or Honduras to train their drug police. We do a broad scope of missions, many of which are never heard about. You'll learn all about them if you make the team."

Booth's eyes widened. This was his calling.

The interview lasted another twenty minutes and then Booth was dismissed. When he stepped out of the office, he took a deep breath. He had breezed through the Physical Fitness Battery. The agent in charge had written him an excellent letter of recommendation. And the interview had flashed by without any trick questions, moving down a more informal avenue once the initial warnings were out of the way. Having met all the prerequisites, all he could do now was return to his station, perform his duty, and hope he was among the few who would be invited to attend the BORTAC selection course.

While making the drive back to Lordsburg, he recalled how he'd come to the Border Patrol almost by default three years prior. He had been finishing up his political science degree his senior year at Virginia Tech and decided to do an internship with the U.S. Marshals in hopes of garnering a future job. Seven of the nine deputy marshals stationed at the office happened to be prior Border Patrol agents. They told him that the Marshals weren't currently hiring, but if he joined the Border Patrol to begin his federal service it would increase his chances down the road.

Booth had taken their advice. He filled out all the necessary paperwork, received an acceptance letter, and then flew to the Border Patrol Academy in Glynco, Georgia, on November 1, 1997. Although the campus had been serene, dotted with duck ponds and pine trees, the next eighteen weeks were the most arduous of his life. Every day began with two hours of physical training—a host of push-ups and sit-ups interspersed with knife defense, ground fighting, and crowd control.

"Immediately you want to see everyone's hands," one instructor had told him. "You want to get everybody immobilized by sitting them down. Nobody gets behind you. You never get pulled into the crowd." With images of future confrontations swirling through his mind, it was off to driver's training where he saddled up behind the wheel of a 4X4 vehicle to peel around the corners of the racetrack, maneuver through obstacle courses, and practice high-speed skids. Then it was a short hike to the firing range or one of the many fire arms training simulators, an interactive video that registered a trainee's lethal hits, his judgment, and his reaction time. None of this would have been so bad if not for the six hours he had spent in the classroom every day, studying immigration law, naturalization law, statutory law, and criminal law. With the Border Patrol being the only federal law enforcement agency to require its agents to be proficient in a foreign language, Spanish was inevitably thrown into the mix. For a non-native Spanish speaker who'd grown up in southern Maine, nightly cram sessions routinely carried over into the early morning hours.

Booth had quickly learned that the Border Patrol Academy was the most difficult of all the federal law enforcement academies. His instructors gave him a simple explanation: The border was dangerous, and growing more so with each passing year. Patrolmen were not only under constant attack by drug traffickers and human smugglers, but also political activists. They hid in bushes with video cameras, even posed as unruly illegal immigrants, waiting to get thumped on by a frustrated agent. During the massive hiring spree in the early nineties, the patrol had been accused of running inadequate background checks on recruits, of hiring men and women unfit to handle border stress and responsibility. Now the academy only graduated the cream of the crop. They weeded out those who had no right guarding the border before they ever stepped foot on the line.

Booth made it through the academy by spending many late nights in the study hall. Upon graduating, he had one week to pick up his life in Virginia and move it to Lordsburg. Unlike the safe confines of the training center at Glynco, the danger in the desert was very real. Assigned to a Field Training Officer (FTO) for the next twelve weeks, Booth's desire was tested further.

"We introduce trainees to the reality of field work," said Field Training Officer Matt Hanna. "The academy is basic training, where you get all the basic skills. When you're out with the Field Training Officer you're applying those skills. We do mock vehicle stops and mock alien encounters. We create situations where they might be under attack, such as being rocked or stoned. At the beginning of our program, we stress conditioning. For a normal field-training day we begin at six a.m. After muster, we check to see what sensors have gone answered in the field, meaning where there is possible alien traffic. We identify those, make sure all our equipment is ready to go, and then head out on foot. Once we locate sign, we spend the next four, five, or six hours tracking. We do a lot of hiking. Because of the environment and terrain that we work in, every agent needs to be able to respond and get to another agent in need, even if that agent is at the bottom of a canyon."

In addition to these long days and what recruits typically refer to as "Death Marches," Booth also had to spend his nights studying for the probationary exams in Spanish and law.

It was a tough few months, but Booth survived his time with his FTO. He also survived the painstaking Spanish oral tests where he had to sit before a panel and ask questions such as, "How long ago did you cross the border and for what period of time were you in the vehicle with the smuggler?" in flawless Spanish. Even after completing all these requirements, his time under a microscope still hadn't come to an end, nor had the learning process. Five and a half months after being assigned to the blistering summer heat of Lordsburg, he partnered up with several journeymen, agents who had mastered everything from tracking to desert survival. The journeyman's job was to fine-tune Booth's skills, as well as rate his conduct, personality, and his work ethic. Instead of feeling uncomfortable during this five-month experience, Booth began to get a taste for what he had in store. Adventurous days hiking solo down trails, tracking groups of immigrants a hundred strong. Heading out on horseback or in an ATV, roaming the desert canyons for smugglers pushing their shipments north. The journeymen he was assigned to all had a minimum of five years' service with the patrol; all were expert trackers. They spent countless hours with him out in the field making sure that once he was released on his own he hit the ground running.

At the ten-month mark, Booth aced his final exams in law and Spanish. By this point, he had both languages down to a science. The journeymen wished him the best of luck, and then set him free. Booth hadn't thought about it for a while, but his original intent to one day join the U.S. Marshals had faded completely by this point. He was twenty-three years old, eager for a long career in the Border Patrol.

Every month Booth spent on the line he grew more proficient at reading sign and understanding the nature of the terrain. His hunger to expand his knowledge and expertise began to grow, especially after having long chats with Ruben Miranda, a confident agent who had gone through BORTAC training just a few years prior. Miranda was always disappearing on exotic details, giving only vague descriptions of his missions upon his return. Booth pressed to learn more, but BORTAC agents were elusive, often mysterious. They drove shiny new sedans, carried themselves as if they could handle any situation, and yet they kept to themselves. BORTAC agents had recently been thrust into the international spotlight when they successfully raided a Florida home to reunite the seven-year-old Cuban refugee Elian Gonzales with his father, but Booth knew that most of what they did was unknown.

Booth wanted to be a part of such an elite team, but because

BORTAC required its agents to have at least three years' time in the service, he applied for the El Paso Special Response Team (SRT) instead. He received training in land navigation, trauma management, interdiction, camouflage, and operations planning by a Special Forces team. The training was comprehensive, but El Paso SRT was nothing like Tucson SRT or San Diego's REACT team, both of which underwent rigorous selection course training and were deployed to hostile situations around the United States. At this point Booth wanted the best of what the Border Patrol had to offer. He thought about transferring stations just so he could be a member of a more demanding regional tactical unit, but instead he bided his time.

Now, a month after his interview at BORTAC headquarters, the agent in charge of the Lordsburg station called him into his office. Booth was informed that out of the 250 agents who applied for BORTAC training that year, he was one of the 80 to have been invited.

A smile spread across Booth's face. The excitement lasted several hours, but was ultimately replaced by nerves. He began to remember all those hellish stories he'd heard about the nature of BORTAC training: sleep deprivation, endless ruck-marches, and ambitious men coming home deflated and defeated. He wasn't quite sure what to think, so he mentally prepared himself for the toughest three weeks of his life. By the time he stepped out his front door two days later, he had made a stern promise to himself—the only way he was coming home was if they sent him home.

Between April and June 1980, Fidel Castro liberated approximately 120,000 of his citizens by allowing them to board boats at the Cuban port of Mariel and set sail for the United States. Although the U.S. had agreed to open its doors to refugees and political prisoners opposed to the Fidel Castro regime, no one had predicted such a mass migration. With thousands arriving on the beaches of south Florida every day, it did not take long for the Immigration and Naturalization Service to become overwhelmed. To get a grip on the situation, INS temporarily placed the Cubans, or "Mariels" as they had come to be known, in their detention facilities around the country. They promised that in time they would all be processed and released to family members or sponsors within the United States.

But that's not how events unfolded. While interviewing the detainees, INS officials quickly noticed a recurring trend—a large portion of the Mariels had jailhouse tattoos covering their bodies from head to toe. Some were hesitant to talk about their past, while others told obvious lies. With their suspicions aroused, officials began running background checks and confirmed their fears. Castro had not only used the accord to rid his country of political refugees, but also an incredible number of convicts and mental patients. As this information reached the press, the topic of what to do with the Mariels became a heated national debate.

While the courts tried to reach some sort of conclusion, the Mariels sat in overcrowded INS detention facilities that were not designed for long-term detention. Literally stacked on top of one another in cramped cells, their anger for the system began to grow. Castro didn't want them back. The United States was extremely hesitant about releasing them into the population. Feeling lost in the system, the Mariels began to riot the service processing facilities.

The Border Patrol attempted to stay on top of the situation. Small tactical teams from the various sectors swooped in to regain control. In many cases, however, the riots were too large for one squad to handle alone. So the Border Patrol began to combine the regional teams, but this only led to a breakdown in command. Each team had its own procedures and protocol. When working together they had trouble deciding who was in charge and how operations should be executed. As a result, some of the missions were handled less than efficiently. It was the final catalyst.

Since the fifties the Border Patrol had been kicking around the idea of creating a national tactical team to cope with emergencies such as riots. They had resisted the temptation for years, not because of the costs involved, but because many people who weren't familiar with special operations tended to fear them. But with riots breaking out at their own detention centers, a few key officials in the Border Patrol recognized that it was time to have a team of nationally recognized, nationally trained, and nationally certified agents who could respond not only to riots at their service processing facilities, but also to any other emergency situation that should arise.

In order to get the first handful of agents trained, the Border Patrol reached out to the U.S. Marshals, which in turn put them in touch with their Special Operations Group (SOG). Established in 1971, SOG was capable of responding to a crisis situation anywhere in the United States within five hours of receiving the call. They had extensive experience controlling violent anti-government protests and riots. In 1973 they had deployed to Wounded Knee, South Dakota, when a militant group had taken control of the area. In 1975 they had flown to Guam to provide security for Vietnamese refugees being relocated. Time and again they had proven their tactical prowess, and, even more importantly, they had their newly established SOG training center at Camp Beaureguard, Louisiana. Their instructors had access to academic buildings and a forty-acre tactical-training area pocked with helicopter landing pads, rappelling towers, and warehouses where SWAT practicals could be hosted. It was a perfect place for the Border Patrol's national tactical team to receive their initial training, and so once SOG agreed to take the first class under its wing—teach them tactical operations and procedures and then release them back to the Border Patrol—the two agencies began deciding upon a curriculum.

In early 1983 a service-wide announcement notified agents that the Border Patrol was taking applications for BORTAC, the agency's national tactical team. Kevin Stevens, who was stationed in Fort Hancock, Texas at the time, jumped at the opportunity. Wanting to be a part of a team that could take him above and beyond his normal duties, he took a series of physical fitness tests; these were followed by a barrage of interviews.

Being one of the forty agents chosen from more than two hundred applicants, Stevens flew to Camp Beaureguard a few weeks later, where he spent the next five weeks training seventeen hours a day in the classroom and in the field, learning land navigation, operations planning, and advanced weaponry. He rappelled from helicopters, deployed to mock riots, and mastered close-quarter battle techniques. "They trained us as they would their own," said Stevens. "But instead of calling those of us who graduated SOG, they called us BORTAC. We kind of became cousins, if you will, to the Marshals's Special Operations Group. In fact we still hold quite a kinship to that unit, particularly those of us from the early classes."

The twenty-four Border Patrol agents who still remained at the end of the course were issued their specialized gear—riot uniforms, flak jackets, helmets, and an assortment of weaponry. They were told to store it in a bag and keep it with them at all times. From that moment on, they were on call twenty-four hours a day, seven days a week. In the case of an emergency, they were expected to be at the airport purchasing tickets with their government credit cards a half an hour after receiving the call. Any additional gear that was needed for the mission would be brought to the site of the emergency by headquarters.

Only two weeks after returning to his station to resume normal duty, Stevens received a call from headquarters. The Mariel Cubans were beginning to riot at the KHROME detention center in Miami. Four years had now passed since the original boatlift; although the majority of the Mariels had been released to family members in the United States, a large number of them had violated their parole and were once again sitting in overcrowded detention centers. Castro still wouldn't take them back. U.S Federal Courts had ruled that since they were not legally in the United States, they had no constitutional rights. With thousands of Mariels trapped in limbo, serving an indefinite sentence while awaiting deportation, the tension had been steadily mounting. Now it had just sprung a leak.

When BORTAC arrived at the facility, they marched through the doors of the main barracks and announced who they were, and that they were there to restore order and control; then they marched out. "The next morning we went in and started bringing people out of the lockdown areas," said Stevens. "Once we got them seated, some of us guarded the group while others walked among them with the command staff at KHROME. They identified the instigators of the riot, and we separated them from the group so they could be moved to other facilities where they wouldn't be in a position to instigate another riot. Once we did that, we got everybody back in their own facilities, in their own bunks, and then just worked to restore order and discipline in the facility."

The riot had been quelled, but the plight of the Mariels was far from being solved. Once BORTAC handed control of the facility back to the guards, it was only a matter of months before they rioted once again. Determined to escape, they set fire to the main barracks and then stormed into the workshop and kitchen to arm themselves with knives and sticks. A group of male inmates forced their way into the women's barracks, attempting to take over the entire facility.

BORTAC arrived just in time. Clad in body armor and armed with shotguns, which fired less-than-lethal munitions such as rubber pellets and beanbag rounds, they promptly restored order. But now there was nowhere to house the Mariels—they had burned their barracks to the ground. Buses were brought in to bring them to other already overcrowded detention centers around the country, but officials realized it was only a temporary solution. With Castro still refusing to sign a repatriation accord, it looked as if many of the Mariels would be trapped in the system for the long haul. To release pressure from the INS detention centers, thousands of Mariels were sent either to the Federal Detention Center in Oakdale, Louisiana, or to the U.S. Penitentiary in Atlanta, Georgia.

Several years passed. With the Mariels locked away out of sight, the press and general public forgot about the Cubans who had sailed to America in 1980. The Mariels felt abandoned, but they still clung to the hope that one day they would be released into the U.S. population. In fact, many of them preferred to die than be shipped back to the island they had escaped. This became evident on November 20, 1987, when the U.S. Department of Justice announced that the United States had come to an agreement with Cuba to repatriate twenty-five hundred Mariels.

Only minutes after television and radio stations broadcast news of the agreement, an irate Cuban detainee at Oakdale accosted a food server in the prison cafeteria. This sparked a burst of aggression, and soon the mess hall was out of control. Although correctional officers managed to restore order, it was evident by the stillness in the air that news of the accord had turned Oakdale into a time bomb. Along with beefing up the number of correctional officers, the warden of Oakdale contacted the BORTAC team in El Paso.[1]

Robert Coleman, who had gone through early BORTAC training with the U.S. Marshals, received the call at BORTAC headquarters. He gathered his gear immediately, and then caught a midnight flight to New Orleans with fellow BORTAC agent Bill Whirly. When the pair arrived at Oakdale Penitentiary at six a.m. the following morning, the situation did not look good. Frustrated over the repatriation accord, inmates had broken into the workshop and armed themselves with makeshift weapons. A group of two hundred hovered in the yard, whispering to one another in Spanish.

"We tried to prepare all day for what we believed to be an eventual attack by the inmates," said Coleman, "and they did attack at five p.m." A group of Cuban inmates made a sudden charge on the front gate, attempting to escape by using force. Robert Coleman and Bill Whirly, along with six Border Patrol agents from the New

Orleans sector who were under their command, responded by launching tear-gas canisters into their midst. Doubled over in pain, the Mariels retreated back into the yard, but unlike their previous riots at KHROME, they were far from giving up. While trying to recover from the effects of the gas, they shifted their focus from escape to destruction. They broke down walls and set fire to buildings. With the prison coming apart at the seams, officials still inside attempted to flee and were quickly subdued by inmates.

Now in possession of hostages, the Mariels mounted another assault on the front gate. Once again, the two BORTAC agents on site responded by firing tear-gas canisters at their feet. The inmates backed off, but Coleman knew it was only a matter of time before they coordinated their efforts and made a massive push. Running low on tear gas, he called several pyrotechnic vendors and had them ship crates of Flash Bang grenades directly to the prison. Immediately after, he contacted BORTAC headquarters and notified them of the situation. By the time he hung up, the inmates had recuperated and were once again inching forward. "We fought them off with some Federal BOP (Bureau of Prisons) help, and some help from the county sheriff," said Coleman. "Basically that fight went on for thirty-six hours."

Kevin Stevens arrived at Oakdale the following morning along with thirty other BORTAC agents. During the night Robert Coleman and Bill Whirly had managed to gain control of the outside of the facility, but the inmates had control of the inside. Along with the FBI and the U.S. Marshals, hundreds of reporters were now swarming around the prison. What would turn out to be the longest prison siege in U.S. history had begun just before Thanksgiving.

"As the FBI tried to negotiate the standoff, we performed perimeter patrol," said Stevens. "Our particular contingent was set up in a large military tent just outside the compound because they needed us to be right there in the event that things got worse." And things did get worse, just a few days into the standoff. The Mariels didn't want to return to Cuba, and until officials could prove the matter was settled, they would continue to hold hostages. This, however, was something the FBI couldn't promise, and so it looked as if things were heading south. BORTAC members were loaded onto trucks, preparing to make a forcible entry into the facility. "If an entry was to go down, our job focused on the barracks facility," said Stevens.

"We were to go in there, breach the barracks facility, make a sweep of it, and try to move through it collecting as many of the hostages and innocents as we could. Fortunately, we never had to respond." The FBI had managed to resume negotiations, promising the Mariels they would receive a fair review and a chance to state their case if they turned over the hostages and surrendered.

After nine days of heated negotiations, the siege finally came to an end. The Mariels released their twenty-six hostages, and then returned the prison to the control of the authorities. For BORTAC, however, the crisis wasn't over. Only two days after Oakdale rioted, Mariels at the Atlanta Penitentiary also rioted. "Once Oakdale was over with," said Stevens, "we kept a part of our contingent there to clean up and restore order, while forty of us were loaded onto a C1-30 and flown to Atlanta. Once again we were on standby as a potential hostage-rescue element."

Although both standoffs were eventually resolved through negotiations, INS officials realized matters could easily have gone the other way. In 1992, Border Patrol agent Lynne Underdown was promoted to assistant district director for detention and deportation in the New Orleans district. Responsible for Oakdale, she worked to keep such an uprising from occurring in the future. "Oakdale is the place in the United States where we send the worst of the worst before it is time for them to go home," said Underdown. "It would be very disturbing to hear the criminal history of some of the people who go through there. We learned a lesson, most certainly the hard way, but we began to take precautionary measures. Generally, we don't send too many trainees to work there because it is very advanced work. There is no bigger priority than making sure our workers are the first ones out when it is time to go."

Beefing up security at the penitentiaries, however, was not the only step taken. The Border Patrol recognized the need to properly back BORTAC and developed a permanent command structure at Biggs Army Airfield Base in El Paso. A commander was assigned, as well as field supervisors who could coordinate operations for the team. They also weaned themselves from the U.S. Marshals. "The Marshals's Special Operations Group taught us what we needed to know, helped make us a unit, and developed our first members as instructors," said Stevens. "Then BORTAC became its own entity."

As its own entity, BORTAC continued to reach out to other agencies to improve their skills. Along with sending agents to train with

the DEA and FBI, BORTAC also began working with the military to
stay on top of the most current advances in weaponry. While many
sectors of the patrol were fighting for a few new pairs of night-vision
goggles, BORTAC was supplied with the latest and greatest in technology. And their training and equipment didn't go to waste. Shortly
after the riots at Oakdale and Atlanta, the agents of BORTAC were
given the chance to test their skills in the jungles of South America.

Soon after arriving at Biggs Army Airfield Base on the morning of
September 1, 2001, Allan Booth was led a quarter of a mile from
BORTAC headquarters to an old-style military H-building where
metal bunks lined both the left and right walls. "You're the first to
arrive," said the man with a clipboard. "Pick a place to sleep. This
will be your home until you get kicked out, quit, or graduate. Drink
some water. We'll get back to you with further instructions."

Booth picked a bed and then began organizing his few personal
belongings in a locker. As the hours passed, other members of Class
15 began to filter in. Most of them looked in fairly good shape; like
him, they had probably been preparing for months, going on long
hikes and doing countless push-ups every morning. He wondered
who would last the entire three weeks and who would quit in the
next twenty-four hours. He wondered if they were all as nervous as
he was, anticipating the hell to come.

By two p.m., everyone had arrived—sixty-one agents instead of
the eighty who had been invited. As it turned out, nineteen had
backed out at the airport. Men were still trying to find lockers and
make their beds when a lanky member of the cadre entered the barracks at three p.m. Everyone was issued a two-quart canteen and a
pair of OD (Olive Drab) green battledress uniforms. They were told
to change and be at headquarters by five p.m.

Class 15 made the quarter-mile march at 4:30, falling into formation behind the main BORTAC building. A few minutes later, a
stocky man in his early forties appeared before them. In a thick
southern drawl, he said, "My name is Charles Whitmire, and I'm the
commander here at BORTAC. I congratulate you all for having the
courage to come out, and I have no doubt that I'm looking at sixty-
one of the best agents in the Border Patrol. These fine men standing next to me will be your instructors for the next three weeks.
They have all gone through the training. They all have extensive

field experience." He began to name them from left to right: Walley Davenport, Jonathan Miller, Charley Sacks, Matt VanGorder, James Wayner, Jim Cody.

Booth swallowed hard. Several members of the cadre had deployed to Lordsburg just a few months prior to help apprehend a particularly elusive group of drug runners. Booth had assisted in their operation, which led to the seizure of more than eight hundred pounds of marijuana. At the time, Booth had felt lucky to work by their side, but now he wasn't so sure. For the next twenty-one days the instructors would do everything in their power to beat down the recruits, strip them of their egos. Now that they knew Booth by name, there would be no hiding in the shadows.

Whitmire carried on, describing the dedication he expected from each and every recruit. Fifteen minutes into his speech, a tall blond recruit in his early twenties began to grow impatient. The afternoon was sweltering, heat vapors rising off the tarmac around them. Booth had grown accustomed to triple-digit temperatures after three summers toeing the line in New Mexico, but many of the recruits from stations with milder climates apparently weren't. After shuffling his feet for several minutes, the blond recruit raised a hand to swipe the sweat out of his eyes. That's when two members of the cadre closed in on him. "What do you think you're doing? When Whitmire talks, when any of us talk, your only job is to listen. Now drop and give me fifty!"

The recruit, somewhat surprised, immediately dropped down and began counting them out. Another recruit two rows down tilted his head to watch the spectacle, and he too was ordered on the ground. And so it went, the instructors circling the group like sharks in the water, until each of the sixty-one recruits was on all fours. This smoke session carried on for the next five hours, through the blistering heat and then into the encroaching cold. By the time Class 15 was dismissed for the night and ordered back to the barracks, Booth found himself wishing he had done a little more in terms of physical preparation. But judging from the sorry look on a few of his classmates' faces, he wasn't so bad off. Already he could spot a few who weren't going to last until the end of the next day.

Booth collapsed into his bed exhausted, but he couldn't sleep. He tossed and turned, wondering what the next three weeks had in store. What had he gotten himself into? he wondered. By the time his eyes finally closed, it was 4:15 A.M.

Instructors entered the barracks at 4:30. It was time to begin a day of hell, starting with the BORTAC physical fitness test. As recruits got dressed and filed out the door, a short recruit with a protruding belly approached an instructor and spoke to him under his breath.

"So are you quitting?" asked the instructor.

"My arms—I barely survived last night. There's no way I can make it through twenty-one days of this." The recruit moved back in the direction of his bunk, his arms hanging loosely at his sides as if they were no longer under his command. Booth did not know his name, nor would he know the names of any of those who didn't last the first two weeks. He was in survival mode. There was no time to talk, to be friendly. It wasn't until after the selection course was over that everlasting bonds were forged.

Booth joined his fellow agents out in the morning heat, where they were told what the BORTAC PT test entailed: Forty push-ups and sixty sit-ups in under two minutes; seven full pull-ups; and a mile and a half run in under eleven minutes. It didn't sound so difficult, but Booth quickly realized how sore he was after the night before. A few of his classmates were holding their arms to their chests, trying to keep their muscles from cramping.

Two hours later, twelve agents had either been disqualified or dropped out. No time was taken to mourn their absence. Those who had completed the test were immediately brought to the firing range—they now had to prove their prowess with a firearm. Out of 360 possible points, they had to score at least a 324. Once again, this would normally be a breeze for Booth, but after the night before and the PT test he just underwent, he didn't know if he could even lift a gun.

The firing range instructor shouted "349," after Booth had taken his last shot. He had made it, but eight others weren't so lucky. The group was thinning out, now down to forty. But apparently that number was still too high, because the instructors rounded up those who were left and brought them out into an open field to crank out an endless stream of push-ups and sit-ups.

"It's Labor Day weekend, boys," one instructor shouted. "Bud Lite is on sale. You don't need this. Go home, call a buddy."

"Yeah," shouted another, "go home, grill a steak, drink a beer while sitting in your favorite recliner; watch some football. You really don't need this, so why are you here?"

Booth blocked out their words. If he let even the smallest shred of doubt into his mind, quitting would become all too easy. He focused instead on the promise he had made to himself, how he was only going home if they sent him home. Apparently, not everyone had made a similar pact. An hour into the mental and physical abuse a curly-haired recruit staggered to his feet. "I can't take this," he moaned. "This isn't for me."

Two others followed his lead.

After five hours, instructors finally gave up on trying to get recruits to leave on their own accord. The class was released back to the barracks where they received their second gear issue—another set of uniforms, rucksacks, flak vests, and two-quart canteens. They were in bed by midnight, and unlike the previous night, Booth was sound asleep by 12:15 A.M.

At 4:30 the following morning Booth learned that the worst was far from over. Out in the heat, recruits were instructed to fill their rucksacks with forty-pound weights and then strap them on their backs. This morning they were making a six-mile road march over hills, across sandy marshes, and through the brush. They had an hour and a half to make it to the finish line. Go.

Booth took off, keeping a steady five-mile-an-hour pace. He crossed the finish line with fifteen minutes to spare and then collapsed to wait for the others. When the full hour and a half was up, however, only eleven recruits had completed the mission. A group of very pissed-off instructors hopped in a truck, rounded up the stragglers, and then dropped them back at the starting line. "You failed your mission," they shouted. "Once again, you have an hour and a half to reach the destination. Now go."

While the bulk of the stragglers took off to the best of their abilities, tripping, staggering, and dragging their feet in an attempt to reach the goal, three agents dropped their packs and said, "I quit." This had been what the cadre wanted. With three more recruits eliminated from training, they rounded up the agents attempting to make the finish line and spared them from making the hike again. It had only been a test, a way to measure their heart, but there was no coming back for the three agents who had muttered those two words.

No one, however, would be allowed to skimp out on the swim test, which came immediately after the six-mile march. Agents were thrown into the pool to tread water for twenty minutes without touching the sides or bottom. By this time, Booth's arms and legs were screaming. He was trying to find another way to stay afloat without using his limbs. His body commanded him to quit, to give up this nonsense, but his mind would not allow it. He successfully treaded water for twenty minutes, unlike six of the agents who were then promptly removed from training. But the pool still had more of his heart to claim: next came drown proofing. This was a touch more difficult; instead of wearing a pair of swim trunks, Booth was now tossed into the pool dressed in his uniform, boots included, to stay afloat for forty-five minutes.

Booth pushed past his physical limits and just kept going. He completed the drown proofing, the hundred-meter swim that followed, and then the fifty-meter swim on top of his rucksack with his weapon in hand. By the end of the day he was not just fatigued, but on the verge of collapsing. His class didn't return to the barracks until one a.m. The twenty-three recruits who remained tore off their uniforms and dove into bed.

Fifteen minutes later a group of instructors came into the barracks and flipped on the lights. "You have two minutes to be outside in full uniform!"

Recruits literally began falling out of bed. Shirts were thrown on backward, pants put on inside out. Men were running into each other trying to get out the door.

When less than a minute had passed, one of the instructors shouted, "Time!"

Recruits staggered out half-dressed, wearily defeated.

"I can't believe you can't do this right. Drop and give me a hundred push-ups!"

Recruits began to drop, but then the instructor changed his mind. "Forget that. I'm taking you on a ten-mile run. Go back inside and get your PT gear on. You have two minutes to get changed."

Class 15 rushed back inside, but after less than a minute had passed, the instructor shouted, "Time." Once again recruits came out half-dressed, wearing one shoe, no socks, and their sweatpants turned around. "You're a disgrace, all of you! I'm going to save the run for later, for when you're actually alert enough to feel the pain. Since there are only twenty-three of you left, you no longer need the entire H-building barrack. I want you to confine yourselves to one corner."

And so the tedious task of rearranging their belongings began at one a.m. Agents could be heard mumbling that this was abuse, and they were right. The instructors were doing whatever they could to keep them awake. The next day, Class 15 began the real training. In the days to come they would be further deprived of sleep and food, and then thrust into stressful conditions for long hours to see how they reacted, applied their skills, and worked as a team. They would be given twenty-klick (kilometer) movements and have twelve hours to complete them. Those who failed would be removed from the course; those who succeeded would then be given more difficult tasks, until only the best of the best remained.

By the time barracks were in order, it was 4:15.

Morning PT was at 4:30.

A small group of BORTAC agents flew to La Paz, Bolivia, in July 1996. After being greeted by DEA officials at the airport, they were taken to the command post, which had been established on the outskirts of the city, and briefed on Operation Snowcap: Deep in the north-central jungles, in a region known as the Chapare, liaisons from the Colombian cocaine cartels had enticed local farmers to grow mass quantities of coca for export. Because it wasn't economically feasible for the cartels to transport thousands of pounds of the coca leaf, hundreds of rudimentary processing labs had been built under the three-layer jungle canopy. At these labs, the coca leaf was mixed with various precursor chemicals to create paste cocaine. Once the paste had been stockpiled, it was picked up by small aircraft and flown to more sophisticated labs in Colombia, where it was transformed into cocaine hydrochloride, a product that could be sold on the streets of the United States.

The Bolivian government's anti-narcotics task force, known as the Umopar, had entered the Chapare several times to destroy harvests and labs, but they had been repelled by hostile peasant organizations. With the country on the verge of economic collapse, the Bolivian government had turned to the United States. Now it was their job to ensure that coca production in the area was shut down. It had been decided, however, that hunting down narco-traffickers would only fuel the peasants' resistance. Instead, they were going to target the processing laboratories—the one location where the coca leaf, precursor chemicals, and transportation all met.

One of the DEA's first priorities was to establish roadblocks along all the routes leading in and out of the Chapare. Their reason for doing this was twofold—to interdict the precursor chemicals used to transform the coca leaf into cocaine paste before they could reach the laboratories, and to teach the Umopar how to create and operate checkpoints on their own. Building successful checkpoints, however, required knowledge and expertise, and so the DEA turned to their friends in BORTAC. "You have to have front and rear security," said BORTAC agent Robert Coleman. "You have to have lookouts at certain distances down the road. Then you need to establish a process for apprehending vehicles that turn and run, and those that try to bust through the roadblock. And then you have to check the vehicles—everything from banana trucks to eighteen-wheelers— and know how to do it right. This all takes knowledge."

Once BORTAC had the checkpoints up and running, manned by personnel from Umopar, they combined forces with the DEA and entered the jungle on search-and-destroy missions. "When you watch [the movie] *Clear and Present Danger,* you think they have these big, sophisticated labs," said BORTAC agent Kevin Oaks, "but when you go out there it's basically just a hole in the jungle. They build big, long maturation pits out of sticks and whatnot, and then they line it with plastic. They dump the leaves in there, and then they add precursor chemicals used to activate the alkaloid in the coca leaf. They put men in there wearing rubber boots, and they'll stomp in these poso pits for twelve, fifteen, eighteen hours, chewing on that coca leaf so they can stay awake. Then they do one or two more processes to turn it into what they call 'Queso,' or cheese, which are these little balls of paste cocaine."

Finding the remote jungle labs was not always easy. "We'd send out reconnaissance flights in the helicopters or in small aircraft," said Oaks, "and we'd discover an airstrip out in the middle of nowhere. We would land and take a look to see if it was connected, and usually it was connected to a network of real small labs. We'd go and try to disable all the labs and collect as much data and intelligence information as possible, and then blow the runway so they couldn't use it."

As imagined, this made BORTAC very unpopular with local farmers, many of whom depended upon coca crops for survival. At the height of the operation, when BORTAC was moving through the Chapare in force, the cartels placed a ten-thousand-dollar bounty on the life of any American law enforcement officer, and offered a fifty-thousand-dollar reward for anyone who could shoot down one of their helicopters. For farmers living on an average annual income equivalent to five hundred U.S. dollars, they were looking at getting very rich in a very short time.

"We were disliked, there was no getting around that," said Kevin Stevens. "You're talking about a country that was extremely impoverished. The people, particularly in the regions we were working in, were jungle folks who were growing the coca leaf. Bolivia has a lot of allowable uses for the coca leaf, and of course internationally, there are medicinal purposes for the derivative of that leaf. So there are a lot of legitimate purposes to grow it. But in an impoverished country the lure of more money if they turned it into something illegal was always there. And these folks had only minimal knowledge of the harm that it was causing. They really didn't understand why we would stop them, so they kind of looked at us as the bad guys."

BORTAC agents kept their guard up. Any time they drove a truck through a town or village, they had to roll up their windows because the local populace would throw sticks of dynamite into the cab. When they sent six- or eight-man teams into the jungle to destroy the laboratories, they usually had to come out the same way and could count on encountering resistance. But when the heavily armed agents didn't prove to be easy targets, many frustrated farmers turned on their own people suspected of supplying law enforcers with information.

On one occasion, a village held a public execution for a young man who was seen talking to the Umopar. The entire village gathered around as they beat him with rocks and sticks until he lost consciousness, and then buried him alive. Among the crowd was another informant, who, upon witnessing the murder, fled the village for the safety of the BORTAC base camp. At dawn the following day, a group of DEA and BORTAC agents strapped on their weapons and headed into the jungle. "When we rode into town we were heavily armed," said Stevens. "I was what's known as a grenadier on the unit. My job was to deploy chemical ordnance at riot situations. The deployment of chemical ordnance is done though the use of standard military grenade launchers, and so that's what I was carrying—but in South America I wasn't using non-lethal munitions. Fortunately, I didn't have to pull the trigger. We recovered the body, confirmed the story, and with the assistance of the informant, who was now hidden in disguise amongst our ranks, we arrested twenty-six or twenty-seven people for the murder of the other informant."

Despite the growing resistance of local farmers, the BORTAC teams stationed in the Chapare managed to regain control of the area. Liaisons from the Colombian cartels fled. Crops dried up. But the cartels were not defeated. Since it was ever more difficult to pull coca paste from Bolivia, they quickly struck deals with coca growers in other countries such as Peru.

In response, BORTAC deployed to a host of Latin American countries over the next eight years, including Guatemala. Along with going into the regions where the coca was being grown, they also attempted to interdict shipments of the finished product while en route to the United States. But with the cartels continuously shifting their transportation patterns, narcotics continued to stream into the United States. And with Mexican drug runners growing more desperate and bold, the majority of BORTAC agents were called home in 1994, where their assistance along the U.S.-Mexico border was needed more than ever.

Class 15 had twenty-three recruits left. All had passed the BORTAC qualifiers. All of them had made it through seventy-two hours of pure hell. It was now time to begin learning the skills they had come here to acquire. Things were only going to get more difficult from this point on.

After their five-mile run, recruits were delivered to the firing range for three and a half hours. Although on this first day they were given extensive training on the basic pistol and shotgun, in the weeks to come they were required to master an assortment of long arms, including the M-4, 223 Rifle, the Heckler and Koch (H&K) UMP, and even a variety of grenade launchers. They trained aggressively, moving forward with speed—shooting on the move, shooting from cover, shooting under stress, shooting at multiple targets in limited time.

"Our people will shoot more ammunition in a training course than most agents will shoot in their careers," said Kevin Oaks, the current commander of BORTAC. "We will burn seventy or eighty thousand rounds in a training course. It's repetition, and you train to failure. People come off the range and they can't even move their fingers. It's one of those things where you have to repeat it, and repeat it, so it becomes subconscious, and then the subconscious comes out and takes care of business."

From the firing range, recruits moved on to the classroom to learn camouflage, first aid, patrolling, tactical tracking, and threat assessment. They were taught land navigation, and how to read cross sections on a map. The only breaks they got from these marathon learning sessions were a couple of ten-minute breathers, where they were ushered outside and ordered to crank out two hundred push-ups and sit-ups.

With time served in the classroom, recruits then had to go out into the field to apply their knowledge. They practiced patrolling, drug interdictions, land navigation, and immediate action drills. "Do your best," their instructor told them. "This training will come in very handy when you conduct counter-narcotics operations along the U.S.-Mexico border. Some of you'll go into an area that's notorious for narcotic smuggling several days prior to your team. You'll dig in along the border, gather intelligence as to who and where the suspects are. You'll set up motion detectors and Hid-site to monitor the area. You need to know what to do, so the rest of your team can come in safely under the cover of darkness.

"You also need to have patience. Sometimes you'll have to sleep in caves, only crawling out on the rocks at night. Days will pass with little activity. Then, suddenly, you will spot a group of heavily armed smugglers leading a pack-train of horses loaded with hundreds of pounds of marijuana. You need to know how to surprise them, identify yourselves. If the smugglers refuse to turn themselves over, you need to know how to use less-than-lethal munitions, such as hand-held flash-bands or sting-balls, to bring them under control. If smugglers retaliate with gunfire, as is often the case, then you will make use of the thousands of hours you've spent on the firing range. Make sure you pay attention, because the training you're getting here and now might save your life, and the lives of your fellow team members, in the very near future."

Booth took such speeches very seriously. He put all he had into training, and when he was finally released at one a.m., he returned to the barracks to wash his clothes, polish his boots, and shower before going to bed. It began to wear on him. His toughest day came on Thursday, just five days into the training. After Class 15 completed its five-mile morning run, four hours of shooting, and three hours of class work, they were turned over to a Special Forces A-team that had been brought in to help train them. On this particular night, the A-team had designed a field training exercise for Class 15 to complete.

"Two pilots have gone down on the McGregor range," said the A-team leader. "Your job is to retrieve them and bring them back here in a reasonable amount of time."

Class 15 took off in full gear, their rucksacks jostling on their backs. They had been going all morning, and since the beginning of the course they had only gotten a total of ten hours sleep. But despite the bad physical and mental shape most of them were in, they covered the five miles to McGregor range quickly and located the two pilots—two aviator bags filled with concrete.

Booth got to work making two makeshift litters out of chain-link fence posts and some rope. When they were complete, the bags of cement were loaded on top of them and two eight-man teams began the task of carrying them five miles back. But about halfway back, things began falling apart. Recruits began tripping over their own feet and falling down. Some of the recruits could no longer hold the heavy litter in their hands, leaving others to carry their weight. Booth tried his best to keep everything together, everyone moving forward, but then the sleep deprivation and dehydration claimed the sanity of one of his classmates.

"Who stole my water bottle?" the wild-eyed agent shouted. "Who stole my goddamn water bottle?"

Both of the litters were set down to see what the problem was. The recruit was screaming that someone had stolen his water bottle, but everyone could see that it was still strapped to his belt.

"Calm down," Booth said gently. "No one stole your water bottle. You have it right there."

The agent looked at his belt, but for some reason he couldn't see his water bottle. Convinced someone had stolen it, he lunged at Booth, trying to rip his water bottle free. When Booth fended him off, he attacked others, shouting at the top of his lungs that thieves were among them.

It didn't take long for Class 15 to realize that their fellow recruit was beyond hope, and so they left him behind to be retrieved by instructors. They carried on with their mission, arriving at their destination shortly after one a.m. By this point, few had any mental or physical strength left. Their rucksacks had rubbed their shoulders raw. The skin on their hands had peeled off from carrying the makeshift litter. They were dehydrated, sore, barely awake. And the agent who had lost his mind was at the focus of all their thoughts. They could relate to him, for a portion of each man still in training also felt like he was losing his mind to some degree. They needed sleep so the same didn't happen to them. But completing their mission for the Special Forces A-Team was still not the end of their night.

Just when they thought they were going to bed, Class 15 was delivered to the Rappel Master's Obstacle course on Fort Bliss. Rising up before them were towers of wood and steel, each fifty feet tall. Although the daytime temperature had risen over 100 degrees, the nighttime was bitterly cold, edging in on freezing. Thirty-five-mile-an hour winds howled around their shivering bodies.

"No one's leaving here until everyone finishes this course not once, but twice," shouted the drillmaster. "And if I see anyone pussyfooting around, I'll make you all do it a third time."

Class 15 didn't return to the barracks until 4:15 A.M. As always, morning PT was at 4:30. After their usual five-mile run, recruits were introduced to Mobil Field Force, BORTAC's method of crowd control. "Since the days of desegregation, the Border Patrol has been known for its ability to break up riots," said their instructor. "BORTAC is the tip of that spear. Because we don't have two or three hundred agents to send out onto the streets, we did away with the age-old method of stomp and drag. Supplied with state-of-the-art equipment such as ballistic shields and protective gear, Mobile Field Force focuses on small-group tactics. In the next week you're going to get a lot of practice separating crowds, both in a prison environment and on the street. You're going to become experts at using less-than-lethal munitions, such as beanbag rounds, rubber pellets, and CS gas. This morning, you're going to get your first taste of CS gas."

Class 15 was ordered out onto a field, and then several CS canisters were launched into their midst. One of them landed right next to Booth's feet. The smoke rose up around his body, engulfing him. At first it appeared harmless, but then his skin began to sting. Soon his entire body was on fire, needles piercing every pore on his body. His eyes slammed shut, and he could hardly breathe.

"Remain calm," shouted the instructor over this hiss of gas. "If you panic, you won't be able to breathe. Just stay calm, take short breaths, and everything will be fine."

The abuse carried on like this for days to come—waking up on less than an hour's sleep to a five-mile run, off to the firing range, classroom time, practicals, and then midnight missions for the Special Forces A-team. Almost every day another agent approached an instructor to utter the words "I quit." Those who stuck it out focused on survival. Recruits spent their few free moments of the day tending to their wounds, which were numerous. Men had holes in their backs from their rucksacks. Feet looked like ground beef. Ankles were swollen and sprained. After lights out in the barracks at night, not a word was spoken. Everyone was hanging on by a thread.

After fourteen days of this hell, the sixteen agents still left filed outside at 4:30 A.M. Apparently, there was no run this morning. A few recruits had smiles on their faces, suspecting that the worst was over. But as Class 15 stood there, watching the sun come up over the horizon, Booth noticed one of the instructors looking off into the distance at a hazy mountain range. In the back of Booth's mind he thought, "Man, that would be a long hike." A few moments later, the instructor pointed to the mountains and informed Class 15 that it was their destination. "A group of drug smugglers is hiding somewhere up in those mountains," he said. "First, you must apply your tactical tracking skills to pick up their trail and find them. Then, at daybreak tomorrow, you must conduct a successful raid on their safe house. It's roughly eighteen miles from here to there, so get humping."

The group didn't complain. The majority of those still left were already members of elite tactical teams such as San Diego REACT or Tucson SRT. They knew that the more they complained the harder instructors would make it for them to complete their task. And so Class 15 got humping, picking up the smugglers' tracks almost immediately. Tactical tracking, however, involved a great deal more than simply following the sign. The recruit who was actually doing the tracking had to be guarded by front and rear security. They also had to assign a radioman and a navigator who used a map and compass to keep track of the team's location.

Moving ahead was slow going, but the team managed to work over two passes and up the side of the mountain by midnight. Knowing they were close to their destination, they crept slowly through the brush and spotted what BORTAC instructors called the Pink House, a dilapidated shack that was a favorite carriage stop and brothel back in the old days. Moving around the perimeter of the house were several of the BORTAC instructors dressed in camouflage. One was mounted on an ATV, and another was glaring at the mountainside through night-vision goggles. They were looking for Class 15 just as hard as Class 15 was looking for them.

The recruits pulled back and broke into two teams. One team monitored the smugglers' activities, while Booth crept through the bush with the second team, scouting for the best route up to the Pink House. Then, shortly after four a.m, Booth was notified that the smugglers had bedded down for the night. "We ended up using a deep arroyo, which is just a dry creek bed, to come under the cover of darkness and sneak up close," said Booth. "And then, at the given time, we got into our line formation. The three rules you use are speed, surprise, and violence of action when you do a takedown. So we used speed, surprise, and violence of action to successfully arrest everybody."

Their mission had been completed, but recruits still had a long day ahead of them. Without even a slight pat on the back, they were brought down off the mountainside and cast out into the desert with a map and compass to navigate eight miles through the heat. Once again men were falling over from dehydration, injuries, and fatigue. Mistakes were being made. They completed the course behind schedule, and upon stepping foot back in BORTAC headquarters the cadre told them they had to do it all over again.

The men didn't argue. Their minds were focused on only one thing—moving forward and completing the mission. But before they could head back out, Charles Whitmire came into the barracks.

"Congratulations!" Whitmire told them. "And welcome to BORTAC. The sixteen of you have passed two weeks of pain and suffering, but in the week to come you'll be getting into the fun stuff—rappelling from helicopters onto various battlefields, conducting air-assault operations, building entries, and making use of the close-quarter battle skills you've already learned. You'll practice day and night, until it becomes second nature. But even at the end of the course, when you're issued a green flight suit, a Kevlar ballistic helmet, and an armored assault vest, your training will not be over. We've been keeping a close eye on you, and know what you are good at, probably better than you do yourselves. As specific operations come about, the deputy commander will begin to call upon you. You will be paired up with BORTAC members who already have extensive field experience. I advise you all to learn from these men, because out on the line or overseas is where you gain your true wisdom. Good job, men."

Booth collapsed into bed, too exhausted to celebrate. He needed all the sleep he could get, because the next day they would be right back at it, only now they would be working in life-threatening environments.

Along with conducting countless drug interdiction missions on the U.S.-Mexico border, over the years BORTAC also experienced a substantial amount of mission creep. Because of their experience in the field, they were asked to train various state and local police agencies in a variety of tactics. They taught desert survival classes to the Bureau of Land Management and the Bureau of Indian Affairs. They continued to return to Latin America, where they helped foreign governments establish elite anti-drug task forces. They even deployed to a host of natural disasters, including Hurricane Andrew, which swept through South Florida in 1992. Their missions were numerous, and yet they remained the most elusive and secretive task force in the country. All that changed, however, on April 22, 2000, when they conducted Operation Reunion.

A small group of BORTAC agents were selected to conduct an early-morning raid on a Florida home to retrieve Elian Gonzales, the seven-year-old Cuban boy who had been found floating on an inner tube off the coast of Florida on Thanksgiving day in 1999. Because Elian's mother (and ten other Cubans) had drowned when the boat they fled Cuba in capsized at sea, Elian had been temporarily placed with his great uncle in Florida instead of being returned home. Elian's father considered this kidnapping, and wanted his son brought back to Cuba. Elian's relatives in America, however, refused to hand him over. And so the battle for Elian began, the entire nation watching and taking sides.

INS had a decision to make: who could rightfully speak on behalf of the child? They sent officials to Cuba to meet with Elian's father, who recounted the day his son was kidnapped by his ex-wife. She had told him she was taking Elian to a picnic, but instead took him to a beach where they boarded a small aluminum boat unsuited for the journey to America. As a result of her negligence, Elian had spent two days in shark-infested waters. It was a miracle that he was still alive. He had been through enough, and he needed to be home with his father.

INS agreed, and they ordered Elian's relatives to hand him over. The family ignored the order and brought the matter to the Florida courts, where they won custody. The INS didn't recognize the court's jurisdiction, and so the family sued for custody in a federal court, which subsequently upheld INS's authorization to decide the matter. With all the cards played, Elian's father flew to America to retrieve his boy. But still the family refused to release him.

When negotiations looked like they were breaking down, the INS turned to BORTAC. "The Attorney General called though the chain of command to the chief patrol agent and said, 'We want you to help the Miami district plan a con-op,'" said Kevin Oaks. "So BORTAC looked at it and went through a bunch of different scenarios. Finally, they got the plan all worked up and decided they were going to do a basic, classical tactical entry on the house and take the child into custody and return him to the Department of Justice."

Planning the entry on the house, however, took several weeks and involved 131 agents from a variety of government agencies. With thousands wanting to prevent Elian from returning to Cuba, including members of the anti-Castro paramilitary group Alpha 66, the agents conducting the raid were expected to encounter resistance upon arriving at the residence. BORTAC was also supplied with intelligence information that suggested the family had hired their own security force. With this in mind, BORTAC officials knew it would be in everyone's best interest to get in and out of the residence as quickly as possible. Accomplishing this would require a show of force—loud commands, large weapons, and menacing presence. They had to intimidate those in the household, show that they meant business, and then be out before any retaliation. They also had to catch the family and its supporters off guard, which meant a predawn raid. "You never take on a tactical challenge unless you know you can execute it," said Oaks. "If you go in there thinking, 'I don't know if we can really do it,' then you shouldn't be doing it. That is the premise we work under. If we don't know we can win, we're not going to do it. We come back another day or come up with another plan."

All the planning was put into effect on April 22. With the family unwilling to return the child to INS authorities, President Clinton personally ordered the raid. "The Attorney General called the commander of BORTAC at the time and gave him the authorization to go, and they went in," said Oaks.

As expected, BORTAC agents encountered resistance the moment they opened the van door in front of the residence. Protestors attempted to form a human wall to prevent their passage, but BORTAC agents moved swiftly around them. By the time they reached the front door, it had been locked and barred from the inside with a couch. Willing to give the family ample opportunity to hand the boy over peacefully, they knocked on the door for twenty-five seconds, the entire time being pelted with rocks and bottles.

When it became clear that the family had no intention of opening the door, the BORTAC agents broke it down with a battering ram and swept into the residence to find Elian. Uncertain as to who or what they were up against, the six agents kept the butts of their Heckler and Koch MP5 submachine guns pressed firmly against their shoulders, the barrels pointing in the direction of their vision as they had been trained. The agents had spent thousands of hours on the firing range with these weapons, and used them during hundreds of scenario-training exercises. If they encountered a threat, they were authorized to take a shot. Until then, they kept the weapons on safety.

An agent entered a bedroom, his body hugging the wall. A child's head popped out of the closet, and then back in. The agent drew closer and opened the closet doors. Elian was inside, being held in the arms of relative Donato Dalrymple. Once the agent saw that there were no threats, he lowered the barrel of his weapon, but by that time photographer Alan Diaz of the Associated Press, who was hiding in the room at the time, had already snapped a photo that would shortly be broadcast around the world and would label BORTAC agents as cold-blooded storm troopers. Few would understand what the agents had been up against—protestors and irate relatives who would do anything to keep the boy in America. They wouldn't understand that every action BORTAC agents took in the residence was for security reasons, and that the raid was handled by the book. All they would see in the photo was a heavily armed agent pointing a weapon at a teary-eyed seven-year-old boy.

BORTAC agents took Elian into their custody and then quickly ushered him outside, where he was handed over to the U.S. Marshals.

Later that day, Elian was flown to an Air Force base near Washington where he was finally reunited with his father.

The actual raid had taken less than three minutes, but the effects were long lasting. In the hours following the operation protestors began rioting on the streets of Miami and in Cuban neighborhoods across America. BORTAC also felt a backlash. "They were trying to get the names of the individuals on the entry team up until the time I left," said Charles Whitmire, who had been the commander of BORTAC at the time of the raid. "There were threats against their lives, threats against the commissioner's life. I provided twelve men for security for the commissioner of the INS, twenty-four/seven, immediately following that because of threats against her life."

BORTAC had not been interested in the politics surrounding Elian Gonzalez. They were ordered to do a job, and they did it with the utmost efficiency. "There was a lot of criticism," said Oaks, "but if you cut everything out and just look at the tactical part of it, all the other tactical experts out there say that it was executed pretty well. There were some minor glitches here and there, but nobody got hurt and we got the right child—because they were worried about imposter children." After their mission was complete, the agents flew back to their stations and waited for the next mission. It wasn't until all the dust had settled from Operation Reunion, however, that they were once again able to retreat into the shadows.

On the afternoon of September 22, 2001, Allan Booth wedged his exhausted body into his pickup and made the drive back to Lordsburg, New Mexico. After sleeping for two entire days in the comfort of his own bed, he once again slipped into his green uniform and headed out into the desert to round up smugglers and migrants illegally crossing the line. Having successfully completed the rigorous BORTAC training, he noticed a difference in the way he handled his everyday duty. His senses were sharper, his instincts more keen. He also noticed a change in the way his fellow patrolmen viewed him. He had gone through the most extensive and comprehensive training the Border Patrol had to offer, and in many ways he was now considered a leader at his station. Agents looked up to him for guidance and motivation. Always under a microscope, he had to be the hardest-pushing guy out there.

As winter settled in, Booth got his first call from BORTAC headquarters. They wanted him to fly to Tucson to help train the next batch of agents trying out for the Tucson sector's Special Response Team. The mission was a far cry from Booth's high expectations, but he gladly obliged and boarded a plane the following week. Then, a few days after he arrived, he received another call from headquarters. The moment he picked up the phone he detected a sense of urgency in the commander's voice.

Two years earlier, in April 1999, a commercial bus traveling from Phoenix to Chicago pulled into a weigh station shortly after crossing the Nebraska state line. A Nebraskan state trooper stepped on board, a routine procedure, but he grew suspicious when the driver couldn't produce the necessary papers. When the trooper asked a few passengers for their identification, he realized none of them spoke English. Upon making the necessary translation in Spanish, the fifty-one Mexican migrants on board admitted that they were in the country illegally and were subsequently arrested.

The situation was unusual. Once illegal workers crossed the line, they often traveled by bus to reach their final destinations, but to have a bus packed exclusively with undocumented immigrants was virtually unheard of. INS was contacted about the matter, and shortly thereafter the Border Patrol's anti-smuggling unit from Tucson traced the bus back to its owner, Golden State Bus Lines, which was based in Los Angeles. Over the course of a two-year investigation, agents discovered that the bus company was conspiring with smugglers to transport up to three hundred illegal Mexican workers from various points along the border to their destinations inland every day.

They had the scheme down to a science. Shortly after aliens were smuggled over the California and Arizona borders, they were temporarily brought to safe houses and hotels. At midnight they were ushered to secluded bus terminals in San Diego and Tucson, where they were instructed to hide in shadows until their buses arrived. With blocks of tickets purchased in advance by smugglers, the immigrants piled aboard. This enabled them to circumvent Border Patrol checkpoints and get into the United States.[2]

For twenty-four months Tucson's anti-smuggling unit had hunkered in bushes, snapping photos and gathering evidence. They had targeted twelve smugglers, all of whom worked for either the "Castillo" or "Pineda" human-smuggling operations. They had also targeted a number of employees working for Golden State Bus Lines, including the company's president, a host of senior managers, and a number of terminal managers. They had all the evidence they needed; now they just had to make the arrests.

When Booth arrived at ASU headquarters in Tucson, more than fifty Border Patrol agents from Special Operations teams across the country were already there, including Tucson SRT, San Diego REACT, and several fellow BORTAC members. With thirty-one high-risk warrants to be served simultaneously, they needed all the help they could get.

The commander of the operation explained the logistics: They were going to break down into five-man teams. Each team would be assigned one house on the list. Because they were dealing with one massive smuggling organization, it was critical that all the warrants be served at the same time. If they went from house to house, someone would have the opportunity to jump on the telephone and start sending out warnings. They couldn't risk a team showing up at the second, third, or fourth house only to discover the suspect had fortified himself in his residence. They didn't want to deal with barricaded suspects—that was a whole different ball of wax. The commander informed them all to learn their targets inside and out.

Booth and the four other members of his team began their intelligence-gathering mission the following morning. In an unmarked vehicle, they parked down the street from their target residence, located in a suburban neighborhood of Tucson. Having planned dozens of similar raids during the BORTAC selection course, Booth knew exactly what to look for. "You try to study the house during both the night and day. If you have the opportunity, you look at it as much as possible to see what cars are there, who's coming and going," said Booth. "You monitor what time the lights go on and what time they go off. Are there toys in the yard—do they have kids? Do they have dogs? Is there evidence of a security system? Do they have motion-activated floodlights? Because we're going in at night, the last thing we want when we step on the front porch is for the whole damn yard to become illuminated. And to get an idea of what we could expect on the inside of the house, we looked at a house down the street that had been built by the same contractor. All these little factors are imperative for the security of the team."

Next came the background of their suspect. Did he have a violent history? Was he known to have guns in the house? Had he ever told one of the undercover officers working the case that he would never get taken alive?

With all this information in mind, Booth and his team began their training. After qualifying on a firing range with the various weapons they planned to use during the operation, they spent long hours each day at Tucson SRT's training facility. Together they entered close-quarter-battle warehouses that had been set up to imitate the floor plans of their prospective residences. At first they conducted the mock raids using "simunitions"—a cross between a paintball and a real bullet—but quickly progressed into live fire. To cover all possible angles, furniture was constantly being rearranged. They practiced moving from the vehicle to the door, from the door into the front room. Various scenarios were tossed at them, to which they had to react without a second thought. "You spend as much time as possible working with your team so you get to know how everyone moves and reacts," said Booth. "We had over three weeks where all we did was shoot. Everything was repetition, preparing for that one moment."

Then, after twenty-one days of training and waiting, the various teams were notified that the United States Attorney had signed the indictments.

The following morning at 4:30 A.M., agents flooded into the pre-staging area set up near the Tucson County Courthouse. Once all their protective gear had been strapped on and their weapons locked and loaded, they piled into a long chain of vans. Over the course of the last several weeks, each team had driven from this exact spot to its destination numerous times. Taking stoplights and traffic into account, they knew exactly how long it would take to reach their residences at this early-morning hour. Because every raid had to be executed at the exact same moment, vans were released in accordance to their drive times. The commander of the operation also stayed in contact with agents in El Paso and Phoenix, where additional teams were being unleashed.

As Booth and his team swept down the nearly deserted streets of Tucson, a touch of light filled the sky in the east. The December morning was bitterly cold, the agents' breaths puffing clouds of vapor in the back of the van. Surprisingly, Booth wasn't cold; adrenaline surged through his veins. In the back of his mind he rehearsed the plan over and over. After thousands of hours of training, he felt more than prepared for the worst-case scenario.

The van came to a stop. Booth checked his watch, which had been synchronized with the other teams—5:58 A.M. The van door slid open and he stepped out onto the street. With an H&K UMP 40 assault rifle in his hands, he led the team quietly up the driveway, knowing the precise location of every obstacle without having to look. Once all team members had positioned themselves on the porch, Booth rapped on the door while another team member boomed, "U.S. federal officers! We have a warrant!"

The team immediately grew silent, listening for any response. They heard nothing, not even feet pattering on the floor inside. They repeated the process after thirty seconds had passed, and still heard nothing. This was the worst part, waiting the three minutes prescribed by law. There was no telling what the suspect was doing. He could be sleeping soundly in bed or taking a position behind a sofa with an automatic weapon. They knocked again, and when they still received no answer Booth forcibly removed the door from its hinges with a battering ram.

They swept into the front room. The floor plan was exactly the same as the home they had studied down the street, and with the furniture arranged just as they had envisioned, they knew exactly where to go.

When the front room had been cleared, two agents moved into an adjacent study while Booth crept toward the master bedroom. He kicked in the door, and found his subject rising out of bed. Booth scanned the room, searching for weapons or additional suspects hiding out of sight. He saw nothing out of the ordinary, and so he moved in to make the arrest. In a matter of seconds, the suspect was in handcuffs.

"Everything went down at the crack of dawn without a hitch," said Booth. "Not a shot fired, nobody injured, no compromises. Everyone we went after, we got. Everything turned out to be excellent, including the raids that went down in Phoenix and El Paso. It was a huge accomplishment, and I couldn't have done it without my training."

After a short victory celebration that night, Booth went back to Lordsburg to once again toe the line. It wouldn't be long, however, until BORTAC called upon him once again, this time to go to Honduras to train their border police in rural tactics. "I have done several different kinds of detail," said Booth. "I've done the high-speed Hollywood stuff—crashing through the door, doing the security at the Olympics. I have also instructed three basic classes. But overall, the most rewarding part of the Border Patrol, in general, is how it espouses its esprit de corps. Border Patrol agents are all very goal oriented. They are very patriotic and do their jobs well. And when you get to BORTAC you are talking about the absolute epitome of that, guys who get up to do their jobs every day. Guys who go out and give everything they have. In BORTAC there is no doubt about the caliber of person you're standing next to, and what you can expect from him. It's just at a level so far beyond what you normally see in your average person. BORTAC is truly a brotherhood. Any one of my BORTAC brothers can call me in the middle of the night no matter where he is or what he needs, and there is no doubt that I would go the extra mile to provide for him and help him out."

Chapter Eight

THE INS DISASTER

"You could say that the Border Patrol is the bastard orphan step-child of the Immigration Service" —Ab Taylor

"I met an old guy who was one of the original border patrolmen from back in the twenties, and this old cowboy was like a character out of a movie or something. He told me, 'Boy, we had control of that border tight down there, but once INS took us over, the whole deal turned to shit.'" —Thomas Hammond

ALTHOUGH Thomas Hammond spent almost three decades working for the INS as an immigration inspector, deportation officer, and, finally, a criminal investigator, he began his federal service on April 2, 1972, as a border patrolman in San Diego, California. At the time, the Immigration and Naturalization Service estimated that approximately 250,000 aliens were working illegally in the United States, but those numbers were rapidly increasing. Many of the Mexican labor brokers who had brought workers legally into the United States under the Bracero Program had flipped over into the human-smuggling business when the program shut down. Every month another smuggling organization opened shop south of the line, charging illegal immigrants a couple hundred dollars for a guided tour north.

Six days a week, Hammond headed out into the field at five a.m. to begin the game of cat and mouse. In a matter of hours, he would usually have rounded up between twenty-five and thirty illegal immigrants and brought them back to headquarters for processing. While he headed home at three p.m., his catch for the day was being shipped back to Mexico by bus. This went on day after day, night after night, and yet the smugglers continued to haul illegal workers north, unthreatened by the notion of apprehension. Growing frustrated, Hammond decided to take a more proactive approach. "Every afternoon in Chula Vista you could see the smugglers lining their vehicles on the streets, getting ready for their evening runs," said Hammond. "They would have a bunch of old, shitty cars parked all over the place, and we would go along with valve-stem removers and try to sabotage them a little bit. The ones we couldn't get, we'd keep under surveillance, and when they loaded them up we would grab them."

Hammond made some major arrests while in the Border Patrol. He liked being out in the field, and he was constantly searching for ways to bring the leaders of smuggling organizations to justice. But he also missed New England, where he was born and raised. Not wanting to detach himself from the battle against illegal immigration, he searched for job opportunities in the INS, which had offices stationed throughout the northeast. After four years toeing the line in San Diego, he got a job as an INS Immigration Inspector at Boston's Logan International Airport.

As an immigration inspector, Hammond's job was to inspect the paperwork of those arriving to the United States through the airport to determine if they were eligible to proceed out into the main terminal, and then ultimately out onto the streets. He was on the lookout for false documents, stolen passports, or criminals using false identification. According to the law, those who didn't have proper identification were not to be admitted to the United States, but Hammond quickly learned that INS was not a firm believer in the rules. "If there was any question at all if they were admissible or not, they just admitted them," said Hammond. "Once they admitted them, they left the area and went on to the middle of the United States or wherever they were going to, and the Boston office never had a problem with them after that. That's the way it was all over the country. It was like shuffling a deck of cards."

This was not the only problem. Hammond learned that detaining someone with improper paperwork was not always in an immigration inspector's best interest. Oftentimes, the detainee had friends or relatives in the United States, who, in turn, would contact their congressional office. The congressional office would then contact the INS, and within a matter of days the immigration inspector who had detained the individual received the third degree. Their job was not to strictly enforce the law, but rather move through the line as quickly as possible and not create any unwanted frustration.

The problem didn't go away as time went on—it only got worse. Former Border Patrol Agent Paul Christensen, who attained a high-ranking INS position during a twenty-six-year career, noticed just how badly the system had corroded by 1990. "Joe Terrorist comes to the United States and presents himself at a port of entry, say LAX out of Los Angeles. Inspectors are supposed to spend only twenty seconds inspecting him—that was the standard three years ago when I retired," said Christensen. "Twenty seconds was all you were supposed to spend. You're in line and I'm an inspector, and you're walking up to me next. You don't have anything out. I say, 'I need to see your passport and your I-94 form,' and you fumble around and get that out. By now I've got maybe ten seconds left, and I'm supposed to check that, type it into a computer that may be down or may be up, and I've got to make a decision.

"Thirty years ago that was not the way it was. The guy stood there, you talked to him a little bit. You looked over the passport to see if it looked like it had been altered or if it was a valid passport or counterfeit, while you were talking to him. You asked him questions about where he had been, and you're looking at stamps to see what type of a traveler this guy was—had he traveled to high drug areas, had he traveled to areas that we're watching, countries that have a lot of terrorists. None of that is going on."

To make matters worse, INS inspectors were considered the cream of the crop at the ports of entry. Working in alternate booths were customs inspectors, who, on the whole, cared little about immigration violations. When illegal immigrants came into the country, there was nothing telling them which line they had to go through, and so in many cases they chose the lines of customs inspectors, knowing that even though their paperwork was incomplete the chances were they would get stamped through. The customs inspector might ruffle through their bags searching for drugs or illicit contraband, but that was a small price to pay for entry into the United States.

"You had these customs inspectors who were a little shady, and they would just walk over and get into their line," said Christensen. "A lot of times you would try to watch for that in the airports, but you can only watch so much when you have flight after flight. Like in Los Angeles, you've got an off-loading plane of three hundred people, and then right behind that, ten minutes later, there are another three hundred. People are stacked up and down the runway to get to the inspection booths. Of course, there is so much politics involved. If you don't hurry up and get these people through, somebody with a little bit of a connection gets mad because they had to wait and calls so and so, who calls so and so's office and complains. Well, that goes down hill and Mr. Director gets a call, and they talk to their people. That's how you ended up with twenty seconds—bang them out, bang them through."

When Christensen was promoted to chief of deportation in Houston, Texas, a part of his new position was to supervise inspections at the airport. While he was learning the ins and outs of this detail, Pan American Airways decided to change a flight that had been traveling between Guatemala City and Los Angeles for years. Everything about the flight remained the same, only now it would be stopping in Houston, in an attempt to gather more passengers.

Christensen was at the airport on the night the first flight came in, and in accordance with the law he informed the immigration inspectors reviewing the passengers to detain everyone who couldn't provide the necessary paperwork. To his surprise, an hour after the plane touched down, half the passengers were in custody. He had no intention of letting illegal immigrants sneak past immigration inspectors on his watch, but that quickly garnered a reaction from the airline, which had to pay for the immigrants' return flights out of its own pocket.

"What happened after detaining half of three flights? Of course, Pan American raised hell with the Immigration Service," said Christensen, "and then they raised hell with the U.S. Department of State—why were we doing this and costing them all this money? And of course the Department of State contacted the INS. My boss was the district director of Houston, and he called us in, 'What the hell is going on?' We told him, and he said, 'Not much you can do about that, I guess. You've got to do what you've got to do.' That flight lasted about a week, and that was that—it went back to Los Angeles. . . . They don't detain anyone in Los Angeles, I don't think. . . . That is kind of an example of some of the stuff that goes on."

When Hammond realized that he would never be allowed to adequately enforce the law as an immigration inspector, he got a job as a deportation officer for the INS in Boston. His mission in this new position was to monitor aliens who were currently undergoing deportation hearings, and then remove them from the United States once they were officially found deportable. But just as with his former position, he learned that INS was far from being on top of the situation.

In Hammond's opinion, it would make sense to hold the individuals until their hearing, and then if they were found deportable, they would be escorted out of the country. INS, however, had set up a different process. If a friend, relative, or employer could post a one-thousand-dollar bond for the alien in custody, the INS would then have the Border Patrol release them on their own recognizance. "It may take a year for them to have their initial hearing, and then if they appeal to the Board of Immigration Appeals it may take four or five years to even hear their appeal," said Hammond. "During all that time they're here in the United States, doing whatever the hell they want to do. They just go get more phony documents and go get another job someplace. They can stay here indefinitely. After 9/11, you saw that the INS was looking for 350,000 illegal aliens that had been issued orders of deportation but they had lost track of them. The reason they lost track of them was because it took the Board of Immigration Appeals and these other entities years and years to even render a decision in their cases. And there is nothing the INS can do—they have no way to take them back into custody. Once they are released on bond, they're out there until their deportation comes down. And if one doesn't come down for eight years, the guy could have moved to San Francisco or New York. They don't know where the hell he is."

While trying to single-handedly keep track of six thousand illegal immigrants as they went through their lengthy deportation hearings, Hammond kept a close eye on what was transpiring along the southern border. Both the Border Patrol and INS had begun cracking down on smugglers by arresting them, bringing them to court, and getting convictions. But they continued to release the illegal immigrants the smugglers had brought into the country. In Hammond's view, this only encouraged other aliens to pay smugglers to lead them north, which in turn created a never-ending supply of up-and-coming smugglers. The problem of illegal immigration got so out of hand, that soon all the cheap-labor jobs in border towns such as El Paso and San Diego had been filled. When this happened, illegal immigrants began migrating farther into the United States in search of jobs. State and local police officers were stopping vanloads of illegal workers throughout the interior of the United States, which happened to be INS's domain. With pressure mounting to bring the problem under control, INS created anti-smuggling units in a number of major cities. This, in turn, opened positions for criminal investigators, who, by definition, were to work undercover to infiltrate smuggling organizations, make arrests, and present cases for prosecution to the United States attorneys.

Hammond jumped at the chance to once again be out there in the field, making arrests. After going through INS's anti-smuggling-unit training program at Glynco, Georgia, in 1979, he got bumped up to criminal investigator and moved to Omaha, Nebraska. During his first several years, he worked closely with the Border Patrol's anti-smuggling units, which were popping up in greater number along the border. Through undercover work, Hammond would discover smuggling groups who were traveling down to the border to pick up illegal workers to fill various jobs in Nebraska or Iowa. He'd call the Border Patrol anti-smuggling units and let them know whom to look out for and when. Then, when the smugglers came across with their loads, the Border Patrol's anti-smuggling units would intercept them for Hammond. This strategy worked quite well in the beginning, but as the years progressed there were so many loads moving north that they could hardly make a dent. Things were spinning out of control, and yet the criminal investigators were getting no support from either INS or the federal government.

The Immigration Reform and Control Act (IRCA) of 1986 was expected to help solve the problem by introducing employer sanctions, an amnesty provision, and increasing law enforcement. It looked appealing to the average citizen reading the morning newspaper, but the law enforcers who dealt with the problem of illegal immigration on a daily basis were not fooled. "The employer sanctions laws were sabotaged from the start by the supporters of the illegal aliens who wanted them to stay here," said Hammond. "The way they did this was by throwing a red herring into the law. After the law was passed, what they said is, 'Look, you can't treat illegal aliens any differently than you treat citizens. If an American citizen can get a job by showing a driver's license and a social security card, if a person is an alien, you have to allow him or her to just show a driver's license and a social security card to get a job also.' Anybody can get a driver's license. And a social security card can be easily counterfeited, or you can purchase one from somebody else and assume his or her identity.

"Say you're some guy who doesn't work, and you've got ten copies of your social security card and you sell those to ten different illegal aliens who earn low wages. One of them is a maid cleaning a hotel, the other one is working in a meat-packing house, the other one is a dishwasher in a restaurant—all these employers are sending this money into your account. Social Security will say, 'Well jeez, how could you be working in all these different places at the same time?' The guy will say, 'Well, I'm an old man and I can't remember now, but I worked all over the country and everything, and you know I'm a Hispanic guy. You guys are just hassling me—I'm just trying to get my social security.' You know what they do? They just give it to him. These people just want to get rid of these folks. They don't want to argue with them or have any bureaucratic problems with them. That's going on all over the country.

"You pull out your social security card and look at it: I mean, anyone can counterfeit it. It's just a piece of paper. It was never meant to need any kind of verification. Before illegal immigration became a problem, the card was just a reminder to a person what their social security number was."

In fact, the employer sanctions implemented by the IRCA actually benefited smugglers. Instead of just providing transportation services, they could now offer the entire package—a ride north, false documents, and a guaranteed job with one of the thousands of employers still eager to get their hands on cheap labor.

The amnesty portion of IRCA also did little to stem the tide of illegal immigrants coming to the United States. The assumption had been that if all the illegal immigrants currently filling the cheap labor jobs around the United States were suddenly granted amnesty then the problem would be solved. The western growers would have their workers, and, in turn, there would be few illegal immigrants fighting to cross the border. What had been overlooked, however, was that the majority of employers didn't want legal workers because along with them came certain responsibilities.

"They didn't want some guy who would sue them, or, if they got hurt, go and apply for workmen's comp," said Christensen. "They didn't want anyone who wanted sick leave or paid vacation time or health benefits. They wanted the illegal aliens who they could pay very little, and abuse them as far as not letting them have sick days or vacation time." The workers who were not fired after being granted amnesty usually left of their own accord. Right away they moved to higher paying jobs, to factories and packinghouses in the city.

To take their place, a whole new wave of illegal immigrants moved into the United States—and many of them hustled just as fast as they could, hoping they too could gain amnesty, even though they hadn't lived in the United States for the designated amount of time.

"That was at least 90-percent fraud," said Christensen. "The Immigration Service caught hell from Congress because they were scrutinizing applicants and denying them, and finally they just gave up and began approving them wholesale." Christensen wasn't the only one who could attest to this fact. According to Ab Taylor, "I bet there wasn't one percent of them that met the requirements of that damned amnesty," he said. "They had to have six to nine years, all this—shit, you couldn't thumb through a thousand of them and find five of them who met all the requirements. The ones who did have family and had been here a long time, it might work. But it ought to work on an individual basis of one person at a time, and not a whole damn swarm."

The last part of the IRCA dealt with increasing law enforcement efforts to crack down on smugglers and employers who hired illegal immigrants, but very little came out of it. For the majority of Hammond's career with the INS, he was one of only four criminal investigators to deal with illegal immigration issues in all of Nebraska and Iowa. He increased the hours he worked, and did everything in his power to prosecute those he found in violation of the law. But with every passing month he found himself more overwhelmed.

"One night in 1995 we were out in North Plate, Nebraska, on Interstate 80," said Hammond. "We were helping the federal Fish and Game checkpoint up there and we caught seventy-five illegal aliens. In one night—that's one night in October. If we had people out there every night, you imagine how many we would catch in a year? When I retired here in 1997, the State Patrol in Nebraska thought at least a thousand illegal aliens were getting smuggled across Nebraska and I-80 every day. Every day! That's 365,000 a year. It's a hell of a lot of people, especially when you've only got four investigators to handle them all. How could four investigators handle 365,000 aliens?"

To make matters worse, Amendment 245(i) was added to the law in 1994, allowing immigrants who had entered the country illegally to become permanent residents without leaving the United States. They could achieve this by having their employers prove that there was a tremendous labor shortage in the U.S. for that particular occupation or by marrying a U.S. citizen.

"All throughout immigration history, if a person came into the United States across the border illegally EWI (Entry Without Inspection) they could never adjust their immigration status here. If they married an American citizen or a permanent resident, they couldn't adjust their status and stay here. They had to go back to their home country, apply for an immigrant visa, go through the visa-issuing process, and then make a new entry into the United States legally; 245(i) did away with all that. What they said to every illegal alien here was; 'If you can find an American citizen or a permanent resident here to marry and pay the INS a thousand-dollar fine, we will just forgive your illegal alien status and give you a green card.' When you do that, aren't you encouraging illegal aliens from all over the world to come over here and fraudulently marry some American citizen, pay a thousand dollars, and then get a green card? Why should anyone wait in Australia or South America or Japan or Europe or anywhere else and apply for an immigrant visa?

"The INS management liked it—they didn't care, because for every illegal alien that came in, they got a thousand bucks. And they used that to run the examinations program—the people who adjudicate the petitions in INS Service Centers. Say you have three or four hundred thousand doing that a year, you could imagine how many thousands of dollars you've got. All that is going into the INS fund, and it is being used to hire more adjudicators and more people to process more applications and more petitions. It was a self-serving kind of deal. Well, Congress knocked it out. And then right before Bill Clinton went out of office, in an effort to conjure up some Hispanic votes for the Democrats in the 2000 election, Bill Clinton got the Congress to pass a three-month extension of 245(i). He brought it back for just three months, and I think about four hundred thousand illegal aliens got their green cards during those four months. They all went out right away and got married. Most of these marriages are bogus, but INS doesn't have anyone to go out and check them. They're running on an honor system here."

As a criminal investigator for INS, Hammond decided to delegate a large portion of his time to investigating fraudulent marriages that had resulted since 1994 because of Amendment 245(i). In one case, a nineteen-year-old exotic dancer from the south of Omaha had married an illegal immigrant from Mexico and then filed for an immediate relative petition on behalf of her newly acquired husband. A few weeks later, she was found murdered in the closet of her home. When the police arrived on the scene, they found no evidence of forcible entry or burglary. Despite having been recently married, she lived alone at the time. The police attempted to track down her husband, but when he couldn't be found, they contacted Hammond at INS.

"I went looking for him, and I found him a couple of weeks later," said Hammond. "He had been living with his brother ever since he went through the marriage with this gal. I found one of her girlfriends who told me that she was getting paid by this guy to go through the marriage ceremony. She was trying to get more and more money from him than was agreed. The chances are that he probably killed her, but the police couldn't prove it."

That didn't stop Hammond, however, from arresting the suspect for fraudulently marrying a U.S. citizen in order to obtain residency status. A few weeks after being detained, the illegal alien's relatives in the United States posted a bond and he was released. "He ended up going through a deportation hearing, and the judge found him deportable," said Hammond. "He appealed that up through the administrative process to an outfit called the Board of Immigration Appeals. Well, they didn't make a decision on the case for about six years—that's how long it takes to get one of these appeals through. Well, they came back and said this was obviously a fraudulent marriage, and that this guy should be deported. Then he filed another appeal to the Eighth Circuit Court of Appeals, which is in the federal courts. He waited for them to reach a decision for another couple of years. Finally, the case came back, and it said, 'No, this guy is a deportable alien.' . . . By that time I was a supervisor, and somebody else went out to arrest him. Lo and behold, when they found him he was married to another American citizen and he had three children. . . . They had to arrest him, and they deported him. But I think he came back; he probably snuck back in and is living in some other part of the country happily ever after."

Cases such as these made Hammond wonder why he worked for

the INS. He was a firm believer that the basic law enforcement function of the INS was to investigate, arrest, and remove illegal aliens
from the United States. But every year the laws grew more lax, and
with the millions of former illegal immigrants who had been natu-
ralized by either the 1986 amnesty program or the 245(i) adjust-
ment program now in a position to vote, it didn't seem as though
law enforcement had a very bright future. This new voting force
had a special interest in relaxing immigration laws, which only encouraged illegal immigrants now working in the country to remain
in the U.S. waiting for future amnesty programs to come about.

Both Hammond and Christensen were spitting into the wind by
continuing to try and enforce the laws, and by 1992 they'd had
enough of it. In order to prove to upper INS management just how
effective enforcing the law could be at solving the problem of illegal
immigration in the U.S. interior, they organized a raid on a large
meatpacking plant in Norfolk, Nebraska, that was suspected of em-
ploying more than a thousand illegal workers. After gathering all
the evidence they needed to make arrests, they garnered the cooperation from a variety of state and local law enforcement officers.
To cover all the bases, however, they still needed additional INS
criminal investigators to support them for the actual raid.

To achieve this, they turned to their superiors for extra funds to
bring in agents from around the country. As usual, Christensen got
the runaround. They sent him from one department to the next,
knowing that no one in a position of authority would delegate the
necessary money to make the operation a success. "Well, I got ahold
of a fairly new guy who wanted to do the job, and he went sneaking
and searching around, and he found ten thousand dollars," said
Christensen. "He went and cut all the travel orders. He got people
from Puerto Rico, New York, and San Francisco to fly in here."

One of their main targets was the plant's foreman, Butch Holton,
a former Border Patrol agent who'd been booted from the agency
for stealing funds and selling green cards. His job at the plant was to
recruit the illegal workers, get them documents, and keep the plant's
illegal practices out of the public eye. Hammond planned to pin him
down, pretty sure he would roll over during questioning. To get
Holton sweating in his boots, Hammond called him a few days before the raid. "I told him, 'We're coming. I'm not going to tell you
when, but we're coming and you're going to be surprised.' He got

----

excited, and he had a heart attack and died," said Hammond. "He knew that it was going to be a big deal, because I had been investigating him and had made arrests out there before."

Despite losing one of their key targets, 186 law enforcement officers surrounded the plant a few nights later. Armed with a criminal search warrant, they stormed into the packinghouse and detained everyone for questioning. By the end of the night, 350 of the plant's employees were found to be illegal immigrants, the majority of whom were processed and then sent back to Mexico within three days.

The true victory, however, came after the operation was complete. The plant was fined one hundred thousand dollars and was convicted by the court for harboring illegal aliens. "They raised their wages $1.25 an hour, and they got them—they got all the positions filled by legal citizens," said Christensen. "It really didn't take that much more. They kept up production, and the cost of meat didn't go up any."

Rather than turning immigration officers away from its doors as they had done in the past, the packing plant agreed to have INS officials visit the plant every month to ensure that no illegal workers were hired. This went on for a year, and even though the plant's managers wanted to keep the inspections in place, INS management shut them down, claiming that they were a waste of funds. The plant's managers took it as a message, and in just a few months the wages dropped and illegal workers moved back in.

"They didn't want to take these people into custody," said Hammond. "When you take all these aliens into custody, you've got a political problem. That's not politically correct to do that. You've got all of the Mexican groups raising hell. You've got the employers raising hell, and they're going to congressmen. And then you've got all these congressmen raising hell because they're afraid they're going to lose a few Hispanic votes. And then the INS directors begin shaking in their boots."

Despite all this, Hammond and Christensen felt like they had made a statement as to the effectiveness of taking action against employers hiring illegal workers, and so they attempted the same type of operation on another large meatpacking plant in Norfolk, Nebraska, during the summer of 1996. They began by investigating the plant, and once it had been determined that they employed more than a thousand illegal workers, they turned to outside help. The United

States Attorney agreed to lead the prosecution, a federal judge issued a search warrant, and almost a hundred law enforcement officers from around the country were detailed to the area to help execute the raid.

Everything was in place, but a day before the raid was to take place, the Omaha INS district director traveled to the meatpacking house and told the manager that an extremely large law enforcement team planned to come crashing though their doors in twenty-four hours to arrest all illegal workers. Because of this, when the operation commenced the following day, the majority of illegal immigrants at the plant had mysteriously called in sick.

Although 265 illegal immigrants had eluded arrest, the INS district director who had forewarned the facility had the gall to hold a news conference to brag about the operation's success. But from that moment forth, never again did he allow any of the criminal investigators to take action against the plant. "The operation made the INS look ridiculous to all the other agencies who had decided to help," said Hammond. "By doing what he did, the district director had broken the Federal Rules of Criminal Procedure. But nothing ever came out of that. . . . What happened was that politicians decided it was in the best interest of these companies to let illegal aliens stay here for cheap labor purposes. . . . You get into each one of these websites for these congressmen, look to see who their donors are, and you'll see all these meatpacking plants giving them thousands and thousands of dollars. What they do is they harass these bureaucratic district directors that the INS has all over the country, and these guys are afraid to do their jobs."

In order to keep everyone happy, the INS came up with a more subtle approach called Operation Vanguard in order to crack down on illegal immigrants working in meatpacking houses in Nebraska. The process began by first requesting that the plants hand over the I-9 forms their employees filled out. Once in possession of the forms, the INS would enter the names of the workers into a database to determine if they were truly American citizens eligible to work. If any questionable workers were identified, INS would then contact the manager of the plant and schedule a time to interview the workers who were suspected of being illegal immigrants.

As expected, few illegal immigrants were apprehended. Warned well ahead of time that INS was coming to determine their status, they either left town or got a job at another packinghouse. It did, however, encourage thousands of illegal workers to assume the identity of U.S. citizens. Because INS did all their background checks on computer, they had no way of knowing that workers in the plants were not who they claimed to be.

"The computer checks on Vanguard would only pick up counterfeit documents," said Hammond. "It would miss all the false claims. As time went by, it would encourage more and more illegals to become false claims. . . . That's a violation of the law. . . . Once they make that false claim, they are forever excludable from the United States; they can't get a green card. But the INS never goes out and checks. I'll tell you, a lot of times if I knew a guy was a false claim in a packinghouse, I would take his birth certificate and make copies of it. I would give it back to him, thank him, and then leave. If I thought he was a false claim I would conduct an investigation after that, and try and find the real person. A lot of times, I would find the person. And sometimes they would be in a New Mexico state prison, or they would be down in Texas somewhere."

On one occasion, Hammond spent almost a year trying to prove that a cattle buyer in Texas wasn't who he claimed to be. After gathering the suspect's information, he launched an investigation to find the real person but came up with no leads. The guy was nowhere to be found and his relatives were all deceased. Not willing to give up, he did a scouting report through the Social Security Administration to get a list of the individual's employers over the years. When the report came back six months later, it named only one employer—the Department of Defense, Air Force Finance Center, Denver, Colorado. Hammond jumped in his car, drove to the Air Force Base in Denver, and visited their Office of Special Investigations. He showed them all the material he had gathered and they ran it though their computers.

As it turned out, the person Hammond was looking for was a sergeant in the air force, stationed in Korea. With this knowledge, he went back to Texas and paid a visit to the cattle buyer. "We arrested him," said Hammond. "He ended up confessing and we deported him back to Mexico. But how many investigators in the INS are going to go to all that trouble? When they run into illegal workers in a packinghouse, if they think the guy won't confess, they just give him back his documents and catch some other illegal alien they can get to confess. But that only encourages more and more of these guys to come up here and do that."

Hammond did his job to the best of his ability, but while attempting to enforce the law, he learned just how uncooperative INS management could be—even in a case that threatened national security.

COME ON IN

The INS Northern Service Center in Lincoln, Nebraska, is responsible for processing various types of applications and petitions that are sent into the INS from aliens around the country. One of the applications they process is a re-entry visa, which the INS issues to permanent residents who plan to be abroad for more than one year, but less than two years, so they can be readmitted to the United States. Just like a passport, the re-entry permit serves as a travel document; it comes in a little booklet that contains the bearer's photograph, relevant information, and the Department of Justice seal.

In 1995, an INS clerical employee assigned to the service center stumbled upon an alarming fact—thousands of re-entry permits issued to permanent residents of Chinese descent were being sent to the same addresses in California. Sensing fraud, the employee pulled one of the suspect applications and set it to the side. Then he went and retrieved the applicant's INS A-file, which contained his fingerprints, photograph, and his history as a permanent resident. When comparing the two, he discovered that all the information in the application matched that of the A-file, only there was one major discrepancy—the photograph on the application didn't match that of the permanent resident. He repeated the process with other re-entry permits that had already been sent to the red-lighted addresses in California, and each one contained a photograph that belonged to someone other than the permanent resident. He put a halt on anything more being sent out to the California addresses, but by that time six thousand fraudulent re-entry permits had already been dropped in the mail.

A few days later, Hammond traveled to the Northern Service Center with a supervisor to investigate the matter. After interviewing the clerical employee who had uncovered the fraud scheme, Hammond found it impossible to believe that the service center didn't properly investigate each application before sending it out—something that could have been done quite easily by cross-checking them to the permanent resident's A-file. But in order to streamline the system and speedily return all applications, INS had decided to forgo such a process.

"When I was over there in Lincoln," said Hammond, "I asked the guy running the operation, 'Aren't you worried about all this fraud? You could be letting all kinds of people into the United States.' He said, 'Fifteen or twenty percent fraud, that's just the way it goes.'" As a result, six thousand re-entry permits had been most likely sent overseas to unknown parties. With their photographs laminated into the travel documents, Hammond didn't suspect that they would have much trouble entering the United States.

Upon hearing all the facts, Hammond knew that whoever had dreamed up the scheme had somehow acquired the personal information of thousands of permanent residents. It was possible smugglers were paying green-card holders to use their information, but more likely it was someone within the INS who had access to the A-files. That made the most sense—those who were behind this knew just how flawed the adjudication process was at the Northern Service Center. To Hammond and his supervisor, this was clearly a case of national security.

Once the United States Attorney's Office agreed to prosecute the case, Hammond's supervisor wrote a detailed report to INS headquarters requesting an investigation. With the ball rolling, Hammond went back to his normal duties, expecting that the matter would be followed up. After a month had passed, he received a call from an assistant United States attorney who wanted to know how the investigation was going. Hammond told him he would find out, and then contacted his superior, who in turn contracted INS headquarters. All three of them were surprised to learn that INS headquarters had closed the case because they couldn't find a criminal investigator in California who wanted to handle it. "It just went away," said Hammond. "They just stopped doing anything on it. That's our headquarters. That case would have put so much bad light on the Immigration Service itself, they didn't want to prosecute. Therefore, they didn't fund it. That's when politics get involved. . . . They controlled investigations, and that's why we didn't get an investigation."

INS headquarters swept the matter under the rug. Their response was to program the computers to detect situations where several re-entry permits were being sent to the same address, but that did little to stop the mastermind behind the operation or the six thousand fraudulent re-entry permits that had already been issued. Supposedly, the names of the fraudulent permits were placed on the lookout so immigrations inspectors could intercept them at the ports of entry. This, however, never seemed to happen. Between 1998 and 2000, the INS only reported having intercepted 1,531 fraudulent re-entry visas. "Here you have the INS, and they're supposed to be running an operation to secure the borders, but here they were—and may still be—issuing all these re-entry permits with somebody else's picture on there. Once they get that document with their picture on it, and they show up at an airport, the chances are the immigration inspectors are going to let them in."

It was situations like this that made Hammond wonder why he had ever left the Border Patrol. "I never got any help from anybody in Washington as far as enforcing the law. You're out there by yourself, and you better watch out for yourself. I remember one time my partner and I were over there on I-80 with a whole truckload of illegal aliens. It was January, seventeen degrees below zero out there, and we couldn't get anybody to help us. In Washington, they had two thousand bureaucrats sitting in INS headquarters. We're down there enforcing the law in Nebraska on I-80 in the middle of January, twenty below zero—two guys."

Chapter Nine

TERROR SWEEPING INLAND

Although none of the hijackers who attacked America on September 11, 2001 gained entry into the United States by illegally crossing the U.S.-Canada border, they very well could have. Terrorists have been doing it for years.

In 1996, Palestinian emigrant Ghazi Ibrahim Abu Maizar made his first attempt to enter the United States by illegally crossing the Canadian border into Washington State. Border patrolmen apprehended him, explained the immigration laws of the United States, and then sent him packing north. That, however, was not the last they saw of Maizar. His second attempt came only a short while later. Although he had no excuses when he was apprehended this time, patrolmen hesitantly agreed to release him on the grounds that he didn't try anything so foolish in the future. But apparently Maizar couldn't take a hint, because he tried a third time in January 1997. The patrolmen who intercepted him realized he would not stop until he entered the United States, and so they arrested him, charged him with violating various laws, and then set the deportation process in motion.[1]

This suited Maizar just fine, because after posting a five-thousand-dollar bond, he was released into the United States to await his hearing. Six months later, after working out the plans to bomb a subway station in New York with fellow Palestinian Lafi Khalil, his hearing came around. The immigration judge found him deportable, but instead of having federal officers escort him to the border, the judge allowed Maizar sixty days to leave the country of his own free will.

173

Maizar did not adhere to the honor system. Instead of leaving the country, he returned to the apartment he had rented in Brooklyn, New York. Excited about his future plans, he began to talk to his new Egyptian roommate, Abdel Rahman Mosabbah, about how he was going to get revenge on America for supporting Israel. He even divulged his ultimate goal—to use terror to force the release of several Arab terrorists currently being housed in Israeli prisons.

On July 30, Mosabbah went to the police, and at dawn the following morning federal agents broke down the door of the Brooklyn apartment. Instead of trying to escape, Maizar and his Palestinian accomplice Lafi Khalil instantly dove for explosive devices that could kill anything within a twenty-five-foot radius if detonated. Luckily, both men were shot in the leg before reaching them.[2]

Charged with building and planning to use a weapon of mass destruction, Maizar received a life sentence. It gave piece of mind to his Brooklyn neighbors, but the high-publicity case only informed other terrorists around the world just how easy it was to cross the U.S.-Canada border.

One of those terrorists happened to be Ahmed Ressam, a weapons expert for the Al Qaeda terrorist organization. Basing his operations out of Vancouver, Canada, he began preparing to bomb the Los Angeles International Airport during the 1999–2000 millennium festivities. By December everything was in place, so he packed the trunk of his Chrysler with explosives and drove it aboard a ferry headed for Washington's Port Angeles.

The only thing that foiled his plot was his lack of cool. Pulling up to the inspections booth in Washington shaking and dripping with sweat, he aroused the suspicions of Customs Inspector Diana Dean. She asked him to pop the trunk, which he eventually did. Inside she found several bags containing white powder, which she first suspected to be narcotics. Ressam was placed in custody, but it wasn't until days later that investigators realized they were dealing with chemicals which, when combined, formed a highly volatile explosive.[3]

Although both these terrorist attacks had been thwarted, it was no thanks to Canada's liberal immigration policies, which have been abused by Islamic terrorist groups for years. Many terrorists enter Canada without visas, and then, in order to avoid deportation, they claim to be refugees and are quickly released into the general population. Because of this, the United States's northern neighbor quickly became the stomping ground for over fifty organizations with known connections to international terrorist groups.[4] Not having to worry about being apprehended, they are free to plot their attacks on the American people. And once all their plotting is achieved, it's just a short drive through an official port of entry or a quick hike through the woods.

Prior to 9/11, there were fewer than four hundred border patrolmen standing guard along the four-thousand-mile U.S.-Canada border, which stretches from Washington to Maine. That's about one patrolman for every ten miles—and it's not an easy ten miles to patrol. Unlike those who patrol the vast, open deserts along much of the southern border, patrolmen in the north are responsible for protecting rugged mountains and wetlands plagued with obstacles that limit methods of travel. Even with all the modern equipment and technology, they confront the same limitations the Mounted Guards did in 1904.

"It's no different than it was fifty or a hundred years ago—the simplest way to cross the northern boundary and not get caught is afoot," said Joel Hardin, one of the first patrolmen to be assigned to Washington's anti-smuggling unit. "If you're halfway smart, and have any ambition at all, you can walk across the border between the ports of entry and not have to deal at all with inspections, documents, or passports. This creates a problem when trying to fight terrorism, but it's not a new problem. Back in the eighties the Immigration Service was concerned about the Middle Easterners who were a part of these small groups. We call them terrorists now, but they were just developing cells in those days. The Immigration Service was not totally unaware of that, but we lacked any public support. We lacked political support for doing anything about it because the U.S. government was heavily involved with developing the Middle East."

That's no longer the case, so why, then, isn't the northern border properly guarded?

At the ports of entry the answer is free trade. With almost one billion dollars of commerce generated every day between the two nations, Congress would not be doing their business constituents any favors by increasing inspections and slowing down traffic to a crawl.[5] And increasing security between the ports of entry would require funding Congress isn't prepared to delegate. "Nothing had been going on up there until 9/11," said Thomas Hammond, former INS Criminal Investigator. "There were people coming in from

China, but the numbers were low, just a couple thousand a year compared to the Mexican border, where you have millions. We figured we were better off directing our resources to the Mexican border."

But now, in an age of terrorism, the U.S. government is rethinking that strategy. The hard part, however, is making change happen. "If they wanted to control every inch of the Canadian border with an eyeball, they would need a million border patrolmen up there," said Hammond.

Shortly after the attack on the World Trade Center, this is what much of America wanted—to secure the northern border, by whatever means possible. In an attempt to fulfill the demand, the U.S. government sent 1,100 National Guardsmen to serve as watchdogs along the border, but it was only a temporary solution. In hopes of solving the problem in the long run, Border Patrol began hastily recruiting, even offering a two-thousand-dollar signing bonus. Despite this, the positions didn't fill up as quickly as the Immigration Service had hoped. Part of it had to do with the salary the INS paid its border patrolmen—on average, they were the lowest paid federal law enforcement agents in the country. And with operations such as Gatekeeper and Hold the Line in full effect, few were excited about sitting on a designated spot for eight hour stretches to *intimidate* illegal crossers. To make matters worse, the Border Patrol was also losing experienced agents to the newly embraced Air Marshals, which not only increased agents' salaries almost two-fold, but also allowed them to return to their hometowns.

The end result was bleak—six months after September 11, only fifteen additional agents had been permanently assigned to the U.S.-Canada border.

President George W. Bush attempted to come to the rescue by issuing the INS $6.3 billion in the proposed budget for 2003—a $1.2 billion increase from 2002. Of the additional funding, $712 million was to go to enforcing the laws of immigration along the U.S. borders.[6] Along with hiring more patrolmen, a large portion was to be spent on surveillance equipment, such as video monitors and sensors. If the United States couldn't watch the entire border with a human eye twenty-four/seven, then they could at least watch it with an electronic one. "There are millions of dollars being spent on one kind of electronic surveillance or another, but the fact of the matter is that it has very little effect on the interdiction of people coming in," said Hardin. "First off, the electronic sensors don't catch anyone. If you don't have someone there to personally take them into custody, they can stand there, moon the camera, and then go on about their business. It sounds good to the public, and in the media it sounds great, but to the guys out there guarding the line it's kind of a joke. It's an extra tool, but by itself it's not enough to do the job."

So what is the Border Patrol to do? The recent trend has been to pull agents from inland stations and reassign them to the U.S.-Canada border. This, however, only weakens law enforcement in the interior of the United States, and every patrolman stationed on the border knows that no matter how effective they are at their job, there will still be those who slip through.

"They have detailed them all to the border and faced them north to intercept anyone who is coming south," said Hardin. "That is their primary function, to intercept anyone coming south." This seemed odd to Hardin, who had guarded the southern border for almost a dozen years with the old fashioned "roving patrol." Curious, he paid a visit to a deputy chief assigned to the Canadian border to find out what was going on. "What about all those people who get behind you—who get behind *us*?" Hardin asked him. "What about all those people who we know are already here?"

"Well, our job is to interdict everyone who is coming in," answered the deputy chief. "We're just hoping and praying that somebody behind us is taking care of those people who are already here."

"Who is going to do that?"

The deputy chief turned his eyes down. "I have no idea."

Hardin didn't need an answer. "There is nobody in the interior looking for these guys," said Hardin. "INS isn't doing it, so nobody else is. This means that the terrorist cells that have gathered and assimilated into the population within the United States in the last twenty years can do as they please. Unless there is some connection made through intelligence sources, they will virtually go unchallenged until something comes up. That's what happens if you line yourself along the border looking out—it makes it pretty hard to watch what is going on behind you."

Under the Immigration Nationality Act, Border Patrol agents are authorized to stop and interrogate illegal immigrants within one hundred miles of any U.S. border or port of entry, which includes all international airports. That's nearly the entire United States, but service policy and lack of manpower keep them huddled in tight along the immediate border. Chiefs of the various sectors have been ordered to keep their agents' eyes locked on the border, and so "Hold them at the line" has become their mantra. This, however, might not be the right approach.

"The Border Patrol presently is gravely, tremendously, increasing the number of agents along the northern border. But it still doesn't change much—just as it is along the southern border, they're trying to cover rough, raw wilderness areas that stretch for most of three thousand miles," said Hardin. "We never did do a very good job on the southern border, and we tried down there for twenty years. For crying out loud, it's best described as a sieve by the people who are hired to protect it. You can't really expect anything but much more of the same along the northern border."

This is a pretty frightening prediction, especially coming from a man who has twenty years of experience dealing with the challenges of protecting America's borders. And he is not alone—many patrolmen understand just how impossible it is to meet America's expectations along the border. But by no means does this mean that they have given up. Although the border might not be able to be sealed, at least border patrolmen can make it difficult for terrorists to cross the line. "In order to achieve this, we have to reform the political atmosphere so we can adequately enforce the laws that are already on the books," said Hardin. "That's the problem that we've always had. We're not allowed to do our job because they don't want us to hurt anyone's feelings; for example, they tell us to catch Middle East terrorists, but in no way should we racially profile anyone. What does that mean? Catch Middle East terrorists but don't racially profile. That's two of the greatest contradictions that there are."

If politicians, lobbyists, bureaucrats, and special interest groups can only stop sabotaging the laws of immigration for self-serving purposes and allow the border patrolmen to enforce the existing laws, illegal traffic along the United States border would drop overnight. Terrorists would no longer be able to ride on the back of the massive waves of illegal workers currently flowing across the mountains and deserts. The Border Patrol's anti-smuggling units would spend less time cracking down on smuggling rings pushing illegal Mexicans over the border and apply more energy to cracking down on the ones who smuggle in Middle Easterners. As it stands, anti-smuggling units consider themselves lucky when they catch illegal immi-grants from countries known for terrorism.

One such streak of luck occurred in December 2002, when San Diego's anti-smuggling unit apprehended an Iraqi national at-tempting to illegally cross the U.S.-Mexico border. After bringing him in for questioning, agents learned that one of his accomplices had successfully made it across the line. The anti-smuggling unit immediately began an investigation, and after learning that the in-dividual was most likely traveling to a relative's home in the United States, they contacted the Department of Internal Affairs. The fam-ily's phone was put under surveillance, and when the suspect called to check in, the anti-smuggling unit traced the number back to its source. "We were able to track down the individual who had eluded apprehension, and he was subsequently arrested in Santa Ana by in-vestigators there," said Juan Estrada, a member of San Diego's anti-smuggling unit. "It took the cooperation of several agencies, but it turned out pretty good."

To make things difficult for terrorists entering over the border, this kind of cooperation must become mandatory. In the past, how-ever, everything has been a turf war. "DEA, they worked on the bor-der with us. Then the FBI decided they wanted to get involved in drugs, so they sent guys down. They were always fighting each other, and they never cooperated," said Paul Christensen, the former bor-der patrolman and INS criminal investigator. "Customs had some drug authority, but they would never cooperate with DEA or FBI. Everybody wanted to make the bust and get the credit. . . . Those were the three major players for drugs in the United States feder-ally, and they were never cooperating. And then you had the ATF (Alcohol, Tobacco and Firearms)—well, they didn't want to cooper-ate with anybody because they wanted to make their busts with guns and explosives. Secret Service, they were involved in counterfeited money and documents, but they wouldn't cooperate with us. We also had responsibility for document fraud when related to aliens; they wanted to get in on that, but they never wanted to share any of the information. And when they had something dealing with aliens, they would call us to help them out, but they still wanted the credit. Same things with drugs—when we'd catch drugs on the border, DEA would come running down and they would take the drugs, be-cause we didn't have any drug authority. All these turf wars, and no-body wants to cooperate."

But when dealing with the very real threat of terrorism, turf wars are the last thing the United States needs. The government has begun to realize this in the wake of America's tragedy, leading to the Department of Homeland Security, which has combined twenty-two agencies and 170,000 employees into one department. It is responsible for protecting American citizens against terrorists attacks, illegal immigration, drug smuggling, and a number of other threats. Three of the agencies included in this lot are the U.S. Border Patrol, Customs, and the Coast Guard, all of which go to great lengths to interdict illegal aliens and drugs. Because they all perform essentially the same duties, it only makes sense to lump them together so their equipment, intelligence, and manpower can all be shared.

One section of the Border Patrol that has made an easy transition into the Department of Homeland Security has been the Miami sector, which is responsible for guarding Florida, Georgia, and both the Carolinas. "We have over 1,700 miles of coastline to protect, which is equal to the border from San Diego, California, all the way to Del Rio, Texas," said Lynne Underdown, chief patrol agent in charge of the Miami sector. "I'm not pretending to say that we make as many arrests as they do along the U.S.-Mexico border, because it is much easier to traverse, obviously, but we have to look at it from a vulnerability- and threat-assessment point of view. Down here we work very closely with Coast Guard and Customs Air and Marine. No man is an island in Florida—it is impossible for any one agency to try to work this area by itself.

"This is the fourth sector I have worked in during my twenty-year career, and the inter-agency cooperation here has really set us up for a very good transition into Homeland Security, because we were already doing it. Just for example, there are eight hundred islands in the Bahamas. The large ones people are familiar with, but the small ones, many of them uninhabited, are often used as staging points for smugglers. And I'm not just talking about smuggling people. I'm talking about smuggling drugs and weapons, as well. Working with the Coast Guard is imperative. A lot of times they will pick up boats on radar, notify us, and then our people out there on boat patrol will go in and interdict. The source countries for this traffic are Cuba, the Bahamas, and the whole Caribbean area—countries, for the most part, which we have no relationship with. And so we don't have a real good feel for what is coming out of there. God bless the United States Coast Guard. They have been phenomenally cooperative with us; without that partnership, we would really be at a disadvantage. They share our mission, and it is great to see a unit that is not parochial and says, 'Hey, let's get out there and get the job done.' It's like a kindred spirit."

In March 2003 a little of this teamwork spread to other sectors of the Border Patrol to stop terrorists from smuggling weapons of mass destruction over the border. In the past, only Customs agents were equipped with hand-held radiation detectors, which are designed to pick up emissions from radioactive isotopes used to build a variety of bombs. But with increasing intelligence that the Al Qaeda network was plotting to smuggle radioactive material over the border and then use traditional explosives to disperse it, something known as a 'Dirty Bomb,' a large number of the detectors were lent to the Border Patrol so that every person or vehicle entering the United States through a port of entry could be scanned.

But even more valuable than the sharing of equipment is the sharing of human intelligence, something in which the Border Patrol has vast experience. "I think with everything we have experienced since 9/11, nationally and internationally, there has been a new appreciation for something the Border Patrol has known all along—the value of human intelligence," said Underdown. "We have always been driven on human intelligence, and I think that the importance of that is finally coming back into focus now. And I really believe it is going to make the difference in us persevering against these terrorist components. You can't just run Homeland Security based on reports and what you think may happen. It is very, very important to have your people out there actually collecting, interpreting, and analyzing intelligence. In the Border Patrol it has always worked that way, because we didn't have enough people to put in every area that had to be worked."

"The Federal government should make the state and local authorities cooperate with them, and they should somehow give them the authority to arrest illegal aliens, even if they have to pay them for each illegal immigrant they arrest," said Hammond. "That's what they used to do in the old days. If some sheriff up here arrested an illegal alien, the INS would pay him so much for each one who was arrested. But then they did away with that, and the reason was because all these special interest groups said, 'Well, it's really not right for the sheriffs to arrest these illegal aliens. They don't have training, and they might arrest someone who is here legally and keep them in jail.' But they're police officers, and if they can investigate a murder, they sure as hell can arrest an illegal alien. . . . Right now in the middle of the United States, they aren't even looking for terrorists. Say Osama bin Laden is bankrolling you—you could come to Omaha from the Middle East, get some false papers, go to a realty agency, buy a house, and then move your entire crew in. Nobody is going to question why you're there. Not local authorities, because it's politically incorrect for them to do that."

Along with sharing information and powers with local, state, and federal agencies, the Department of Homeland Security must also eliminate the speedy inspections currently conducted at airports and ports of entry. "The inspectors have to be allowed to spend more time actually talking to people coming in," said Christensen. "You want to look at the documents and make sure they're not altered, or counterfeit. It's also important to have a conversation with the people, especially if you're good at it. When you talk to the individuals you can tell a lot by their demeanors, and a lot of time that can lead to the secondary referral where they inspect their documents much closer. They need to do more of that. Everyone has to realize when you are dealing with people other than those from major Western countries, you don't know who anyone is because of counterfeit documents."

No one expects the Department of Homeland Security to solve existing problems overnight, but many of those in the patrol feel that their experience and capability in the field will play an essential part. "The leadership in DHS has a very keen appreciation for our traditions and our training, and they understand why the Border Patrol works so well as an entity," said Underdown. "We've been told that they do not want to disturb that. I think they are analyzing the best of what every agency has to offer and then will weave it through all of the agencies. From the Border Patrol, they certainly notice our comradeship and esprit de corps. I know our people in headquarters have been very involved in 'think tanks' in terms of brainstorming partnership forums that will decide how everyone should not only identify with DHS, but also have an appreciation for their individual identities. That will be the challenge—not to destroy existing cultures but take them and build on them. I think we are going to be the centerpiece for that in the Department of Homeland Security. I am always going to be a Border Patrolman first, no matter what rank I go past that. That is our identity, and we cling to that with fervor. It's a passion that is almost indefinable. I could be in a crowd of people who are working for different components of the Department of Homeland Security, and I can pick out the ones who are a part of the Border Patrol. It is something about how they carry themselves; it's a confidence that no task is too difficult. It's very emotional for me—a spiritual devotion that no geography, no title, no external cosmetic change is ever going to alter. It becomes a part of you, because you have earned it."

Whether or not the Department of Homeland Security will eliminate the bureaucratic red tape that has plagued some of these agencies for years, is unknown. There are mixed feelings running though the Border Patrol. "I guess it's going to be a magnificent, overblown, incredible bureaucracy," said Ab Taylor. "I'm sure right now everyone who has a friend in politics is jumping on the bandwagon, because when they open up something new like that, all these professional politicians in the civil service began to shake and move and run around to get the good jobs. Along with it, I hope they pick some people who make a difference.

Joel Hardin, on the other hand, has higher expectations. "One of my biggest hopes is now that they have split the INS and the Border Patrol it will further remove the politics involved. In the past, on one side you had benefits, and the other side you had enforcement. They have split them up now in the new department, so we won't have the same person running both sides, which is good."

Whether or not the immigration laws are reformed and the Border Patrol is utilized to its full capabilities under the new department, patrolmen will continue in their sworn duty to protect America. Seven days a week they will continue to hike across arid, rocky terrain plagued with rattlesnakes, just as they did during the days of Pancho Villa, Prohibition, and the Great Depression. They will continue to encounter heavily armed drug smugglers, bandits looking for easy prey, and the Mexican military out to test the boundaries. And, most of all, they will continue to embrace their esprit de corps. "We have a great pride in what we do," said Ab Taylor, "and we sincerely feel that we are keeping the country from being overrun. Morale is often low, because we never have enough money to do the job, but we still bust our butts. We are a dedicated, proud bunch of men."

Notes

— ▪▪ —

CHAPTER ONE: THE COWBOY DAYS

1. Skeeter Skelton, "Jeff Davis Milton," *Shooting Times Magazine,* (November 1978). Available at: *Dark Canyon* www.darkcanyon.net/jeff_davis_milton.htm, unpaged.

2. Ibid, unpaged.

3. Ibid, unpaged.

4. John Myers Myers, *The Border Wardens.* (New Jersey: Prentice-Hall Inc., 1971), p. 15.

5. Marian L. Smith, *A Historical Guide to the U.S. Government.* (New York: Oxford University Press, 1998). Available at: www.ins.usdoj.gov/graphics/aboutins/history/articles/ OVIEW.htm, unpaged.

6. Myers, op. cit. p. 15.

7. Ibid. p. 16.

8. Ibid, p. 18.

9. Ibid, p. 19.

10. Ibid, p. 19.

11. Leon C. Metz, "United States Border Patrol," *Handbook of Texas Online,* www.tsha.utexas.edu/handbook/online/articles/view/uu/ ncujn.html, unpaged.

12. Jim Tuck, "Democrat to Autocrat: The Transformation of Porfirio

Diaz," *Mexico Connect*, at:
www.mexconnect.com/mex_mex_/history/jtuck/jtporfdiaz.
html, unpaged.

13. Myers, op. cit. p. 20.

14. "The United States Border Patrol, Introduction," *United States Border Patrol*, at: www.usborderpatrol.com/border1.htm, unpaged.

15. Joe Griffith, "In Pursuit of Pancho Villa 1916–1917," (August 27, 2002). Available at: www.hsgng.org/pages/pancho.htm, unpaged.

16. "The United States Border Patrol, Introduction," *United States Border Patrol*, www.usborderpatrol.com/border1.htm, unpaged.

17. Haldeen Braddy, *Cock of the Walk Qui-qui-ri-qui!: The Legent of Pancho Villa*. (Albuquerque, NM: University of New Mexico Press, 1955), p. 128–132.

18. Griffith, op. cit., unpaged.

19. Ibid, unpaged.

20. Metz, op. cit., unpaged.

21. Myers, op. cit. p. 32.

22. Ibid, p. 35.

23. Ed Pyeat, "Lon Parker. . . . April 26, 1892–July 25, 1926."

24. Ibid, unpaged.

25. Ibid, unpaged.

26. John Myers Myers. *The Border Wardens*. (New Jersey: Prentice-Hall Inc. 1971), p. 58.

27. Leon C. Metz, "United States Border Patrol," *Handbook of Texas Online*, www.tsha.utexas.edu/handbook/online/articles/view/uu/ncujn.html, unpaged.

CHAPTER TWO: A NEW DILEMMA

1. Julian Samora, *Los Mojados: The Wetback Story*. (London: University of Notre Dame Press, 1971), p. 38.

2. "The Bracero Program." Available at: www.farmworkers.org/bracerop.html, p. 36.

3. "The Bracero Program." Available at:
www.farmworkers.org/bracerop.html, p. 41.

4. John Myers Myers, *The Border Wardens*. (New Jersey: Prentice-Hall Inc., 1971), p. 77.

5. Fred L. Koestler, "Operation Wetback," *The Handbook of Texas Online*, www.tsha.utexas.edu/handbook/online/articles/view/ OO/pqp1.html, unpaged.

CHAPTER FOUR: THE ART OF SMUGGLING

1. Edward M. Brecher and the Editors of *Consumer Reports* magazine, "The Consumers Union Report of Licit and Illicit Drugs: Chapter 59. The 1969 marijuana shortage and 'Operation Intercept,' " (1972). Available at: *Schaffer Library of Drug Policy*, www.druglibrary.org/ schaffer/Library/studies/cu/CU59.html, unpaged.

2. Sebastian Rotella, *Twilight on the Line*. (New York: W.W. Norton and Company, 1998), p.135.

3. "United States vs.Verdugo-Uriqdez," *GunCite*, www.guncite.com/court/fed/sc/494us259.html, unpaged.

4. Terrence Poppa, "Epilogue, from Drug Lord," *The Nimby News*, nimbynews.com/epilogue.html, unpaged.

5. Bruce Carey, "Senator says government has evidence," (July 1997). Available at *Federation of American Scientists*, www.fas.org/irp/news/ 1997/38955055-38959546.htm, unpaged.

6. Esther Shrader, "Federal Agents Under Siege in the Southwest," *Los Angeles Times*, (March 12, 2000).

7. Diana Washington Valdez, "Border Patrol Team Investigates Mexican-Soldier Confrontation," *El Paso Times*, (March 24, 2000). Available at *Mexico Border News*, www.dslextreme.com/users/ surferslim/update2.html, unpaged.

CHAPTER FIVE: A PARTIAL SOLUTION

1. Sebastian Rotella, *Twilight on the Line*. (New York: W.W. Norton and Company, 1998), p. 125–26.

2. Ibid, p. 126.

CHAPTER SIX: GROWING SENTIMENT

1. William Branigin, "Questions on Military Role Fighting Drugs Ricochet From a Deadly Shot," *Washington Post*, (June 22, 1997). Available at *Drug Policy Forum of Texas*, www.dpft.org/hernandez/ wp 062297.html, unpaged.

2. Kevin Sullivan, "Billions Worth of Drugs Entered U.S. by Tunnel," *Washington Post Foreign Service*, (March 1, 2002). Available at *Corruption on the Border*, www.customscorruption.com/archives_page_3.htm, unpaged.

CHAPTER SEVEN: TRAINING THE ELITE

1. Mark Hamm, *The Abandoned Ones: A History of the Cuban Prison Riots at Oakdale and Atlanta*. (New York: Northeastern University Press, 1995), p. 3–4.

2. "California Company Indicted for Immigrant Smuggling Operation," No author available. (15 November, 2002). Available at: KFMB-TV, www.kfmb.com/topstory.php?storyID+5018, unpaged.

CHAPTER NINE: TERROR SWEEPING INLAND

1. Michael Kapel, "Three Strikes and You're In," *The Australia/Israel Review*, (October 23–November 20, 1997). Available at *Australia/Israel & Jewish Affairs Council* at: www.aijac.org.au/review/1997/2215/ notebk2215.html, unpaged.

2. "Hebron Man Convicted by US Federal Jury," *Associated Press, Jerusalem Post*, (July 24, 1998). Available at: *The International Policy Institure for Counter-Terrorism*, www.ict.org.il/spotlight/det.cfm?id=115, unpaged.

3. Hal Bernton, Mike Carter, David Heath, and James Neff, "Chapter 12: The Crossing," *The Seattle Times*, (June 23–July 7, 2002). Available at: http://seattletimes.nwsource.com/news/nation-world/ terroristwithin/chapter12.html, unpaged.

4. David Phinney, "Staging Terror from the North?" Available at: http://abcnews.go.com/sections/world/Daily/News/canada991228.h tml, unpaged.

5. Ibid, unpaged.

6. Rebecca Phares, "U.S./Mexico Border: Bush administration seeks budget boost, federal troops, for border security," *Central America/Mexico Report,* (February 2002). Available at: *Religious Task Force on Central America and Mexica,* www.rtfcam.org/report/volume_22/No_1/article_10.htm, unpaged.

Index